KP
CRICKET GENIUS?

The Biography of
KEVIN PIETERSEN

by Wayne Veysey

Know The Score Books Limited
118 Alcester Road
Studley
Warwickshire
B80 7NT
01527 454482
info@knowthescorebooks.com
www.knowthescorebooks.com

A CIP catalogue record is available for this book from the British Library
ISBN: 978-1-84818-701-6

Printed and bound in Great Britain
By TJ International, Cornwall.

Acknowledgements

I would like to thank:

My wife Emma for her wise words and support.

Woody and Beamish for making me smile.

All those who helped the researches, especially Clive Rice, Errol Stewart, Simon Jones, Graham Ford, Jamie Fleet, Mike Bechet, Wayne Scott, Richard Logan, Micky Arthur, Graham Thorpe, Shaun Pollock, Jonty Rhodes, Rod Marsh, Doug Watson, Grant Rowley and Shaun Udal.

And everyone at Know The Score Books for all their help.

Wayne Veysey
March 2009

CONTENTS

FOREWORD

by CLIVE RICE

KEVIN PIETERSEN HAS BARELY scratched the surface of his cricketing potential. There is a huge amount still to come from him. If Kevin improves his focus and concentration at the crease he can be up there with the top three cricketers who have ever played the game. That is a huge statement, but he is that good. He can beat Graham Gooch's record as England's leading run-scorer, that's for sure. He can beat Sachin Tendulkar's record for the most Test hundreds. On faster wickets he can even beat Brian Lara's record for the highest individual score in Test cricket. Kevin is capable of scoring 500 runs in a Test innings.

He has to understand he is good enough to do that and to do so would take application. When you see the great players they get a whole lot of 200s. Kevin has got one Test double-hundred, but you would like to see him regularly extending his scores into 200s and 300s. That will be his next step. It comes pretty easy to him. If he bats for a day he will have 200 and have murdered the opposition. Then, when he gets to 200 he has to do what Brian Lara has done and stay in there and get 300 and then 400. When Kevin gets to 400 then we know he has got the concentration to last longer and get 500. It won't take him long to do it. He kills good attacks and murders mediocre ones.

Kevin's downfall is often over-exuberance. I think he can go where no batsman has gone before if he can improve his concentration and learn to hit a six followed by a single rather than three sixes in an over, or one to bring up a century. He does occasionally play some stupid shots at that stage of his innings, like when he got out for 97 in Jamaica against the West Indies in February 2009 by slogging it straight up in the air. Those stupid mistakes are not made between 0 and 10. They are made because of his confidence at 90.

Confidence can be both his greatest strength and greatest weakness. A good attack bowling well on a slow pitch clearly is a bit of a hindrance to him because of the pace he likes to get his runs. When he is a little bit bogged down, that doesn't appeal to him. He clearly likes the ball coming on nice and fast because the faster it is, the further it goes when he strikes it. On the faster wickets he has to be ultra-patient over one-and-a-half days. Then we will see some huge scores from him.

When you look at the England batting line-up he is the best batsman by far. Andrew Strauss is a fine player, but KP is your out and out matchwinner because he can play all the shots. When he goes into bat he can win you the game. Opposition teams are scared of him. When you see the great batsmen, like Viv Richards and Graeme Pollock, those guys can rip you apart. When you see Kevin walk into bat, you know it is no different to Viv, Graeme, Greg Chappell, Barry Richards, Brian Lara or Gordon Greenidge. When they walk in, you know there is a problem.

Kevin has developed a lot since I first saw him as a 17-year-old at a schools' festival in South Africa after which I first brought him over to Nottinghamshire in 2001. He has tightened up his game. It can still be tightened up some more. He has developed some amazing shots and changed how he is looking to score. When you come out of the schoolboy ranks you certainly find the mens' game a lot different. Good players will find out your faults pretty quickly and exploit them. You then have to work on them until you eliminate them. That's what Kevin has done. During that initial stage he eliminated those faults quickly by hard work and application.

We still keep in touch regularly by text and occasionally by phone. When I see him play I send him a text about what he is doing and what his targets are. Whatever he wants to set himself, as long as it is reasonable, he can do it. That will all be in his head. He loves the game. Sure, he loves the publicity out of it, but he is passionate about cricket, about winning and about being centre stage. For him, it is about staying in that position and keeping the passion going. You don't want it to be too easy for him. You are talking about a Rolls-Royce here. How long does he want it to go on for? I know if he applies himself he will play until 36-37 years of age easily. Maybe even 40. His longevity revolves around setting these high standards and looking after himself.

I don't see what he is like in the dressing room now, but it is no secret that Kevin needs careful management. If you are managing him you tell him he is number one. You need to confirm in his mind he is in the side as a matchwinner. You have got to boost his ego in terms of what is going on all the time. You boost it and boost it again. Because his ego is boosted, he can perform at his best. You have to be astute with him. He is a hard man to impress. If your advice is good he will respect you a lot more.

I thoroughly enjoyed managing him. But then I had the experience of handling Eddie Hemmings, Derek Randall and Chris Broad. Randall, my goodness, he was a loony on the field. How do you handle him? There were times when Eddie Hemmings was impossible. The toys would come out of the cot and he would throw huge strops. I would say to the other guys, "Leave him, I will deal with him." I would have to refocus him and settle him down.

I've always known Kevin as a seriously confident guy. In the dressing room that probably upsets people. But I would rather have a guy 110 per cent confident like him than a player who is 70 per cent confident, because he will not win you the game. The thing about Kevin's attitude us that it upsets mediocrity, it upsets those players who like a nice, comfortable existence. It certainly affected some people at Notts because of some of the mediocrity that existed there. They couldn't handle him. Often people can't handle guys who are confident.

Kevin was outspoken, no doubt about it. You can take it seriously and react to him or divert his attention from being stupid. At Notts, he was a young guy coming into professional cricket trying to prove himself and get recognition. In the dressing room, he would make stupid comments that would upset people. They might not have done so well during the day's play and Kevin would brag a bit because he had been successful. He would try to get people's attention because of the fact he had done well by saying, "I won the game," or, "Did you see that reverse sweep for six?" The other guys couldn't do it, couldn't make that shot. Well, he would brag that he could. That all quietens down as you get older. And getting that recognition isn't a problem for Kevin anymore.

Kevin has grown up and matured and that's why I was really disappointed when he lost the England captaincy. The team was transformed when he took over. There was no doubt. I have no idea how he lost the captaincy and I haven't spoken to him about it, but there was clearly a dispute between Kevin and Peter Moores. Kevin probably might not have been diplomatic enough, but was that enough for the ECB to strip him of the captaincy? I'm not so sure. The captain runs the show on the field and the coach runs the show off the field, prepares the team and offers guidance. Kevin seemed to be doing a good job. If Moores wasn't, and the guidance and ideas he was offering weren't good enough, then only he should have been sacked.

When England went to the West Indies for the Stanford tournament in October 2008 they didn't play very well. I sent Kevin a text saying, 'You can't switch your form on like a light'. Then the team played badly when they got to India against India A. He said it didn't matter because they would turn it around. To me, they were getting complacent. Having done well in England they should have continued that in the West Indies and walked away with the bucks. They should have started out like they meant it against the India A side and then taken the form and confidence into the one-day internationals and Tests. It's such a shame it ended the way it did. Kevin never really had a proper go of it. At least losing the captaincy will allow him to concentrate totally on his batting and reach new heights on that side of his game.

I'm proud of the role I played in bringing Kevin from Natal to Nottingham. When you find a diamond and it is a big one that is one hell of a special feeling. I'm delighted that I was able to give the guy a chance of entertaining every cricket supporter in the world. I knew full well that in South Africa he wouldn't be given a chance because of the stupid quota system. When I look back to the times my and Kevin's home country were banned from playing Test cricket in the 1970s, it was a sporting tragedy that the world were denied seeing the talents of Barry Richards, Mike Procter and Graeme Pollock at the highest level. They would have been fantastically entertained. South Africa would have challenged the West Indies for the title of best team in the world. Without any doubt.

It would have been another tragedy had Kevin stayed in South Africa and fallen victim to the quota system. If he was still there now he wouldn't be an international cricketer. He would be a surfer on Durban beach. Can you imagine the sporting world without KP now?

INTRODUCTION

LOSING THE CROWN

THE SECOND DAY'S PLAY has finished in the Test match that proves to be Kevin Pietersen's third and last as England captain. In dreary conditions that are more Manchester than Mohali, the venue for the denouement of a draining tour, India have been squeezed out for 453 following a commendable fightback by an Andrew Flintoff-inspired England. Despite poor weather forecasts for the three remaining days of the game, the visitors still have a narrow chance of the victory which would level the two-match series.

The mood in the dressing room is reasonably upbeat. England had looked dead and buried only hours before. But the captain is not happy. He is at loggerheads with the coach, Peter Moores. They are barely on speaking terms, as a long-running rift that dates back 18 months reaches boiling point at the climax of a decisive Test. The issue? Pietersen doesn't rate Moores as a coach and blames him for failing to provide adequate tactical support and inject fresh ideas as India chased down 387, the fourth highest last-innings chase in Test history, in the previous match at Chennai several days earlier.

Unusually for an overseas Test, there is a large gathering of powerbrokers from the England and Wales Cricket Board in Mohali, a consequence of the sensitive nature of the re-arranged series following the Mumbai terrorist attacks of 26-28 November, which left over 100 dead, and the need to show solidarity with the players. Chairman Giles Clarke, chief executive David Collier and managing director Hugh Morris are all travelling with the team and they become increasingly aware of the complete breakdown of the relationship between captain and coach. Pietersen tells Morris that he has serious misgivings about Moores' abilities and, such is the ferocity of the criticisms and the urgency of the situation, a series of meetings are scheduled over the next few evenings at the Taj Hotel, the team base in nearby Chandigarh, while the match is still going on. Crisis talks would ordinarily be unthinkable in the middle of a series-defining Test which hangs precariously in the balance, but these are extraordinary circumstances. Over the next few nights, several meetings are convened involving Pietersen, Moores, Morris, Clarke and Collier to discuss at length how the damage can be repaired.

Morris, Clarke and Collier are shocked that Pietersen and Moores' relationship has completely disintegrated only four and a half months into the captain's tenure. "The management were trying to work out, 'How do we address the problem with our coach?'" said a senior ECB source. "Has the captain got too big for his boots? Does the coach do 90 per cent of his job well? Does the captain need specialised support?" Indeed, one suggestion was that Pietersen could be offered the help of a part-time tactical guru or consultant to help guide him through the murky waters of international captaincy, former captain Michael Vaughan being touted for the position. The ECB are looking for time. Morris' instinct is to get all parties back to London, for the dust to settle and then bang a few heads together and work out a clear path forward. Collier suggests that Pietersen composes a detailed email strategy, outlining his vision for the future and how he envisages the team developing during the Ashes year of 2009.

To a backdrop of disharmony and emergency meetings and in the wake of an emotionally sapping six weeks, Pietersen arrives at the crease on the third day with England in a perilous position. Andrew Strauss and Ian Bell have been dismissed only seven balls into the innings and the visitors are 1-2. Pietersen needs a big innings to re-assert his credentials after scores of 4 and 1 in Chennai, the worst return of his 45-Test career to date. What happens? He plays with insatiable *joie de vivre* in a breathtaking 144, swiping Harbhajan Singh into the stands with his trademark switch-hit and scoring at a fearsome lick that keeps England in the game, before his dismissal late in the day prompts a collapse. With it go England's hopes of victory. It is uncanny how Pietersen tends to score a century in any innings of extra significance. In Mohali, he demonstrates once again that his ability to block out distractions is astonishing; superhuman even.

It would prove to be one of his final acts as England captain. A week later, an email lands in the inboxes of Morris and Clarke, the leaked contents of which sparks one of the most dramatic sporting fall-outs of modern times. In an attempt to engineer Moores' dismissal, Pietersen ends up engineering his own as well.

PETER MOORES strongly recommended Pietersen to be the England captain. This may seem remarkable in hindsight, sifting through the wreckage of the most cataclysmic captain-coach head-on collision in English cricket history. But when Michael Vaughan resigned in tears at a hastily arranged press conference at the national performance centre in Loughborough, Moores felt Pietersen was the best man for the job – above Andrew Strauss, the other realistic candidate, and above the rank outsiders Alastair Cook and Robert Key. Kevin was Pete's man. Moores was one voice of the five-strong group who selected the captain – the others were the England and Wales Cricket Board's managing director Hugh Morris and the three man selection panel of Geoff Miller, Ashley Giles and James Whitaker – but the coach's opinion counted for the most.

As details emerged of how Pietersen attempted to overthrow his line manager less than five months later, Moores could be compared to an especially dumb turkey voting for Christmas. Yet there was a great deal of logic to appointing Pietersen, even taking into account his maverick tendencies and controversial past. Kevin was an indisputable first choice in all three forms of the game, he was an experienced international widely respected by team-mates and opponents, he was the right age and he wanted the job. For Moores, however, there was more to granting Pietersen his support than the player's captaincy credentials. He was also convinced it would improve his working relationship with England's star player.

Moores and Pietersen had not seen eye to eye from the moment the fresh-faced coach was promoted from within to succeed Duncan Fletcher. Moores had the medals (a county championship with Sussex), the coaching badges and bundles of energy. He was the heir apparent and so convinced were the ECB that he was the right man they did not even bother to interview him or consider other applications. Pietersen was not so easily impressed. Moores had been a mediocre player who made his reputation as a coach in county cricket and, although Pietersen had done the same during a run-laden four-year stint at Nottinghamshire, he did not have a high regard for the county game, or mediocrity of any kind. As a South African-reared alpha male, his coaching mentors had been Graham Ford and Clive Rice, wise heads who shared his background and had backed him to the hilt when he was struggling to make the breakthrough in his homeland.

Pietersen had not been a Fletcher disciple in the same way as Vaughan, Marcus Trescothick or Paul Collingwood were, but he respected the Zimbabwean's knowledge of batting and his southern African mentality. Fletcher's quiet yet insightful direction was also appreciated by Pietersen, who has not been formally coached since Rice spent dozens of hours tinkering with his technique in the nets during Notts' pre-season tour of Johannesburg in April 2001. Mick Newell, the long-time Notts coach who worked with Pietersen for four years, says: "We weren't coaching him. He can play shots and innings that no-one else can. You just try and manage him, make sure he is as happy as he can be and make sure he can go out there and perform, which he did." Pietersen possesses the aura of a once-in-a-generation genius. Everyone I have spoken to in researching this book also insists he is the hardest worker in the England team. His preparation is immaculate, he trains ferociously hard and leaves nothing to chance. Generally speaking, he is happy to take responsibility for his own game and be left to his own devices. At international level, he sees the coach's role as more of a business consultant.

This was in stark contrast to Moores' idea of what a coach should be. He likes to be the man in charge. His coaching is all about hard work, practise and challenging the players to be better, fitter and stronger. Laudable ambitions but not necessarily ones tailored to elite athletes. Moores could also be uncompromising, to the point of bloody-minded. After a physically and emotionally draining one-day international against New Zealand in Napier ended in a tie, Moores insisted that the exhausted England players had a full-on training session immediately afterwards because the following day would be spent travelling. This did not go down well. The coach's obsession with physical training and unwillingness to give the players much down-time was beginning to grate. Pietersen grew to feel antipathy towards Moores' methods, as did his captaincy predecessors Vaughan and Paul Collingwood, who were, coincidentally, Kevin's two best friends in the England team. This manifested itself in some negative body language. When Moores addressed the players, Pietersen would sometimes undermine the coach by looking the other way.

Despite their chalk-and-cheese backgrounds – one, a flamboyant extrovert with the international stats to die for, the other, an ECB man to the core with the stats analysis to die for – Moores felt that by working closely together, he could finally get Pietersen on side. With their common purpose and shared ambitions, they could sort out their differences and forge a far better relationship than when Kevin was a member of the rank and file, went his thinking. If he could win over Pietersen, all the other doubters would follow. It was Moores who insisted that the pair met at a Northampton hotel – one of the few examples of them meeting each other halfway – to thrash out the issues before Kevin formally accepted the offer of the England captaincy. Pietersen wanted a big say in how the team was run and asked Moores to take more of a back seat, a demand that was tacitly accepted. It was an uneasy truce, but a truce nonetheless.

All appeared fine and dandy in the early weeks of Pietersen's leadership as a revitalised England took advantage of South Africa's end-of-summer lethargy to handsomely win the Oval Test and administer a 4-0 hiding in the subsequent one-dayers. Pietersen appeared comfortable wearing the crown. His sense of timing and occasion was typically acute as he scored a masterful even 100 in his first innings as leader. Kevin hugged and hyped his players in public and made some smart moves that belied his pre-England captaincy experience, which amounted to a single Notts second-team game in 2002. He persuaded Steve Harmison back into the one-day fold, rejigged the team (Owais Shah to No. 3

and Andrew Flintoff to No. 5), backed his hunches and injected an increasingly downtrodden dressing room with barely concealed joyousness. Most importantly of all, his batting seemed unaffected.

Pietersen and Moores had the momentum of instant success, but cracks soon began to appear. The Stanford Twenty20-for-20 was never about the three hours of action, it was always about the money, but it was a concept that the England players had trouble with from the start. Aware that the British economy was collapsing by the day, they seemed frightened to seize the opportunity to be dollar millionaires and in the build-up to the game got distracted by talk about the money, the conduct of Allen Stanford and the facilities at the ground. Pietersen admitted afterwards his team had not been thinking solely about cricket, a damning indictment of their preparation and a subtle dig at the coach. In the aftermath of defeat, it was to Vaughan that Pietersen turned, not Moores. He flew to Vaughan's holiday home in Barbados to discuss where England had gone wrong. It was the former Test captain, not Moores, who had become Kevin's chief counsellor and guide.

It was in India that things really started to unravel. England were on the wrong end of a walloping in the one-day series, sliding to a 5-0 defeat as India's army of explosive batsmen found new ways to bludgeon England's bowlers to smithereens. Pietersen felt he was not being given sound enough advice from the expensively assembled England backroom staff and outlined his concerns to Morris for the first time during the one-dayers. The murderous attack on Mumbai, the cricketing capital of India, averted the possibility of a humiliating 7-0 shellacking, but leadership of a different kind was now required from England's captain. Despite the threat of further atrocities Pietersen was brave enough to encourage his team to resume their tour of the subcontinent. Key roles were played by Morris and Reg Dickason, the ECB security adviser, but Pietersen undoubtedly showed statesmanlike qualities in insisting that England return to India while other players were more wary, which will be investigated in detail later in the book. It was an extremely demanding situation for Kevin, but his reputation as a leader was much enhanced by the time the entire squad arrived back in India. This was to have a crucial bearing on later events. Emboldened by the praise he received both in England and in India, where he was given a hero's welcome, Pietersen was confident that his power base had increased. "He thought he was untouchable," said the ECB source.

The aura of indestructibility came crashing down within a month. When Pietersen flew back to London on Christmas Eve after an incredibly draining tour, there was little opportunity to put his feet up after the crisis talks that had taken place during the Mohali Test. He had a series of face-to-face meetings at Lord's with Clarke, Collier, Morris and Moores, during which Pietersen made it clear that he felt his relationship with Moores was beyond repair. In one meeting with Morris and Collier, names of a replacement coach were even discussed. Pietersen nominated Graham Ford, the Kent and former South Africa and Natal coach, who had been such a big influence on his own career. Kevin was not involved in selecting the touring party for the trip to the West Indies starting in late January, but he lobbied strongly for Vaughan to be included as one of the specialist batsmen at the expense of either Ian Bell or Owais Shah before flying to his native South Africa for a sailing and surfing holiday with his wife, Jessica Taylor. Moores spoke out against Vaughan at a highly charged meeting that went on for five-and-a-half hours later that day. When the tour party was announced on 29 December, the names of Shah and Bell were in it. Vaughan's was absent. Pietersen and Vaughan are in regular phone contact and Kevin's response was to call his friend and apologise.

On New Year's Eve, Pietersen sent the strategy email that had been requested. The language he used was as withering as his treatment of the world's bowlers. Kevin wrote: 'I can't lead this team forward to the West Indies if Peter Moores is coach.' Twenty-four hours later, Pietersen's desire to force out Moores became public knowledge in an article in the *Daily Telegraph*. The story, headlined 'England captain Kevin Pietersen in ECB crisis talks over coach Peter Moores', had been evidently leaked. Although the *Telegraph* ran the exclusive story on the front page of their pull-out sports section, the paper could not be accused of over-playing it, nor were the facts completely right. 'It is not inconceivable that [Pietersen] could issue an ultimatum to the board,' it said. Pietersen had already done so in his inflammatory 'it's me or him' email to Collier and Morris.

Given that only two parties were aware of the contents of the email, the leak could only have come from the ECB, Pietersen or someone closely acquainted with Pietersen to whom he had relayed its general details. The ECB vehemently deny it was them. Pietersen swears it was not him. Privately, all parties are certain that the source was Vaughan, a *Telegraph* columnist, despite his subsequent denials. "It was an emotional response to not being picked," said one insider. "Vaughan though it would help to get rid of Peter Moores."

It would prove to be a massive misjudgement. What Pietersen and Vaughan had not grasped was that they felt more strongly about Moores' methods than those who had not been Test captains and worked as closely with the coach. In his email, Pietersen had said: 'The whole of the team think he is no good. The whole of the team want him to go.' Never one for half measures, he wanted Moores' assistant coach Andy Flower and other support staff removed as well. A more diplomatic man would have gently sown the seeds of discontent. Pietersen planted the entire contents of the garden at the ECB's door.

The ECB's reaction to the *Telegraph* story, which was swiftly followed up in all the cricket press (although some papers chose to focus, wrongly, on the angle that Pietersen wanted Moores out because Vaughan had not been selected), was not to comment on it publicly in the hope that it would go away or, at the very least, dampen the flames. They were briefing cricket correspondents that it was not true but their failure to issue an on-the-record statement of denial was interpreted in some quarters as an admission of its veracity. At this stage, Morris was still hoping to broker a truce between the captain and coach. He spoke to Moores in person and rang Pietersen while he was on holiday in Africa on 3 January.

But Pietersen helped to write his own death warrant. Three days after the story appeared in the *Telegraph*, he became the first party involved to speak on the record about it, via his column in the *News of the World*. Ostensibly, the quotes were not especially revelatory – 'Obviously this situation is not healthy, we have to make sure it is settled as soon as possible' – and Pietersen did not refer to Moores by name, but his words put the story right back to the top of the agenda. The ECB could not legitimately deny the story any longer.

A few critics have subsequently claimed that the ECB were just as much to blame as Pietersen, for allowing the column to pass through its censors unaltered. Yet the governing body's power to vet player columns is only a partial one. The arrangement between the powerful Professional Cricketers' Association and the ECB is that the players, or more typically their agents, are sent the column or quotes by the ghostwriter and then it is emailed to Lord's. The ECB were understood to be 'concerned' about Pietersen's comments and notified the player's agent, Adam Wheatley, of their apprehension. This was either disregarded by Wheatley, thinking the quotes were relatively tame, or not outlined in strong enough terms by the ECB, who do not have the power to censor columns, as dictated by central contracts. Pietersen was clearly not blameless. Michael Vaughan was smart enough to relinquish his lucrative column with the *Daily Mail* soon after taking over the England captaincy. Pietersen, whose deal with the *News of the World* is worth £100,000-a-year, was not.

The ECB top brass were 'dismayed' by the manner in which Pietersen had added fuel to the fire and recognised they had to act decisively. During the pre-Christmas tour to India, Pietersen had revealed his problems with Moores to four senior players, firstly Strauss and Collingwood, the pair he was closest to, and later Flintoff and Harmison. He claimed they all pleaded with him not to resign as England captain. Morris checked the accuracy of these claims on the same Sunday that Pietersen's column was published. He did not speak to all of the England players, just a coterie of the senior citizens – believed to be Strauss, Collingwood, Flintoff, Harmison and Alastair Cook – as well as those same members of the backroom staff that Pietersen clearly didn't rate, Andy Flower et al. The message that came back from the players was two-fold. "They said, 'Pietersen was probably right to argue Peter Moores was not good enough to be our coach,' but they also said, 'Pietersen doesn't have the skill set to be our captain,'" said the ECB source.

Morris spoke to Pietersen again on the Sunday but found him unwilling to give any ground, not surprisingly for a man who, in the words of Ford, "doesn't take a step backwards for anyone". Morris knew he had to step carefully with the combative Pietersen. "The absolute priority was to keep him in the team," added the source. If Moores was expendable, Pietersen the batsman was not. When Morris reported back to Collier and Clarke, the feeling was that Pietersen, for all the promise he had shown as a captain and the leadership he had displayed in taking the team back to India, could not be allowed to do what no England skipper had done before and effectively sack his immediate boss. By the Monday, Clarke was letting it be known that the ECB were now considering not just one position, but two.

It didn't help Pietersen's cause that he was issuing ultimatums from 6,000 miles away. He was not aware of the mountain of media coverage in England that had been afforded to his rift with Moores. Day after day, it was dominating the back pages of the newspapers. The story had legs and it was out of his control. Pietersen was scheduled to attend a meeting at Lord's on Thursday, January 8, the day he was due to arrive back in London, but the ECB were not prepared to wait. The time for bridge-building had passed.

On the Tuesday evening, Morris called a teleconference of the 12-man executive board to tell them he was proposing to remove both Pietersen and Moores. Support was strong among the 10 members who joined the hastily-convened conference call (two were unavailable). There was no disagreement. English cricket has been run by committees for generations and the feeling of this one was that a single opinionated interloper, no matter how supremely talented, could not just march in and demand root-and-branch reform after just three Tests at the helm.

Pietersen did not see the axe falling. He was at his parents' home in the leafy Durban suburb of Westville that evening with his mother, father, eldest brother Tony and his brother's three children when Morris phoned to say the ECB had accepted his resignation at an emergency board meeting. "I said, 'Excuse me?' They said, 'We've accepted your resignation,'" recalled Pietersen. "I said 'on what basis has it been accepted?' They had no answer. Next, I received an email from the ECB saying, 'Your resignation is of immediate effect'." Pietersen was not even aware that he had tendered his resignation, but the ECB's lawyers had assured Morris that the wording of his email strategy amounted to the same thing. His reaction was more of shock and despondence than anger. Pietersen took 20 hours to confirm his 'resignation'. But he swiftly texted friends and team-mates with news of his imminent departure. It is believed that one of these contacts then informed Sky TV, who broke news of the double-departure the next morning. Just over an hour before Strauss was unveiled as the new England captain at the Oval, Pietersen issued a defiant statement saying he was standing down even though he felt he had 'much more to offer as captain'.

Had he not made such a radical proposal coated in such forthright language in his email strategy, Pietersen would probably still be in a job. Had he played the political game more sensitively and made more diplomatic noises about how he viewed Moores' abilities, he would still be in a job. Had the ECB acted decisively when the story broke and insisted that Pietersen came back to London to thrash out the various issues, he would probably still be in a job.

Pietersen had not aided his own cause. Aside from his email, Pietersen was guilty of three mistakes – his friends being indiscreet; going on the record in the *News of the World*; and being in the wrong place at the wrong time as the story spiralled out of control. He had also been poorly advised. It would surely have made sense for Pietersen to have aborted his African holiday while the captaincy crisis escalated and returned to Britain with his wife, who was to appear in ITV's Sunday night entertainment show *Dancing On Ice*.

Nevertheless, the admission by Dennis Amiss – the ECB's vice-chairman – that Pietersen was forced to resign on the convenient pretext that he lacked the support of the senior players was depressing. As was the concession that once the information was in the public domain that the captain wanted the coach out, it was going to be impossible to resolve amicably. "His position was untenable because of the media coverage," said the source. "When he saw the press coverage he had to resign. He accepted that he had to go."

Although Pietersen verbally assured Morris of his long-term commitment to England, an especially thorny issue because his central contract had not been signed at the time and he could have operated as a freelance and thrown himself into the full six-week Indian Premier League programme during April and May, the ECB wisely recognised the need to cushion the blow for their most prized asset. Lord's arranged for private security and armed guards to protect Pietersen from the media hordes when he arrived at Heathrow Airport via Durban and Johannesburg. They also laid on a chauffeur-driven private car to whisk the former captain to his home in Chelsea. By luck, rather than judgement, English cricket had kept the best batsman in the team and were able to appoint the man they now felt was best equipped to be captain – Strauss. Pietersen's era as England captain had been too explosive for a governing body that is still utterly conservative in its nature. Pietersen had been too much for the ECB to handle.

AFRICAN BOY

KEVIN PIETERSEN IS A man of contradictions. Widely misunderstood yet exceptionally uncomplicated. Incredibly confident yet deeply insecure. Popular yet disliked. Cocky yet humble. Fiercely loyal yet castigated as a traitor. Tall and strapping yet possessed of a thin, reedy voice that wouldn't be out of place in a kindergarten. He is the African boy who stabbed three lions on his bicep and became unequivocably the most riveting cricketer to have played for England in the modern era, and perhaps ever.

His cricket career has been extraordinary, characterised by fierce clashes with hierarchy, immense achievement and the growth of a mostly unmerited reputation for being a monster of egotism. It is true, however, that Pietersen does not quite fit in with people around him. He seems to lack a number of the familiar traits and opinions you would expect to find in a true blue Englishman, never more apparent than in his very un-English chutzpah and all-embracing self-belief.

The reason for this is simple. Pietersen is not now, nor has ever been, an Englishman. He might have English blood in his veins, but he is not an Englishman through and through. To be six foot four and carry yourself as if you were ten foot four makes you noticeable among the English; a society that tends to discourage any kind of Billy big-time immodesty. No-one has ever accused Pietersen of modesty, however. And even from a distance, you cannot mistake Pietersen for a run-of-the-mill anybody.

He was born in South Africa, the son of an English lady and an Afrikaner man. Kevin Pietersen may stand out amongst his English peers, but his upbringing was typical among white South African boys. It was a strict, religious childhood spent mostly outdoors. As a boy, Kevin, like all of the Pietersen offspring, was required to speak only Afrikaans on Wednesdays. On Sundays they attended church twice, once in the morning and again in the evening. They said grace at every meal. If the boys misbehaved, they were caned with an army stick by their father.

"That's the way kids are brought up in South Africa and I think it's fantastic," Pietersen told the *Observer* in 2006. "Discipline is good. It taught me that I didn't have to have what I wanted; that what I needed was different from what I wanted. If you were naughty, you were punished. There was none of this 'sit on a step and cry your eyes out'. Clout. Job done."

If the Pietersen boys got out of line at school, they would be disciplined by their teachers – caning was still allowed in South African schools in those days – and again by their father when they got home. When Kevin bunked off school to watch the 1992 Cricket World Cup on television with his mates, he was caned at school and, when his mother quizzed him about some marks on his back when he had a bath that evening, he was subsequently caned again by his father. "I can honestly say it didn't do me any harm," Kevin said. "It grounded me and my brothers well. I respect Dad for the way he disciplined us and I think caning should still be allowed now."

He was raised in Pietermaritzburg, which was then the capital of the province of Natal, and which later shared its post-apartheid title as capital of the (newly created) province of KwaZulu Natal with Ulundi. Pietermaritzburg's capital city status is slightly misleading. With a population of 230,000, it is completely overshadowed by Durban, South Africa's third-largest city and a thriving industrial centre, which is an 80 kilometre drive south along the speedy N3 freeway. British author Tom Sharpe, who lived in Pietermaritzburg during the 1950s, described the city as "half the size of a New York cemetery and twice as dead". It is more notorious for being the location where Mahatma Gandhi was forced to leave a whites-only train carriage in 1893 in a humiliating incident which became the source of his embrace of passive resistance.

Although founded by Boers, Pietermaritzburg has strong British connections, evident today in the splendid late Victorian architecture in the heart of the city. It is an area dominated by fine period buildings, none grander than City Hall, which, built in 1893, is the largest red-brick building in the southern hemisphere. Wander through these streets by day, as I did, and, when the sun isn't shining, you could almost be in a spa town in England. It is easy to see why it is jokingly referred to as The Last Outpost of the British Empire by South Africans.

Pietersen grew up at a time when the winds of political change were sweeping through the country. With the abolition of apartheid in 1993, the days of white rule were numbered even though Pietermaritzburg was less affected by the change of government than most places as it had been a liberal city and not a stronghold of the National Party. Not that the young Kevin was a particularly keen student of politics or current affairs. "The changes that occurred in the country were huge, but when it was all happening, the enormity of it passed me by to an extent," he said.

KEVIN PETER was born on 27 June, 1980, the third of four boys. The Pietersen parents converged from neighbouring continents and similar working class backgrounds. His mother Penny was born in Canterbury in Kent, moved to Lancashire when she was five, grew up as a Bolton schoolgirl and emigrated with her family to South Africa when she was 18. Her own father, Norman, a coal miner, had got a job working in the local mines. Penny later met her Dutch-born Afrikaner husband, Jannie, while he was in the army in Pretoria doing his national service. Kevin's maternal grandfather had been an ardent England cricket fan, but did not live to see his grandson play international cricket.

To be born white in Pietermaritzburg in the second half of the 20th century was a fortuitous accident of birth. In what had emerged as a pleasant if somewhat commercial city, life was mostly comfortable. There is an atmosphere of general prosperity, which is far removed from the strife and disorder – some might say, excitement – of larger settlements. For the Pietersens, it was especially comfortable. Jannie was a director of a civil engineering firm and worked long hours to support his family. Kevin's formative years were spent in a generous sized 1970s style bungalow in an affluent Pietermaritzburg suburb. Like many homes in the more desirable parts of South Africa, it had an enormous back garden, nearly an acre in size, and a large swimming pool.

Kevin's competitive instinct was honed by hours and hours of sport played in these spaces against elder brothers Tony and Gregg and younger sibling Bryan (Penny, it seems, got her way in the naming of the children as all four boys were given English names). He led an outdoor life from an early age, swimming competitively with his brothers in the family's pool and throwing himself into sport all year round. At school, he would mainly play cricket, rugby and athletics. At home, it was a case of anything goes. The boys would watch Wimbledon on television, grab their rackets, draw up a court in the garden and play tennis. After the FA Cup final, they would kick a football around. They would devise triathlon routes around the neighbourhood and race one another. Squash was also a major sport in the Pietersen household. Jannie and Penny both played to a high standard and Pietersen pere would take the third of his sons with him when he played squash with friends. There, with a squash racket, the infant Kevin revealed his outstanding co-ordination of eye, hand and wrist. "Kevin would sit watching me with my headband around his head, my wristbands on and hitting a squash ball against the wall. He had amazing hand-eye co-ordination for one so young," recalled Jannie. "You could give Kevin the biggest present in the world on his birthday, but it wouldn't have the same impact as giving him a ball."

A true outdoor childhood, one in which every day can be spent roaming in a T-shirt and pair of shorts, is one that the average Brit, used to a dreary climate, might find difficult to comprehend. It was almost impossible not to be vigorous and sporty; there was so much opportunity to be outdoors playing sports, and little time for anything else. It was something the Pietersen boys, who often needed only each other as opponents, took as a natural part of life. A sunny climate and living in a green belt area surrounded by fields and forests could only encourage a healthy lifestyle. Even school and church were seen as opportunities to play more sport. 'I didn't truly know the meaning of religion at this time – to me, church was fun,' wrote Pietersen in his 2006 autobiography. 'Church meant mixing with friends and it meant begging Mum and Dad for us to be allowed to go to church early because we could then play a game of football beforehand.' Pietersen is no longer a churchgoer, but he remains a believer. His eldest brother, Tony, is a minister in Waterfall, a quaint, hilly town near Durban.

Tony and Gregg were always regarded by those who knew the Pietersen family as the more upright characters, cautious and noble like their father. By contrast, Kevin and Bryan were considered the 'rough diamonds'. The relationship between the brothers was always good. The only times they ever had words or fights was when they argued about who scored which try or whether someone was out or not. Kevin looked up to Tony and Gregg, in particular, and they were strong and likeable role models who took pride in their little brother's successes. The two older brothers are also 'big units', like their father. As a youngster, Kevin learned to watch his back. When his parents closed their eyes to say grace at meal times, Tony and Gregg would try to nick the sausages – or whatever – from Kevin's plate. He soon learned to stand up for himself.

Kevin's manic desire to win was fostered by his father. Jannie was not worried about his sons – who were each separated by two school years – knocking lumps out of one another. Indeed, he actively encouraged it. "One of my principles was that the boys should try to win," he said. "They had to work extremely hard if they wanted my full support. My message was that the boys had to be self-motivated, and if they were, they would kick me into gear also." From a young age, Kevin's enthusiasm for sport was characteristically relentless and competitive. That driving impulse to win – to be the best, to play the game hard and well and often, to practise repeatedly, to think carefully and cleverly about strategy and technique – was always there. Penny believes Kevin stood out from his brothers in that, although not talent-wise. "All the boys were similar in ability at sport when they were young, but Kevin had the greater heart for it," she recalled. "He was always in there to win. He would walk though a brick wall to get what he wanted, but was never overbearing. He would come in from school, get changed, get something to eat, do his homework and then grab a bat and ball and go out to play. He took control of his own life."

Kevin's junior school was Clarendon, which he attended between the ages of five to eight. It was here that he first came into contact with Graham Ford, who became a big influence on Pietersen before carving out a top-class career for himself as a coach with Natal, South Africa and Kent, finding himself in contention for the vacant post of coach of the England national cricket team as this book went to print. Ford, who also hailed from Pietermaritzburg, was then a sports master at Clarendon, which concentrated on athletics and swimming rather than cricket. "He was one of the guys who stood out, even though he was just a little pip at junior school," says Ford. "Even at that age, you could see his competitiveness, particularly as a swimmer. He was a very good swimmer and wanted to be first all the time. He was one of those guys who was not shy of getting stuck in and doing the hard work. I didn't coach him at that stage, but you could really see he had the desire and drive."

Digby Rhodes, the father of Jonty Rhodes and who was headmaster at Clarendon when Kevin was a pupil there, does not have 'cricket memories' of Pietersen at that stage, but recalls an unruly nature. "Kevin was quite a hellion," says Rhodes. "I wouldn't say he was a vindictive boy, but he knew what he wanted and knew his own mind, very much so. You know how young children look at something and say they want it? He would just go after it. He prepared his path of what he wanted and made sure he got it."

Jannie Pietersen, the disciplinarian Afrikaner, did not believe in spoiling his children. What rewards the boys got, they had to earn. While their friends would strut around in Nike trainers and Patrick boots, the Pietersens would have to make do with more modest footwear. All pleas to their parents for upgrades would fall on deaf ears. Jannie had a saying that he would drum into his sons, 'Buy what you need, not what you want'. Kevin had to wait to receive his first cricket bat. His father wanted him to earn it. "Money was never wasted and I never had anything fall at my feet," said Pietersen. "I remember my Dad promising me my first cricket bat when I scored my first 50, and it came when I was eight, playing against ten-year-olds, when I was being coached by Digby Rhodes. Off we went to King Sports and I proudly purchased my first Duncan Fearnley colt bat."

Kevin had begun to play in organised games towards the end of his time at Clarendon, even though cricket had always been second best to swimming up until that point. He started to take the sport more seriously at Merchiston, the all-boys primary school that the Pietersen brothers attended from 8 to 13. Merchiston is a semi-private state school where fees for non-boarders, as the Pietersens were, are around 12,000 rand (£800) a year. Established in the late 19th century, it has strong academic and sporting traditions and has been a breeding ground for generations of Natal and South Africa sportsmen. And one adopted Englishman. The facilities are excellent. Nestled in its sweeping grounds are half a dozen sports pitches and the premier pitch by the main building even has floodlights and hosts non-schools fixtures. In Britain it would be unthinkable for a state primary school to have a proper, floodlit cricket ground. When I visiedt in early December, the last day before the boys broke up for their six-week summer holiday, the cricket-mad pupils were having throw-downs from their coaches in the nets, as Pietersen would have done 15 years previously. Dave Beetar, who is now the headmaster, knows Kevin from when he was rank-and-file teacher who coached the school's Under-11s team. He recalls: "I had two seasons with him. Kevin was a chap in your team that you needed. He was an outstanding cricketer and had huge talent. You couldn't afford him to be sick or unavailable. He was very competitive, a real driving force, but he wasn't one of the top dogs. Kevin was always there, not a late bloomer so much – the talent and ability was there – but it came later in life for him. There were other boys who stood out more at that stage. His contemporaries were hugely talented."

The best athlete at Merchiston every year is honoured with a place on the magnificent oak board in the school assembly hall. Among the winners of the prestigious 'Sportsman of the Year' title are Jonty Rhodes (1982), his brother Clinton Rhodes, who also played first-class cricket (1984), and Grant Rowley (1991), who was older than Pietersen and would become one of his best friends. The winner in Kevin's final year at the school in 1993 was Matthew Cairns, a gifted cricketer and rugby player who would play a lead role in the Pietersen story. None of the Pietersen brothers, super sporty though they were, made it to the honours board, which reiterates the calibre of the place. Rob Fuhri, head coach of Melchiston cricket academy and a former coach of the school's Under-9s and Under-10s sides, says: "This is an unbelievable school with very talented kids and Kevin was just a normal Merchiston schoolboy. He did play for the first team here, although I would never have thought he would become what he has."

Kevin made his mark in other ways. "He wasn't scared to let the rip on the field," says Beetar. "The aggro was there. Adversity was a huge driving force for him. That has always been him. If he wasn't selected as an opener or number three, his attitude was: 'I'll show you what for'. That's one thing about Kevin that hasn't changed. He can put his money where his mouth is."

It was an attitude that didn't always endear him to others. Even at such a young age, Pietersen dealt in confrontation. "He was always at loggerheads with people," adds Fuhri. "What always struck me was he had his own character, his own personality and did things his own way. I don't think he has ever done things different to that. KP is his own man. He was always like that. He was self assured. Why must he fit into a little box?"

Though not especially tall for his age, Kevin carried himself in a way that put some noses out of joint. He had a bit of a strut. "Sometimes in the way he walked around people could think he was cocky," says Beetar. "He had a proud walk, which can be misconstrued. His father walked the same and so did his brothers."

Yet Pietersen was no cocky loner. "Kevin was fiercely loyal and had a strong core of friends and strong family ties," confirms Beetar.

What Pietersen could always be guaranteed was the close support of his family. Jannie, Penny and the four boys were "extremely close-knit", according to Beetar and, despite the sporting rivalry that was actively encouraged, there was also genuine delight in one another's successes. If they were not competing, then they would invariably be cheering one another on. Kevin's parents threw themselves into all aspects of their children's lives. Penny was on the mother's committee at Clarendon and Jannie was chairman of the board of governors at Merchiston, where he was remembered as very hands-on. "I knew his parents well," says Rhodes, who still teaches full-time at Merchiston. "They did a lot for the school. Penny was extremely active and I remember Jannie on the sidelines at sports events being very supportive and encouraging all the time." Every weekend for the Pietersen parents became a pilgrimage, criss-crossing the country by car and plane in pursuit of trophies and the joy of the game. "For a while our lives revolved around the boys' sport," said Jannie. "I remember clearly one weekend flying to Johannesburg to watch Gregg swim and then flying down to Port Elizabeth to watch Bryan swim in different championships. Meanwhile, Penny stayed behind to watch Kevin and Tony in what they were doing. It was very important to the boys for us to be there and that sort of weekend was typical for us."

Academically, Pietersen was above average at primary school. Even at what is commonly regarded as one of Pietermaritzburg's finest prep schools, he was a good scholar. Rather than differentiate between A to E grades, Merchiston would fast-track the A grade boys and call them 'express', so as not to stigmatise the lower achievers. Pietersen was in the top 25 per cent who formed the 'express' group. However, Charles Griffiths, a teacher at the school since 1981, maintains Kevin did not stick in the memory for either his academic or cricket skills. "I remember all the Pietersen boys as swimmers. Kevin was a normal young boy. He didn't stand out as being a trouble-maker or brilliant sportsman or brilliant academic."

In many ways, the young Kevin was characterised partly by great sporting potential and partly by his sheer ordinariness. Greatness was a long way away. And, for this son of Africa, it would not come easily.

LATE DEVELOPER

THERE ARE MANY CRICKETERS who step onto the up escalator at schoolboy level and make serene, inevitable progress to international level. Their talent is never in question. The transitions are all seamless; from schoolboy to club cricketer, from Under-19s to county or state pro, from representative sides to Test matches. It is all laughably easy. So is their progress in authority; school captain, Under-19s captain, county or state captain . . . international captain. Mike Atherton was one who followed this path in the modern era. David Gower another. Ricky Ponting, Brian Lara, Hansie Cronje and Graeme Smith did the same in their respective countries. For them, it was just a matter of time. Their worth was vividly apparent for all to see. They were the chosen, appointed and annointed ones.

There are other cricketers who clamber to the top of the escalator step by agonising step. It is a precarious journey and each stage conquered is a kind of triumph over the doubters, a victory for the cricketer's strident inner determination to show 'em all that he really is the best. He has to show John Wayne-style true grit and a never-say-die attitude merely to make the grade.

Kevin Pietersen's journey through high school cricket was like this. It was a painful one. At times it felt as if he had to climb the escalator with his teeth. Not for him the ease of belonging that comes to the gifted few. He had to scrap and fight for recognition and then scrap and fight some more. To paraphrase Shakespeare, some are born great and others have greatness thrust upon them. Pietersen had to work at achieving greatness.

With sport ingrained in the very fibre of the Pietersens, Kevin could not have hoped for more inspiring surroundings with which to pursue his love of cricket than Maritzburg College. Established in 1863 soon after Pietermaritzburg had been converted from a Boer village into a Victorian market town by the British colonists, the school has grown in both size and reputation to become one of the finest of its type in Natal, if not in South Africa. Ostensibly a state school, as the South Africa government pays the wages of half of the 60 full-time teachers (the parents pay the other half), it has the traditions, facilities and academic, cultural and sporting achievements of the very best private school.

Maritzburg College oozes history. You can feel it as you turn from College Road into the wooded school grounds, up the winding driveway, through the security guard-manned barrier and round to the immaculate lawns that surround the magnificent red-brick front buildings. Wander around the main reception and there are dozens of photographs charting the school's history and ornate honours boards listing its finest sportsmen and academics from each year. A conference room just a few giant Pietersen strides from the front desk, known as the 'hearth', is a kind of shrine to the most decorated modern-day sportsmen to have trod the school's squeaky clean corridors. Among the framed shirts and pictures of famous old boys, the centrepiece of one wall is a signed Pietersen shirt (XL and emblazoned with his initials and Test match number – 626) from the 2005 Ashes-winning series. To the left, in homage to Pietersen's stunning century at The Oval, is a billboard from the regional paper, *The Witness*, which states in capital letters: 'College Old Boy Wins The Ashes'. This is a school that celebrates its heroes. And there have been many. Phenomenally, Maritzburg College has produced more than 180 international sportsmen – believed to be the most by a single South African school – including 23 South Africa captains, two in cricket (HG Deane and Jackie McGlew), and, of course, one England cricket captain, plus statesmen, soldiers and the renowned liberal Alan Paton, who wrote *Cry, the Beloved Country*. Yet amidst all the grandiose architecture and nostalgia there is a sense of purpose and confidence about the place which the less fortunate might regard as arrogance. Kevin Pietersen fitted in well.

Generations of Pietermaritzburg's brightest, sportiest and luckiest children have made the two-mile journey from Merchiston to Maritzburg College. It was never in question that Kevin would follow his two older brothers Tony and Gregg – as would younger sibling Bryan – and do the same. He was born a white South African, part of the country's elite, even at this crossroads in its history, and his father worked hard to give the four boys the best possible education. Fees at the school are not cheap by South Africa standards – 19,000 rand (£1,250) a year for a day scholar – but inexpensive compared to the country's elite private schools, which charge around 130,000 rand (£8,500) for a boarder. Although the balance of power between the white colonists and the black natives was beginning to alter before Pietersen went to high school it would be some time before the changes would filter down to the younger South Africans. Apartheid officially ended when Pietersen was 13. Clarendon and Merchiston, his first two schools, had been whites-only (as were his first visits to the beach, journeys on public transport and so on) and there were only a smattering of non-European faces during his four years at Maritzburg College. "I don't hate anybody, but this was a system that was in place as I was growing up, something that thankfully is now a thing of the past in South Africa," said Pietersen. "By the time I was getting older the races started to mix together. It goes without saying that no-one should be treated differently because of the colour of their skin, but when you're young you don't really question the system you are growing up in. I guess you are brainwashed to an extent, but then things started to change. It was odd at first to see non-European faces around us. That's how unnatural the system was." He had black friends outside, and later, inside, school.

Jonty Rhodes, another Merchiston and Maritzburg College old boy, was head boy in 1987, captained the cricket first X1 for two years and set batting records that still stand today. He says: "As white boys growing up in South Africa we were quite privileged. We were given opportunities that were not given to the black boys. Maritzburg was a normal college, but the facilities were amazing given that it was a government school. We took all this for granted. My days at school were awesome. Maritzburg College has a great tradition and a lot of guys had strong family ties to the school. Because of the tradition in the school you could find youngsters to come to the nets with you and help you with your cricket, although in those days there were no turf nets – we had to practise on concrete."

Pietersen arrived at College, as his seat of learning is generally called, in 1993 as a fine all-round athlete and loved it from the off. He had represented Natal Schools at rugby, squash and cross-country running and particularly excelled at swimming, in which he had represented the province through the age groups. As with Michael Owen at football, Pietersen acknowledges the advantage of having two older brothers to drag up his own performance. But at high school, aged 13, he was forced to concentrate on just two sports. College policy is that each pupil chooses one winter sport and one summer sport. Kevin opted for cricket and rugby. He was a natural at both, as a nippy full-back noted for his kicking skills in rugby and an all-rounder, particularly proficient bowling off-spin, in cricket, and preferred the camaraderie of team sports to the more lonely individual pursuits at which he was equally proficient.

Yet his development was stunted by two factors out of his control. He had suffered a serious accident when he was 12, falling off a climbing frame and breaking his arm. It took a long time to heal and when it did, he broke it again in exactly the same place while playing rugby. When there were complications in the healing process, doctors decided to break the arm for a third time. The result was that hyperactive, sports-mad Kevin spent over six months on the sidelines. His progress was also hindered by his misfortune that he was one of the youngest in his school year. Born on 27 June, he made the cut-off date by just three days. In those days, the school year began on 1 July. It has since been changed to 1 January. This meant that Pietersen was always playing catch up. Mike Bechet, College's forthright, long-time Director of Sport whose duties include coaching the first cricket X1, says: "He didn't set the world alight through the age groups. Not as a batsman or as a bowler. He was young for his year, which put him at a disadvantage."

Pietersen didn't play a great deal of organised cricket through his teens. Unlike a British cricket-mad youngster, there was no junior or colts cricket to hone his game as only the senior boys were allowed to play in club games. He would play around 13 games a year split between the two summer terms and although he was always in the College 'A' teams through the age groups, there was no thought of fast-tracking him into the first team. Indeed, extraordinary as it may seem in hindsight, Pietersen's progress lagged behind many of his schoolmates in his mid-teens. "In the second to last year he was playing Under-16," says Bechet. "Most of his peers in the same grade were in the open division of age groups playing second or first team cricket."

Maritzburg College has an excellent reputation for cricket and the standard of the schoolboys was high. Fifty-over or timed games would be played on Saturdays against most of the country's best schools. Rivalry between schools and among team-mates was intense, with competition for places fierce. Because of College's reputation as a sporting school, their opponents put in a huge amount of preparation during the weeks leading up to their games, often considering the match the highlight of their sporting year. This meant that almost every weekend the College boys would have to face psyched-up opponents, and there was no room for making mistakes.

It was the dream of every cricket player in the school to make the first team and receive the cherished red, black and white striped cap. Even better was to play at Goldstone's, the immaculate first X1 ground and the jewel in the crown of College's dozen pitches. With its manicured oval overlooked by steep trees, modern two-tiered pavilion and rows of US High School-style benches on the grass bank to the side of the square it is an exceptional facility in which to play school cricket, far better than most club grounds. The modern fuses with the traditional. Ignore the harsh southern hemisphere sunlight in this oasis of calm and tranquility and you could almost be at an English private school cricket ground, perhaps Eton or Millfield. Yet emblazoned on the fence opposite the pavilion are the names of over 20 sponsors and it is unlikely Eton has a colossal braai, a traditional southern African barbeque, behind the scorebox, large enough to feed an army. Goldstone's draws in big crowds. Hundreds will watch a regulation Saturday match and temporary stands are brought in for one of the eagerly anticipated fixtures against College old boys. Astonishingly, one such game in December 2008, shortly after I visited, drew a crowd of 12,000.

Hard work high standards and a rugged culture are the cornerstones of the school's ethic. A winning culture is bred into the boys, almost surreptitiously. Bechet has decorated the whitewashed walls of the spacious home dressing room with 44 inspirational slogans (I know because I count them), including one entitled 'How we ARE going to be successful' that is adapted from Steve Waugh's autobiography and lists 12 maxims promoting excellence. Other slogans range from the mundane – 'Stay a strong unit and enjoy each other's successes' – to the more motivational – 'The difference between a successful man and others is not a lack of strength, not a lack of knowledge, but rather a lack of will'. Great performances are highlighted. On the inside of the dressing room door is a list of the pupils who have scored a century or taken a five-wicket haul at Goldstone's. There is a Pietersen on the honours board – but it is younger brother Bryan, who took two five-wicket hauls for the first X1 there in 1999 and 2000. Kevin's name is not in evidence. The opposition dressing room is equally spacious, but its walls are completely bare.

It was at Goldstone's that Pietersen played much of his first serious cricket. Somewhat disadvantaged by being so young for his year, Kevin played only half a season in the first X1 in 1997 before matriculating, gaining promotion from the second X1 as a bowling all-rounder only after Matthew Cairns, the team's leg-spinner and a brilliant schoolboy sportsman, emigrated to New Zealand midway through the year. "I thought he was a solid cricketer, a good all-rounder," says Bechet of Kevin. "But I hadn't picked him because in my opinion – and the buck has to stop with the coach – at the time Matthew Cairns was a better spinner than Kevin and had taken more wickets through the age groups."

It was a decision that rankled with Pietersen, who made his feelings clear in his autobiography. 'I was only kept out of the first team because the coach, Mike Bechet, had something against me – or so it seemed to me,' said Kevin. 'It's funny now because he tries to claim me as one of his successes and asks my mum for shirts and things, but I will never have any time for that man. I reckon he showed a real bias towards Matthew Cairns, who was a real teacher's pet. It was only when he emigrated to New Zealand that I finally got my chance in the first team.'

Despite Pietersen's criticism of what he believed was Bechet's failure to recognise his ability, the two never had crossed words at College. Discipline and mutual respect were values drummed into Kevin at home and they were reiterated at school. Bechet would select the team on a Thursday night and pin the X1 on the noticeboard. Omitted players would be called into his office and told why they were not in the team and what they had to do to get back in. Bechet tells me: "Kevin would never knock on the door and say, 'Why am I not in the team?' He wasn't quite as brash when he was a kid because the system doesn't allow you to be like that. There is respect for elders here, good manners. I'm sad the school's not in session here at the moment because when you walked up to my office you would have to have said, 'Good morning' 200 times. Everyone would have said, 'Morning sir' to you. And if you had got out of your car there, someone would have come up to you and said, 'Morning sir, can I help you?' We are a traditional school."

Although Pietersen couldn't make the first team at school, he was being monitored closely by Graham Ford, who had moved on to a new job coaching the Natal Colts side and ran age group sessions at the indoor academy for the province's best young players. Pietersen was in his sights. "We invited him to sessions here from when he was about 14," says Ford, speaking in an administrative office at the vast Kingsmead Test ground in Durban. "He showed a lot of talent and we were quite excited about him. The school first team didn't pick him initially, but we still kept him in our squads, so he was in his age group squad for Natal, but wasn't making the school first team. He was in the [Natal] Under-19 squad when he was 16. He operated more as an off-spinner and was one of those we felt could go through to play provincial cricket, although at that stage we didn't think he would achieve what he has managed to achieve. I certainly saw him as a guy who could cut it as a first-class cricketer."

It took Bechet longer to be convinced. The problem was two-fold. College had a strong top six batting line up, including schoolboy star and Kevin's good friend Grant Rowley, and Pietersen was not the awesome ball striker he is today. Far from it. He was tall but weak and, by his own admission, this hindered his batting. The gulf between 16 and 18 seems immense to a schoolboy and Kevin was not one of those teenagers who looked as if he had reached puberty in one effortless bound and become a man overnight. 'I loved my batting, but I didn't have much strength and couldn't hit the ball very far,' he recalled of that time. 'I couldn't hit sixes and could barely hit fours.'

Bechet has a slightly different take on it. Pointing at a photograph of the 1997 College first team, which includes Springbok rugby World Cup-winning fly half Butch James, he says: "I wouldn't say Kevin's physicality held him back at school. He was one of the tallest guys in the team – he was 6ft then. Look at Butch James stood next to him – he is skinny too. But he has got helluva big and strong. You can see he has trained hard. He has always had a very good work ethic. He concentrated at training and practised hard. I can see since he has left here and cricket has become his career that he has gymed a hell of a lot. He is a highly conditioned athlete."

That process had in fact already begun. By the time he turned 17 Pietersen had started to bulk up by working out and having two stints on the muscle-building drink Creatine. As this neatly coincided with Cairns emigrating he was finally granted his chance in the first X1. After so long spent champing at the bit, many teenagers would have been overcome by tension. Not Kevin. He was merely intent on making up for lost time. His debut was against an extremely strong Old Boys X1 coached by Ford and which included a string of Natal first-teamers, including the established opening pair Mark Bruyns and Doug Watson. Pietersen was completely unfazed. Coming on to bowl with Bruyns and Watson in full flight, he completed his 10 overs for a miserly 24 runs and nipped out two wickets, including Bruyns for 130 (out of a total of 228 for 7). "He played against quality players and went for very little," says Ford. "That's when everybody started jumping up and down about his off-spin and saying, 'Gee, this is something special'. The way he walked into that first game for College was, 'No, I'm not intimidated in the slightest'. From our point of view, that showed he had the temperament to play in front of crowds and against bigger names."

In Pietersen's second game, he smashed a quickfire 61 at number seven after College had made tortuous progress for most of their innings. He then bowled 11 overs for 13 runs, taking one wicket, as Pretoria Boys' High School hung on for a draw. Impact had been made.

Kevin continued to make significant contributions in every game with both bat and ball and ended up topping the first team batting averages for the 1997 season and coming fifth in the bowling averages. In 11 first team games, he scored 279 runs at 46.5, including two fifties in the lower middle-order, and took 18 wickets at 17.9 apiece. Cairns, incidentally, topped the bowling averages with 27 wickets at 14.2, but scored just 55 runs in his four innings. DR Jury, the cricket master, wrote this of Pietersen's contributions in his end-of-year 'Critique of First X1 players': 'With the departure of leg-spinner Cairns at the end of the first term, he came into the first X1 and played as if he had been there all season. A talented young all-round cricketer, he finished top of the batting averages, which is something to be proud of at any level of cricket. A disciplined and dedicated batsman, his 61 against Pretoria BHS and 59* against Kearsney were mature innings, the latter placing College in a winning position. As an off-spin bowler, he bowled with intelligence and aggression and his eighteen wickets were of tremendous value to the team. His Natal selections were strongly deserved.'

Bechet's tone was equally measured, and similarly noticeable for its absence of eulogy, in Pietersen's 1997 College co-curricular report, which I have also seen. Bechet wrote of Kevin: 'He forced his way into the 1st X1 in the second half of the season and he put together a string of consistent performances with the bat and the ball. His selection to the Natal Schools A side was most deserved and he was awarded Honours for his efforts.'

The manner in which he grabbed his opportunities by the scruff of the neck was an early indication of Pietersen's ability to resist setbacks. Undoubtedly, this has been helped by his colossal self-belief. "Kevin has always had that," says Bechet. "He has always been an in-your-face cricketer, an in-your-face sportsman. I don't want to use the word 'cocky' in an ugly sense, but he was always confident in his own ability. That's what's got him there. If the side were four wickets down and staring down the barrel it wouldn't worry him. His attitude would be, 'Give me the bat and I'll score the runs.' His personality has always been one of arrogance, which I believe is what you need to be a top class anything. If you haven't got a stop-at-nothing 'I'll show these buggers' attitude, you are not going to cut it in international sport."

What chances Pietersen got, he grabbed with both hands. He quickly burst from nowhere into the Natal schools, South Africa schools and Natal Under-19s sides after scoring an assured 70 in a Natal schools trial. In late 1997 Kevin represented the Natal schools side at the prestigious Nuffield Week in East London, a cricket festival traditionally ripe with talent-spotters. It was during a one-day game that he was watched for the first time by Clive Rice, a towering figure in South Africa cricket who combined being a national selector with a role as chairman of schoolboy selection. Rice says: "When I saw him play, I thought, 'Hang on, I like what I see. Number one, he is an athlete. Number two, I like the way he strikes the ball. Number three, he can bowl and if he works on it, it can happen there as well.' At school he was batting in the lower middle order and wasn't really given the right opportunity, but he could play and I liked what I saw. He could strike the ball so well."

Ford adds: "Ricey asked all sorts of questions about the lad. It was quite an achievement to play for Natal Schools and South Africa Schools and yet not to have been in the school first team for half of the year. We had been quite surprised [he didn't make the team]. We thought he had real ability. But Maritzburg College was a tough first team to get into [with] some really good batsmen, like Grant Rowley who was always churning out runs, so their batting unit was quite settled. Kevin couldn't break in as a batter. So he was competing for a place as a bowler. Unfortunately, I think he should have been competing for a place as an all-rounder."

Bechet is remarkably candid about the mistake he made in failing at first to pick Pietersen. Does he feel he held him back? "No, not at all," he says. "When his book came out, I was criticised by Kevin. It was on page 52, I won't ever forget. It was bugging me, so I got up in the middle of the night and had a look at the school's old book of stats. My wife got up and said, 'What are you doing?' She's a bit of a cricket widow, but knows her cricket. I said to her, 'Look at these stats,' showing her the stats of Kevin and Matthew Cairns from College. 'Which one of these two is the better player?' She said, 'That one,' pointing at Matthew Cairns. My responsibility is to pick the best available eleven at any given time. I don't let personalities get into it. It is about performance, performance, performance. This is a very hard school. There are 1,100 kids here and the most we've had at any one time is 38 teams of eleven players. All the cricketers want to play in the first team. If I had said to Kevin Pietersen in the first term, 'Come and bat number eleven and don't bowl and field fine leg to fine leg', he would have done that because he wanted the striped cap. That's an honour. Everyone wants it. But it would have done nothing for his cricket. At the time I'm very convinced I picked the right guy and I'm very convinced that when I brought Kevin into the side it was the same story. He had done nothing special as an Under-16 cricketer to warrant selection straight into the first team."

Bechet is no mug. He is a legendary figure in local circles, part boot-camp instructor, part mentor and part cricket coach. Sitting in a two-room office crammed with memorabilia and collectibles, from signed shirts and caps – even Pietersen's signed first X1 cap is here – to autographed thank-you notes and posters from famous and not so famous old boys, it is clear that he is a cricket fanatic who is popular among the thousands of boys he has influenced. For many of them he has been both a sporting coach and a coach for life, a massively influential third parent. He did not have that relationship with Kevin. Where perhaps he erred was in pigeonholing Pietersen as a spin-bowling all-rounder. Although Bechet insists he had "a good top order" and "six guys who were better batsmen than him", Pietersen's performances when he was finally promoted proved his worth on both fronts. Indeed, he was one of only four players from College who represented Natal Schools in 1997. The others were batsmen Rowley and E Nel and seam bowler J Piennar.

Nevertheless, it was far from clear yet that Pietersen would waltz into first-class cricket. He had not even scored a hundred during his four years at high school and even his greatest admirers did not see him as a genius-in-the-making. "I had Jonty Rhodes here five years before him and Kevin was nowhere near his standard," says Bechet. "Technically, Jonty wasn't a great player either, but he had a strong mind, lots of guts and belief. Different type of man – people's person, amazing fielder, infectious, smiley, no controversy – probably more humble than Kevin. I didn't see a potential genius at all in Pietersen." To prove the point, he tells me that in 1987 Rhodes scored three hundreds and a 99 in four consecutive games opening the batting. There is a scorebook in a framed box in the Hearth with the page open to a first X1 game on 28 February 1987. Rhodes batted through the innings to compile an unbeaten 162 out of Maritzburg College's 205-5 from 52 overs, which remains the highest individual score at the school. Pietersen was a long way off making such an indelible mark.

Some at College viewed Pietersen as equally adept at rugby although the school was so strong in the sport that he could not break into the first or second XV in his favoured position. Rugby master Mr Whitear wrote of Kevin in his 1997 College co-curricular report: 'A very adept fly-half who excelled at ensuring his forwards played ahead of the gain line. His goal and line kicking was of great benefit to the team. A very valuable member of the side.'

Being good at all sports ate into Kevin's studying time. He was a solid, though not outstanding student. He got a C grade aggregate in his final, matriculation year which put him in the bottom half of the 1997 graduates. Out of 212 boys, 113 got A or B aggregates and 57 got, like Kevin, C aggregates. Pietersen got C grades in Afrikaans, Geography and Maths and Ds in English, Physical Science and Technical Drawing. Ironically, given his early career change of allegiance from the motherland to the land of his mother, his weakest subject in his June 1997 mock examinations was English. 'Kevin does not have natural ability in this subject,' wrote his English teacher, Mrs Clark. Bechet insists that College played a big part in the person that Pietersen is today. He says: "This school is big on leadership and accountability for yourself. You're born with genes, but we can influence attitude. This school is a particularly competitive school. College played a big role in shaping him as a person, I've got no doubt in my mind. Not me. College, the system. There is a pecking order here. You serve time here. You come here, you're nothing. 'You run here, you sprint there. You're not allowed to stand there. Better stand to attention here.' Each year you go through it and get a few more liberties until you get to matric and land. How you land determines what sort of person you are. This school doesn't allow flashiness. That came later."

When school was over, Pietersen had a few options open to him. College wanted him to do post-matric because he was young for his year and there was also talk of him going to university. Pietersen, however, had other ideas.

"As time went on I wanted to play cricket more and more, but never knew if it would lead to a career or not," says Kevin. "When I was 17 I decided to give it a real go and see where it led me." Crucially he had the support of the two most important people in his life: his parents. Penny Pietersen recalled: "He was clever enough to go to varsity, but he wanted to play cricket, so we set him goals and said that if he achieved them he would be able to carry on playing cricket. Each goal we set him, like playing for Natal under-19s while he was 17 and things like that, he achieved, so eventually we said, 'Go for it and see how far you go.'" Ford was impressed by the teenager. "He didn't look for the easy options. Most kids would have settled for another year at school and being the hero. There was no way he was going to go back. He wanted to go into the big world and play proper cricket."

Kevin Pietersen was ready for the big, wide world. Was it ready for him?

FITTING IN

THE JUMP FROM SCHOOL to the real world can be a giant one for those adolescents who do not stroll off to university or embark on a glorious, exploratory period spent travelling the world. Suddenly, they have to get a job and earn money. Life will never be the same again. For some it is an anxious time of self-doubt and self-discovery. For cricketers who have not already been snapped up by a county or state team especially so. Not Kevin Pietersen. He doesn't do navel gazing. He could have gone to university and had a riotous time. He could have stayed on at college for another year and been king of the hill. But Kevin didn't just want to be the high school star. He was aiming far higher than that. Still six months short of his 18th birthday, he had a clearly defined goal. The boy who did not make the Maritzburg College first X1 until the final term wanted to be a professional cricketer and he was prepared to dedicate every ounce of his body into achieving his goal.

It is a measure of Pietersen's reservoir of self-belief that he was not daunted by the size of his task. It is far harder to make the first-class grade in South Africa than it is in England, where there are 18 counties and a pool of around 400 professional cricketers. When Pietersen matriculated there were 11 provinces competing in domestic first-class cricket, although Natal was considered strong enough to field two teams, an A and a B side, which tended to be a mixture of up-and-coming players and seasoned campaigners.

Pietersen was well known to the Natal coaches. He had played for all the age group sides from Under-13s upwards as an off-spinning all-rounder and it was a natural progression from College to the Natal academy, which sounds grander than it actually was. "He wouldn't have earned anything at that stage," says Graham Ford, who left Natal in 1998 after six years as coach to join the national side. "There wasn't a lot of money around at that time. Natal would have contracted about 10 players and a couple of the others would have been pay-as-you-play type contracts. It was semi-professional. Most guys held down jobs and played cricket." Starting on the bottom rung of the ladder was no get-rich-quick scheme. Yet Kevin was fortunate in other ways. By now the Pietersen family were living in the upmarket suburb of Westville, a town about 20 km inland from Durban, in order for Jannie to be closer to work and Kevin was able to live at home without the pressure of bringing in money. Secondly, the academy is based at the iconic Kingsmead stadium in central Durban and the facilities are world-class. There is an indoor cricket school, superbly maintained outdoor nets and, of course, the Test ground itself, a mix of old and modern with its grass banks and steepling stands. It is an inspiring arena and, with the east coast humidity freshened by the breeze from the Indian Ocean, provides ideal conditions in which to play cricket.

Natal also had a squad bursting at the seams with top internationals, which would prove counter-productive in the long-term, but Pietersen turned it to his advantage in the early days. Rubbing shoulders with internationals like Shaun Pollock, Jonty Rhodes, Lance Klusener, Dale Benkenstein, Andrew Hudson, Errol Stewart, the Zimbabwe all-rounder Neil Johnson and the West Indies fast bowler Eldine Baptiste had a beneficial effect on the teenage Kevin. It was a rarified environment in which to learn his trade. Ford explains: "He was pretty smart in watching what the successful guys did and made sure he got out and did the same. I remember he used to spend hours watching Lance Klusener practise. Lance used to spend a lot of hours on the bowling machine hitting balls, practising his ball striking and boundary options and that's what made him such a fine finisher in one-day cricket. Kevin used to watch him and once he had finished his session of about 45 minutes he would go into the bowling machine net and practise what Lance had been practising. Klusener's big thing was, 'Okay, if they're going to bowl to me at the death what are my boundary options and I'm going to practise nailing them.' He would go for hitting straight down the ground and cow corner (deep mid-wicket). Every ball that was bowled at him by the bowling machine he would either hit it straight or cow corner, the two areas that are open on the field. Kevin would go in and practise the same thing."

The nets at Kingsmead provided a tough examination for any young cricketer, even one imbued with as much bravado as Pietersen. "I know it is uncomfortable for young guys coming to the nets at Kingsmead," says Pollock. "The wickets are the bounciest and quickest you are going to get in South Africa and are also quite green, so they are not the easiest to bat on. All the batsmen got tested with the short ball. Kevin would take it on and he got himself in trouble. He was always a confident guy, although probably not as confident as he is now. I remember playing a pre-season game with him. We were chasing 280, he came in at number nine, we got together, had a big partnership and won the game. He could bat, no doubt about it. But you wouldn't guess then he would go on to average 50 in Test and one-day cricket." In fact, Pollock felt that, in his late teens, Pietersen had more potential as a slow bowler. "He came in pretty much as an off-spinner who gave it a bit of a smack down the order. I always thought he had a hell of a future as an off-spin bowler. His action was really good and he got a lot of purchase on the ball. We thought he was going to be a really good spinner."

At Maritzburg College, Pietersen had played alongside Grant Rowley, a batsman a year older than him who he would describe in a GQ interview in 2006 as "a very good mate who is a better player than me". This was not false modesty. Rowley had been everything at school that you would expect Pietersen to have been. He was voted Sportsman of the Year at Merchiston, the prep school both attended, and at College captained the first X1 and opened the batting with great style and success. He was earmarked as a future star. He was the golden boy, the David Gower of his generation, not Kevin. Rowley had stayed on at school for another year so the pair joined the academy at the same time and were among a group of four graduates from College recommended by Natal to Berea Rovers, one of the strongest clubs in the province, based only half a kilometre from Kingsmead. Pietersen and Rowley played league and knockout games at weekends for Rovers while training with the academy during the week and competing for places in the two Natal teams. Wayne Scott, the long-running chairman of Rovers, who is a highly respected cricket figure in the province (South Africa coach Mickey Arthur was the best man at his wedding), says: "We had a good structure with good cricketers and the boys obviously wanted to play with the best. You could see they could play, particularly Grant. They stood out. Grant always had more ability than Kevin. There is no doubt about that. Kevin had to work harder to get where he is. In fact I'd say he tried harder. Kevin would have loved to have been as free-flowing a cricketer as Grant." If this sounds ridiculous when you watch Pietersen rip world-class attacks to shreds today with a repertoire of strokes possibly unrivalled in the game, it was an opinion shared by many shrewd observers at the time. "He left school as a promising cricketer, not really outstanding to be honest," recalls Phil Russell, the former Derbyshire coach who succeeded Ford at Natal. "He had very good hand-eye co-ordination and was a more than average off-spinner at the time." No mention of his batting.

With their similar backgrounds, ages and goals, Pietermaritzburg boys Pietersen and Rowley formed a close bond and began training together. Rowley, a strapping, genial figure possessed of a vigorous handshake, tells me: "We would train in the mornings with Natal four or five days a week and were always the ones who, after the nets, would go indoors with a couple of bags of balls for the bowling machine. We would then come down to Rovers to have a net there, so would sometimes be practising twice a day. On top of that, Kevin would actually go home during the middle of the day and go for runs around where he was living in Westville with his parents. If there was a [formal] Rovers practice, he would go to the Virgin Active gym."

Pietersen didn't just push himself. In a sign that he might be something other than mere footsoldier material, he pushed his mate, too. "I remember there was one run where he left me in the lurch, about 300 or 400 metres behind, and he was pushing himself by shouting at me at the top of his voice and actually motivating me. He was one of those guys who was so driven he would drive other people."

At Natal, Ford devised a pre-season training race around Kingsmead for his players to hone their fitness and competitive edge. Gold, silver and bronze medals would be awarded to first, second and third on the rostrum. "We used to have a circuit which involved running up and down the steps inside the stadium and doing a lap of the ground," explains Ford. "It was a fun competition done in a great spirit and the chaps would try to get a place higher than the previous time. When Kevin joined the squad he used to get the gold medal, which put a few noses out of joint. He would come first most times without a problem." This was no small achievement when you consider he was competing with some serious athletes. Jonty Rhodes was as nimble as a hare and arguably the greatest fielder of all time, while Errol Stewart was a brilliant all-round sportsman renowned for his dedication to fitness. Doug Watson, a South Africa A opening batsman and another Maritzburg College old boy, was tough as teak and as competitive as they come. Watson recalls: "Kevin usually got gold. No-one remembers who came second. There used to be a couple of us who would push him hard. I wasn't the quickest, but I pushed myself and it helped Kevin reach new heights. There was a good rivalry and competition to see who would win the gold medal. It was almost like trying to win gold in the Olympics. You had to strategise and plan when to go flat out and when to hold back. He never wanted to come second. For me to get the gold medal from him I had to shoot him on the start line. That was the same in anything – touch rugby, football – anything he played he always wanted to win. That was the fire he had at that stage. He is 6ft 5in and a hell of an athlete."

The training runs became insanely competitive. Pietersen was so driven to get the gold medal he would do the circuit again in his spare time. Speaking from his office in the second tier of Kingsmead Ford gestures out of the window to the immaculate ground outside and tells me: "The Natal team could be playing here in a match and you would see him come and do the course on his own, making sure he was super, super fit. He practised to win it, but he wanted to be in the best possible shape anyway so he saw that as something beneficial to his fitness. Any fitness work he wanted to be out in front."

Mike Bechet believes Kevin's dedication was moulded partly by his elder brother Gregg. "Gregg was a very good swimmer. I know his mother used to take him to training at 5am every day. Gregg's self-discipline with the swimming might have dropped a pebble in the pond with Kevin." There was also an element of Kevin repaying the faith that had been shown in him and his brothers by their parents, Jannie and Penny. "The parents have given them every opportunity and have supported them in their dreams and quests to be good sportsmen. There has been nothing left untapped. If the kids had to be taken there, fetched here, dropped there, whatever, they have always been very behind their kids. The boys have been very lucky. Their parents are not rich. They've had to work for their success and definitely didn't spoil him. He didn't have four bats and all brand new kit or anything like that. They were a close knit family, the six of them were like this (gesturing togetherness)," Bechet adds.

Pietersen's work ethic was by now impressing some influential observers. "It's what you need if you want to make it in cricket," says Ford. "He was prepared to get out and do the extra, lonely hours on his own. Quite often kids don't mind practising if it's all laid on and set up for them. He was prepared to do it on his own. He had made up his mind to get somewhere and was always going to get there, no matter what. He was extremely self-motivated. He showed real toughness and it certainly helped in his fielding. He would throw himself around. I suppose he had grown up with role models like Jonty, especially having gone to Maritzburg College, where both he and Jonty had come through the system. The fielding aspect, diving, throwing yourself around, being athletic, was what he had grown up with, plus the fact that his father was a rugby player. The backyard battles and scraps with the brothers, obviously he used to take a few knocks and had to be fit and strong to survive. That all contributed. He never, ever allowed any situation to intimidate him." Watson was similarly struck by Kevin's desire. "He is one of the hardest workers I have ever seen. I remember he was fiercely determined to succeed. He trained hard on his fitness and practised hard on his cricket. He would be there on his own hitting balls. I don't know how Graham Ford had a shoulder left the number of throw downs he did."

It was Pietersen's off-breaks, and not his rapidly improving batting, that catapulted him into first-class cricket at the age of 17 in March 1998, beating his mate Rowley by eight months. Astonishingly this was less than six months after Kevin made the College first X1. To put it into context, this was as much to do with the paucity of decent spinners in the province as anything else. South Africa has struggled to produce a decent spinner of note since readmission to the Test arena in 1992 and the cupboard was as bare in Natal as it was everywhere else. Kevin's debut was a fairly uneventful one. Selected for Natal B against Easterns in a three-day game at Kingsmead, the home side had the better of a rain affected match. Pietersen bowled 37 overs in the game, more than any other Natal bowler, and took one wicket, that of Easterns' veteran number three, Craig Norris. Kevin was selected for only one more first-class game over the next year, against Griqualand West B seven months later, which, coincidentally, saw Rowley's debut. Pietersen was promoted to number three, but failed to make the most of this opportunity. Although he followed up his first innings 3 by hanging around for 57 balls in the second innings for a patient 16, he was completely overshadowed by Rowley, who opened the batting and compiled a three-hour half-century, and another former Natal Schools team-mate, Jon Kent, who scored a brace of unbeaten 80s. Kevin's 21 overs with the ball again only yielded a single wicket. "At that stage I saw him as an all-rounder who could bat in the top five," says Ford. "I then got appointed assistant coach for South Africa and before I left there was quite a bit of talk about this all-rounder who could bowl some good off-spin."

During this period, Pietersen was doing most of his bowling in club cricket. Berea Rovers, who competed in Natal's 60-over Premier League, provided the perfect apprenticeship for an aspiring young cricketer. They were a far cry from the hackneyed image of enthusiastic amateurs having a jolly time on the village green before drinking the clubhouse dry. This was a real team imbued with a hard-core competitiveness whose ambitions matched Kevin's. "We were ultra competitive," recalls Scott. "We hated losing. We were the worst losers in the league, I'll be honest about it." This suited Pietersen, who was also in love with the pursuit of excellence. He was whisked straight into the first team, which was then captained by Scott, after leaving school. He started off batting at six, but soon established himself at three or four in a strong top order that included Rowley and Errol Stewart, a seasoned campaigner for Natal and a batsman-wicketkeeper who played six one-day internationals for South Africa. It was here, under Scott's captaincy and guided by the wily Stewart, where Pietersen began turning himself into a truly formidable cricketer. Their ability was enough to win his respect – his own ability had the same effect on his colleagues. "You often find with an out-of-school cricketer that they are scared to give their wicket away and play with great caution. He was totally different," recalls Scott. "Some players would come into bat and say, 'I hope I can get through the first five overs, then the next five and play a few shots.' Kevin was never like that. He had total confidence in his own ability. That first ball, he was going to bang it. He wasn't just going to shoulder arms and let it go through to the keeper. He had the presence about him to always score runs freely within a framework. I'm not talking about hacking. He played good shots. He was never as unorthodox as he is now and not quite as powerful. But one thing that always stood out to me was he backed himself 100 per cent to score runs week in, week out. It might not always happen, but his mindset was so strong. There was total belief."

Pietersen soon began displaying the ferocious batting talent that had lain largely untapped during his high school years. Stewart says: "There was one particular match in which he really caught everybody's eye and he made a huge impression on me. It was a club game in which I batted at number three and he came in a number 4. I was on 60-70-odd when he came to the crease yet he still beat me to a hundred. And I was not a slow batter by any means. I stood at the other end and watched with awe. Let's be honest – club wickets are never the best – but he was unbelievably destructive and the ball disappeared to all parts of the ground. He just hit it so cleanly. It wasn't one particular shot that worked for him on the day. He had a full array of shots. He played in the same way he does now. He was very strong on the leg side, had a fantastic eye and great hands."

For good measure, Pietersen followed up his ton by taking five wickets. "He was invited down to the Natal nets on the back of that performance. I had the ear of the coach Phil Russell at that time and I said to him, 'You should be looking at Pietersen. He has not just produced an incredible display of batting, but bowling as well.' I wouldn't for one second say it was because of what I said, but I like to think it was a catalyst to get him down there. At first-class level he was a late developer, but at club level he produced some excellent performances."

Rowley recalls an even more astonishing Pietersen tour de force. "It was a Castle Cup game at Kingsmead for Rovers. I batted three, he batted four. He got 150 off about 90 balls, some of the best hitting I think I have ever seen. There were two Natal B opening bowlers. He was walking down the wicket to them and pulling short arm jabs into the stands – and they are big boundaries. It was unbelievable to watch. I back myself to hit boundaries, but I was just hitting singles to get him back on strike."

The cockiness, outrageous confidence – call it what you will – that had been spotted by Pietersen's teachers when he was at junior school was beginning to manifest itself in Kevin's approach to cricket as the match-winning performances began to pile up. He was a crack player in a crack team at this level and his sense of adventure was emboldened by batting with the likes of Rowley, who remembers: "Sometimes we would try and outdo each other. We both play similar games, quite expansive, and I remember a game at Rovers against Chatsworth, which was a one-and-a-half day league game. We batted first, did quite nicely and Kevin and I both got runs. We bowled Chatsworth out quite cheaply. In those days, you could actually bat again to play time and get points. Kevin and I would normally bat four, five, six back then, but Wayne Scott sent us up front to open the batting. It was quite a laugh. There were express bowlers coming in – not your Dale Steyn or Brett Lee, but they were bowling 130kph, which, on club wickets in Natal, you have to respect – and Kevin has walked out in a cap. Normally, you would always wear helmets because of unpredictable wickets, but he wore a cap, confident as ever, and absolutely murdered them. He made a mockery of the opening bowlers. He was hitting a four almost every ball. There were fielders on the boundary and he was finding the gaps, it was just brilliant to watch."

Pietersen was not only getting a reputation as an explosive cricketer, but also a confrontational one. "He was a chirper, a sledger of note," recalls Scott. "He wasn't quiet," laughs Rowley. Sledging is the systematic abuse of batsmen, done for the sole purpose of talking them out. Others call it banter. Steve Waugh euphemistically termed it 'mental disintegration'. Pietersen didn't just do his chirping from his usual station in the point or gully region. Unusually, he even did it with a bat in his hand. Scott says: "When he was batting he would say [to the bowler], 'Is that the best you've got?' or 'Don't just bowl that because we're mates.' It's unusual for a batter, but that's the way he was – not when he first joined us, but when he was 19 to 20, a bit more established and had the ability to practise what he could preach. Once he crossed the line, he became as competitive as it gets. People will tell you he was arrogant, but he backed it up." In the dressing room, Pietersen was equally voluble. He felt comfortable at Rovers. He was a key figure in a successful team – Rovers were twice crowned Premier League champions at the turn of the millennium – and playing with old College buddies who were as desperate to win as he was. "He was always geeing the blokes up," said Scott. "A lot of it was crap, just to generate banter. He was a big talker and a big Mickey-taker. He enjoys the fun element of cricket. Cricket was always going to be his life. No two ways about it. He loved his cricket, he loved pitching up for games. Yes, he was controversial, he was cocky, he was arrogant. He was all of the above. But if he was on your team, boy, you knew you had someone on your side who could stand up for you."

Pietersen was no mouthy, village slogger – all brawn, no brain. Even at that time his mind operated as a personal cricket computer, storing and downloading information in various files of his brain, ready to be accessed and printed out when the time was opportune. The teenager who had been brought up with tales of Jonty Rhodes' amazing feats at his junior and high schools watched what the successful players did and incorporated it into his own game. A big influence on him was Stewart, an extremely popular member of the Rovers and Natal sides and who, Pietersen later admitted, was one of the two cricketers he "particularly admires", the other being Shaun Pollock. Stewart not only talked Kevin up to the Natal selectors, he also advised him and demonstrated to him the art of building an innings. "Kevin was not the best player in the [Rovers] side. Errol was," recalls Scott. "Errol was a mentor for Kevin. Kevin always had the potential to achieve, but he always had the potential to get out because of the way he played. If Kevin got a quick 30 or 40 and walked off saying, 'I didn't get as many runs as I wanted, but I contributed', Errol would always try and be not out at the end – whether it be 60, 70, 80 or 100. The prize was not to give your wicket away. When he played for Berea Rovers you could see the level that he brought to us and the value that he had for the youngsters in the team."

To Pietersen's credit, he did not get carried away with the many social opportunities that cricket offers, as many players of his age do. Perhaps this was partly down to lack of finances (at the same age Andrew Flintoff was boozing his hefty Lancashire contract up the walls of Preston's public houses). More probably it was because of Kevin's disciplined upbringing. Religion was still a major part of his life and this curtailed many late night carousing opportunities. "He was never a big drinker, but he enjoyed a beer," says Scott. "When he came out of school he enjoyed a pint or two. He couldn't afford Jack Daniels and coke in those days. He loved a beer after the game, loved to socialise with the boys, but he didn't particularly stay until 8pm or 9pm like us, getting stuck in. A lot of the time, straight after a game on Sunday, he would go to mass. Him and his brother Bryan would be off. The folks would like the kids to be there every Sunday."

Even at this age, Pietersen's confidence and self-trust was unusual. It is a quality that can wind others up. Pietersen, certainly, has alienated many people over the years, particularly in his younger days and particularly in the self-interested world of county cricket. Others have been secretly frightened by his boundless self-belief. Dennis Carlstein, the Natal manager from 1990 until 2002 and a father figure to many of the young players of that era, says: "He was always a confident boy, even to the point of over-confident. He talked himself up and believed in himself to an unusual degree. He was that sort of guy."

It seems that Kevin was not a genius of skill at this stage – far from it – but what was emerging was a cricketer of extraordinary faith in his own ability. A genius of self belief, you might say.

The problem for Pietersen in his late teens was that, while he was thriving against first-class standard cricketers, playing in first-class cricket was proving a far tougher nut to crack. In 1998, post-apartheid South Africa, desperate to address the imbalances of the apartheid years with 'positive discrimination', introduced the controversial quota system which insisted that provincial sides should include a select number of 'non-white' players. This undoubtedly stymied Kevin's progress. It was perhaps his misfortune that he was still considered a bowling all-rounder by the Natal powers-that-be, even though his club performances were suggesting otherwise. Nevertheless, when he was recalled to the Natal B side in February 1999 and given a run of three consecutive first-class games Pietersen was not shunted down the bottom of the order. He batted at No. 6 in two games and at No. 7 in the other, so he could hardly complain that his batting performances for Rovers had been ignored. The results were mixed. Five innings yielded 123 runs, although Pietersen top-scored with a quickfire 60 in one game against Easterns B, a knock that included three sixes. He was more successful with the ball, deceiving some decent batsmen with loop and turn and emerging with a couple of cheap three-wicket hauls. As the South African summer came to an end, Pietersen could at last feel that he had won over the Natal selectors with some steady, although far from spectacular performances.

Yet as the 1999-2000 season got underway, Pietersen found himself back at square one. It would prove to be the beginning of the end of his relationship with Natal, and South African cricket in general. Despite appearing to make a breakthrough towards the end of the previous campaign, he was omitted from the Natal B side for their opening two first-class games of the new season, suffering once again from the new quota system. This was a huge kick in the teeth for Kevin, who felt he had done enough to stay in the team on merit. Upon his return to the side he bludgeoned an unbeaten 30, took a single wicket and this was enough for him to be promoted up the ranks. Twenty-one months after making his first-class debut and aged 19-and-a-half, Pietersen was finally selected for the Natal first team in the longer form of the game in December 1999. It was a high profile match in which to make his bow – a four-day game against the England touring side. 'This was a big occasion for me,' wrote Kevin. 'It was the biggest match of my life until that point. Here was the England cricket team playing against my team at a time when I was trying to make my way in the game.' Pietersen owed his selection partly to his own burgeoning talent, but mostly to the province's desperation to unearth an effective slow bowler. He took his place in an inexperienced side that had rested its biggest stars. He replaced Robbie MacQueen, an off-spinner who had played for South Africa at Under-19 level, but was struggling to make the grade at senior level, and was paired in a two-pronged spin attack with Gulam Bodi, a 20-year-old Indian-born left-arm wrist-spinner in the Paul Adams mould who was playing only his second game for the state.

Playing at Kingsmead in front of a sizeable media presence, as well as his family and old College mates, Pietersen grabbed his opportunity with both his hands. He came to the crease when Natal were 203-7 and rallied the tail with the kind of destructive hitting which he had been producing on a regular basis for Berea Rovers but of which there had been only fleeting glimpses at first-class level. Batting at No. 9 against a strong England attack of Andy Caddick, Andrew Flintoff, Alex Tudor and Phil Tufnell he walloped 61 not out off 57 balls, including four sixes. "I played in that game and I remember he hooked Caddick into the stands with a front foot pull," says Watson. "It was a pretty audacious against a guy who was probably England's best bowler at the time. People were saying, 'Geez, that guy can play.'" Scott adds: "He was awesome. I remember sitting with my mates and he was pulling the fast bowlers off the front foot easily, like it wasn't the biggest stress for him in the world. He came in at number nine and stood out like a sore thumb."

Pietersen also caught the eye with the ball as England opted for batting practice in response to Natal's 310 and dawdled to 421 off 164.2 overs. Kevin sent down 55.5 of those, partly because of an injury to Bodi, and took four wickets for 161 runs, his best return in first-class cricket. Notably, his victims were the cream of the England top order – Michael Atherton, Nasser Hussain, Michael Vaughan and Chris Adams – and they were classic off-spinner dismissals, too. Hussain and Adams were bowled through the gate, Atherton was stumped and Vaughan was caught behind. Pietersen then impressed Hussain further by having the chutzpah to approach him afterwards to ask about playing cricket in Essex. The England captain, though, didn't quite twig Kevin's motives. "He thought I meant club cricket and gave me the number of his brother Mel, who played for Fives and Heronians in the Essex League," said Kevin. "But I had bigger aspirations than that. I was thinking of county cricket perhaps, at that stage, as a non-overseas player because of my British passport. Even then I knew my mother's nationality could open doors for me and I was inquisitive about the opportunities that might await in England." Hussain recalls the conversation with wry amusement. "I still laugh when I think back to my first tour as England captain when this young lad, bold as brass, came and sat beside me in the visiting dressing room. I had enough on my plate to worry about with my own team at that stage, so probably I wasn't thinking straight and told Kevin to try my brother Mel's club in Chigwell. He had his eyes on much bigger fish."

After his outstanding display against Hussain's tourists, the rest of the season was an anti-climax for Pietersen. His reward for smacking a run-a-ball half-century against international bowlers was to be demoted to No. 10 for Natal's next game when the big guns were back in harness. Kevin stayed in the side for the last four first-class matches of the summer, but was played as a bowler and, although he took some useful wickets, he did not make the most of his few opportunities to shine with the bat. Carlstein remembers a particularly poor display against Gauteng at the Wanderers a fortnight after the England game when Pietersen batted at No. 10 and scored four in both innings. "He was shocking," says Carlstein. "He tried to hit everything and his technique was all over the place. In the early days he didn't look like the batsman he is now. He was a mediocre batsman and although he was keen on his bowling, I didn't think he was that good." As winter beckoned, things were looking bleak for Pietersen. Wisely, he had formulated a plan B and was ready to put it into action.

TROUBLES ABROAD

BY THE AGE OF 20 it is usually clear whether a sportsman is going to make the professional grade. Indeed, the very cream of any major sport are usually to be found making big inroads at the very highest level, being hailed as prodigies, with huge futures of global domination ahead of them.Michael Owen had scored *that* goal against Argentina aged 18. Wayne Rooney starred in Euro 2004 aged 18, while Michael Atherton was an England captain-in-waiting at 19. India's star batsman of the modern era, Sachin Tendulkar, who also holds the record for most runs in Test cricket, debuted at 16 and scored his maiden Test century in the following summer's series in England. The man Tendulkar toppled from head of the Test run charts, Brian Lara, was captaining Trinidad & Tobago by the age of 20 and made his Test debut that same year. In basketball, Kobe Bryant was selected as an NBA All-Star at 20, while in rugby, Jonny Wilkinson's boot won the 2003 World Cup final for England at the age of 24 after he had been the fulcrum to Clive Woodward's approach to the game for the preceding three years following his call-up to the full England squad at the age of 18.

Shortly before he turned 20, Kevin Pietersen's career was still barely out of the starting blocks. He had achieved little in 10 first-class games for his state side apart from, ironically, a fine display against Nasser Hussain's England tourists. Even in the one-day arena his performances had been modest.

Like most young southern hemisphere cricketers Pietersen was keen to develop his game by playing a season's club cricket in England, a traditional rite of passage for would-be international players for generations. It was especially relevant for him as his mother's English nationality provided him with a back-up option should his progress stall in South Africa. In late 1999, as Kevin found himself in and out of the Natal first X1 and B team, he put the word about that he fancied spending the next South African winter in England. By chance, it was Cannock Cricket Club who came in with an offer. Jamie Fleet, the club's current chairman and Mr Fix-it, was responsible for bringing the young unknown to England after making a long-distance call to Doug Watson, the Natal opening batsman who had been Cannock's overseas player for two seasons in the 1990s. "I got in touch with Dougie and asked for a recommendation for a player," Fleet remembers. "We weren't particularly looking for a South African. We talk to various people in the close season to see who is available. Dougie clearly knew what was happening at Cannock, knew what the facilities were like and could tell the [new] guy. He recommended Kevin. It was in December 1999, after Kevin had just scored runs against England's touring side and Dougie said, 'There's a guy in the next hotel bedroom to me who is interested in coming to the UK. You might have seen something in the press about him. His name's Kevin Pietersen. I'll go and ask him if he's interested and I'll call you back.' He phoned me back, I spoke to Kevin on the phone and said, 'Are you interested in coming to Cannock?' He said, 'Yeah, what's available?' I quoted some figures and we discussed arrangements. The next thing you know the flights are booked."

The deal was that Pietersen would be paid £100 a week, plus receive free accommodation and return air fare in exchange for committing himself to a 22-week season that would primarily be made up of Saturday league games, Sunday and occasional midweek matches. He would also be expected to help out with junior training at the club on a Monday night. Furthermore, Cannock promised to find Kevin 20 hours of work around the club each week, an agreement which would later become a major bone of contention for the player.

Pietersen had barely set foot in the land of his mother's birth and the one where he would eventually rise to the highest cricket office in the land when he was collected at Heathrow by Fleet in April 2000. The only time he had spent in England had been a couple of short holidays when he was a child. Yet he was far from nervous when he arrived for his first overseas assignment. "He was confident," says Fleet. "Kevin's always been confident. When I picked him up he asked a lot of questions, we talked about things. He wasn't the type of person who made you think, 'Oh God, we've got a right guy come over from South Africa.' Kevin was perfectly normal and we made him feel at home."

Located close to the Black Country just to the north of Birmingham, Cannock has its roots as an industrial, coal mining town although it has become increasingly affluent in recent years and is now a popular commuting area for the larger metropolitan bases of Birmingham and Wolverhampton. Pietersen's home for five-and-a-half months was Cannock Cricket & Hockey Club, a seven-day-a-week multi-sports arena which specialises in the two sports to which it bears its name and is located only a few miles from a somewhat unprepossessing town centre. The club lives and breathes sport. I visit on a Tuesday lunchtime in late November and, although it is fairly quiet apart from a few business conferences and members slugging it out on the squash court, the sporting facilities are immaculate. There are three well maintained cricket grounds, a trio of state-of-the-art Astroturf pitches, all-weather cricket nets, a bowling green and tennis courts. The club's nerve centre is a two-storey building that, although functional rather than especially charming, radiates purpose and good health. It features two bars, a restaurant, 13 changing rooms, three squash courts, fully equipped gym, aerobics studio, toning suite, sauna and steam room. All of these were available for Pietersen to use free of charge during his spell at the club. The facilities were not too dissimilar to what Kevin had been used to at Berea Rovers. Moreover, they were practically on his doorstep, for the site also houses the two-bedroom flat that he shared with Graham Wright, an Australian who ran the bar and played alongside Pietersen in the first team.

Although Pietersen said he was "immediately impressed" with the facilities at the club he was less enamoured with his lodgings. "When they took me to my residence I found I was staying in a single room above a squash court," he said. "For me, a person who had always led an outdoor life, it was quite a shock. Totally not what I had expected . . . coping with my little room in this little town."

Until now, Fleet has refused to respond to the criticism, but he is keen to put the record straight. "In fact, the 'room above a squash court' is a two-bedroom flat with kitchen, lounge and bathroom," he says. "It's got a washing machine, it's got a cooker, it's got satellite television. It is not actually above the squash court. It is adjacent to it."

Fleet, the type of dedicated man who is the lifeblood of such sports clubs across the country, bristles at the notion that Kevin had been shortchanged. "We had to deal with a young lad from South Africa in the best way possible," he continues. "My wife did his washing for him the whole time he was here. Kevin came to our house for meals. For the first two to three weeks we – predominantly my wife and I – mothered him. We have three children of our own but had to make him feel at home, we had to try and find him accommodation, make sure he knew all the first team players, had the right kit, help him if he wanted help with anything such as phone home, use the internet or the bank. It's not in the middle of the city, that's one thing, but you've got a McDonalds, two pubs half a mile away. You can walk into Cannock town centre from here."

Having visited both Berea Rovers and Cannock, there is little difference between the two clubs. Indeed, if anything, Cannock is the more impressive. Perhaps Pietersen, who was far from a man of the world at that stage and was living abroad and away from his friends and family for the first time, was merely suffering from chronic homesickness. Fleet says: "As time progresses, they find their own friends . . . girls . . . you know. This club is a multi sports club. We play hockey all through the year, organise mixed hockey festivals, a lot of late night parties, lots of opportunities to meet people. He knew the craic. The bar serves food six nights a week. He wouldn't have necessarily got free meals, but he wouldn't have had to pay a lot for them. You get to know people, you work the channels, you work behind the bar. There's a buffet, it doesn't all get eaten . . . you go out with the first team, three of whom are married guys with kids, for a curry; 'Don't worry Kev, we'll get this'. That's how it is."

Although Pietersen recognised at Cannock that "people looked after me and I didn't have too much to moan about", he did not mention those who helped him, which was interpreted as offensive in some quarters. Fleet's wife, Marian, is more blunt about the supposed tough conditions that Pietersen had to endure. "My husband and I tried really hard to make his time as pleasant as possible," she says. "I would welcome anyone to inspect the flat – not room – that Kevin stayed in. It's not the Ritz by any means, but I would have no problem allowing my boys to stay in a similar flat if they were ever lucky enough to be offered the chance to play cricket in South Africa, and I am an overprotective mother."

In comparison to Watson, his friend from Natal and one of his overseas predecessors at the club, Pietersen's digs were the height of luxury. "In his first year, Dougie lived in a caravan on the ground by the scorebox," says husband Jamie. "We ran the electricity out of the scorebox into his caravan. That was all we had available. Dougie was more than happy. He stayed in there and had some good times. He was by himself, a young lad. Dougie accepted it and came back the second year, when he went from a caravan to a bedsit, so it can't have been all that bad."

Not that Pietersen was totally restricted in his living arrangements. When the Fleets went on holiday for a fortnight in the summer, they asked Kevin to house-sit. He was also paid to do a few jobs around the place, such as mowing the lawn and painting one of the rooms. "My son said he broke his bed which I hope to this day was purely because it was a slatted bed and my son was quite small then," laughs Fleet. "We will put it down to the fact the bed was too small for him."

Pietersen's criticisms of Cannock in his 2006 autobiography were not restricted to where he put down his head at night. "I worked as a barman in the Cannock clubhouse and I met some very nice people there who I still keep in touch with to this day," he wrote. "I look back on it now and it seems a world away, what with those horrible Black Country accents I had such trouble understanding. I was very much an innocent abroad. But I did run into some trouble when I wasn't paid what I reckoned I was owed for the work I did behind the bar. I still haven't been paid that money now! As far as I'm concerned Cannock didn't honour their agreement with me."

Unsurprisingly Cannock have a slightly different take on events. Fleet admits that the club did owe Pietersen money, but it was outweighed by an unsettled phone bill that he had run up during his summer in Staffordshire. Fleet says: "He may well have not collected the money he was owed for bar work, but if you count the money outstanding for phone calls to South Africa, we believe we are on the positive side. I guess the outstanding phone bill was approximately £200 and Kevin would not have been owed £200. It is a pittance really."

The dispute was not sorted out at the time because Pietersen left in a hurry three weeks before the end of the season after being selected for Natal's pre-season tour of Western Australia.

"If he had stayed we could have sorted it all out," says Fleet. "He could have sat around the table with us and said, 'You owe me this'. We could have showed him the phone bill, shook hands and said, 'Okay, Kev, let's forget about it'. You could call it selective recall."

Such was Pietersen's haste to hotfoot it from the Midlands and the breakdown of their relationship that he did not even bother to tell the Fleets about his departure. "I just heard he was leaving and that was it," says Fleet. "He didn't tell me directly, no. Perhaps at that point Kevin was busy preparing himself for the next stage of his career."

Pietersen was also disappointed that the club did not live up to its promise of providing him with 20 hours of work each week. He would make this plain to his team-mates in the first X1 and friends he made at the club. Indeed, such was his anger that, somewhat cruelly, he took to calling Fleet, the man who, along with his wife, had given up so much of his time to help Kevin settle at Cannock, '20 hours' behind his back. Fleet maintains that it was not always possible to live up to the promise he had made to him. "We were going through a change in management at the time and the hours weren't always available," he explains. "We tried wherever possible to ensure Kevin got work opportunities. My wife got him some coaching at one of the local schools and he coached my youngest son. He was a very good coach – natural with the kids. He didn't perhaps want to do some of the work outside. He would much prefer to be working at the bar. It was just getting the right balance. He preferred to be working in the evenings rather than during the day. He had other cricket commitments – he was out trying to have trials with the counties. But I don't think he ever ran out of money while he was over here. It was a completely normal situation. With hindsight, you'd say, 'Kevin Pietersen, England captain, you'd pay in gold to have him at your club', but he came over as a young, unproven 19-year-old. To have gone out on a limb to do things for him would have been extraordinary."

Although Pietersen later said he did not much like his time at the Staffordshire club – "by the end of my time at Cannock I hated the place" – despite the team winning the Birmingham League for the first time in its history, in some ways it was the most significant period of his career. Not only did it introduce him to English cricket and conditions, it was on these shores that he converted to being a specialist batsman. Cannock had two stalwart spinners, Laurie Potter, their captain who had played county cricket for Kent and Leicestershire, and Guy Bulpitt, who bowled slow left-arm for Staffordshire. Pietersen's off breaks featured only as a back-up option. "It was probably a bad signing for the club," says Bulpitt. "We had two left-arm spinners and probably didn't need an off-spinner as well. He wasn't a bad bowler, although he wasn't exceptional. He just went to a club that already had two spinners."

Potter remembers that Pietersen was desperate to be recognised as an all-rounder. "He would ring me up on Friday nights quite regularly and ask if he would be bowling on Saturday," he explains. "I would say I was just trying to make decisions that would benefit the team. Nine times out of 10 Guy and I would bowl rather than Kev. It didn't cause problems, but it used to be frustrating for Kev. He said a couple of times, 'I have come here to play cricket and if you don't give me a proper chance I may as well not be here.' I don't know if he meant it or not. He was probably just letting off steam. Even though he was talked about as an off spinner-batsman I felt pretty clearly, and this is not being wise after the event, that his batting would be more valuable to us. Not that he was a bad bowler. I and a number of others in the club felt that his batting was going to be his strong point."

Nevertheless, Potter was impressed by the chutzpah of the club's overseas pro. "To me, Kev saying he wanted to be more involved was a good thing. Some players would do as much as they could to get out of something. He wasn't like that. He was almost demanding attention for his bowling because he felt he had to bowl. He often said, 'I have to bowl'. He said it was an imperative part of his game and overall package. At the time he was looking for everything that would make him a better cricketer. As a captain I didn't have a problem with that. You want people to be ambitious and to do their best."

Despite the club's reluctance to throw Pietersen the ball he still managed to take 16 wickets at 25 apiece. At the same time, he batted regularly at number four behind Potter and the former Worcestershire and Nottinghamshire batsman Anurag Singh, and scored 485 league runs at an average of 48.50. "He was very good under pressure," remembers Bulpitt. "He performed better when it mattered most. Even at 19 or 20, he scored runs when the team needed them. You could see him visibly rise to the challenge. He would finish games off for us. Once, he finished a game with three sixes and walked off in a strop because he had not bowled much earlier."

Interestingly Pietersen's stand-out performance for Cannock came when his parents flew over from South Africa for a few days to visit him and take in a league game at Harborne. They had promised their son a bottle of champagne if he scored a hundred. Pietersen, showing early signs of his flair for an occasion, responded to the inducement by taking four wickets in Harborne's 199-9 declared and then belting five sixes in an 88-ball unbeaten 107 as Cannock raced to victory by seven wickets. Further motivation had been provided by the presence in the opposition line-up of a fellow South African. "He was their pro, a good bowler and proper quick, especially for the Birmingham League. Kev whacked him everywhere and won the game for us in 25 overs," says Bulpitt.

It would be Pietersen's only century of the season, proof that he was an exciting talent, but still a long way off the finished article. By comparison Adam Gilchrist, another southern hemisphere batsman in the aggressive Pietersen mould, had smashed seven centuries during the summer he spent playing for Richmond in south-west London in the late 1980s. And he was only 17 at the time.

"It became clear his batting was exceptionally strong, but if I say I expected him to go on to have such success, I would be lying," says Potter. "I thought, yes, he would become a top county cricketer, but difficult to say more than that. In the Birmingham League there is not the quality of pace bowling. If there are any quick bowlers they are playing first-class cricket anyway. That's always a factor when it comes to judging players. There was nothing to indicate the level he would reach." Moreover, there were concerns about whether his flamboyant style would cut it at professional level in English conditions.

"Technically then he was exactly the same as he is now," says Bulpitt. "He was quite unorthodox and we wondered whether he would be able to hit perfectly good balls through midwicket when he made the step up."

Fleet was equally sceptical. "I'm not going to say he was a world-beater. Kevin was not exceptional when he was here. His records show it. Kevin looked a very good player, but he looked no different to Dougie Watson had done – though Dougie hit the ball along the ground more than Kevin did. Dougie was what I would consider a quality opening batsman, who could grind out a hundred."

What stood out at Cannock as much as Pietersen's ability was his sheer ambition, which stood as tall as his skyscraper physique. It was not a trait that he felt compelled to hide and, in English club cricket, where the stiff upper lip and traditional reserve is still commonplace, it was not always appreciated by his team-mates. "He got on fine with most people but at times he would wind them up and at times people didn't agree with things he did," Potter says. "He was focused and knew where he was going to go and how he was going to get there. He was a confident chap in a way that was typically South African. He was a young, strong personality, fairly outgoing and didn't make it a secret that there was an opportunity for him potentially within the game in England, as his mother was English. He spoke about it freely in the dressing room and was negative about the quota system and negative about the opportunities he would have in South Africa. Anyone who has that determination would, at times, upset people. I don't think people always found him easy-going because he saw things his way.

As a 19-year-old you felt he had a bit of bite about him and he would go along the line that he felt was right. That's not a bad thing for a sportsman to have. He knew Cannock was only a stepping stone. We have had young pros that just want an experience of a summer here. Kev had a different idea. He had higher expectations." Fleet adds: "He had his agenda. He wanted to become a better player and saw Cannock as part of that."

Bulpitt has some sympathy with Pietersen's uber-professional approach. "It is an English thing not to like ambition, especially someone as obviously ambitious as Kevin was. You could fall out with Kevin if you wanted to. He is that kind of person. You have to take him for what he is. He says what he thinks and is quite open about what he wants. That upsets some people, who are not used to someone displaying such open ambition. A few people at the club had cross words with him. He was an outspoken lad. He was promised things and would say, 'They have not lived up to their word on this or on that.' He wasn't just playing for fun. He saw it as his career and he took it really seriously."

Curiously, there is no photographic record of Pietersen's season at Cannock, which Fleet says was "the pinnacle of this club's history". It celebrates its 150th anniversary in 2010. In the bar of the clubhouse, there is a team photograph of the 2000 Birmingham League champions, the only title in their history, but Pietersen was not present as it was taken late in the season and he had already returned to warmer climes.

His comments in his autobiography six years later have left a bitter taste in the mouths of many Cannock stalwarts. "Not only me but several people in the club feel quite let down by his comments," says Fleet. "He was convenient with some of the information. But it sells a story, doesn't it? Unfortunately we are made to look like cowboys. But we are not. We wouldn't have won the Birmingham League if we were cowboys. I'm disappointed he has that perception of the club and that he went public about it without telling all the facts. He picked up on the negative side and didn't pick up on the positive things. The book is full of inaccuracies. Kevin doesn't refer to the help that my wife gave to him and the help that other people gave to him. He doesn't refer to me taking him to Heathrow so he could go back to South Africa to talk to his family and Natal in the middle of the summer and sort his own financial position out. He paid for the flights, but I took him to Heathrow and someone else at the club picked him up from Birmingham airport on the way back. I know the number of overs Kevin bowled and the number of hours he got to work were a pain. We tried to find alternative work and put notices advertising for one-on-one coaching with him. That isn't mentioned, the level of commitment that other people made."

When Fleet had dinner with Pietersen's parents at the club in mid-summer there was no talk of any problems that their son might be experiencing. "You'd have thought they would have mentioned it to me if there was an issue," he says. "We had an enjoyable dinner and they were a nice family. That's what is so disappointing. If it wasn't for Cannock Cricket Club and the opportunities he had here to meet certain people then who knows what would have happened? He could have gone to Essex and might not have made it there. He might well have done. But this club put him on a stage. He met some people who could have joined the dots. He had the cheek to comment about the Black County accent with the accent that he has got! I'd like him to go and stand up at the Sports Personality of the Year in the West Midlands and go and criticise the accents of the people there. That sums up in many respects the unnecessary dig at Cannock Cricket Club and the West Midlands. It was part of him growing up, it was part of him becoming the player he is today."

Attempts have been made to heal the rift that has developed, but even though Pietersen still keeps in touch with some of the Cannock players he has brushed all overtures aside. "We asked him back a few times through his agent before he became a really big superstar – to sign the odd shirt and give a speech or this, that and the other – but he refused. We were just told 'Kevin doesn't want to'. It is up to Kevin.

What would be nice is if Kevin Pietersen ate some humble pie. Perhaps he might just come back here to our 150th anniversary in 2010 and acknowledge that Cannock was part of his success. I'm quite willing to write him out a cheque for his bar work and draw a line in the sand."

Jamie's wife, Marion, is even more forthright. "We really believe in the saying that what goes around, comes around," she simmers. "You should always be good to people on the way up as you meet them on the way down. He was a nobody when Cannock gave him the chance to come to England, he should remember that. I think Kevin believes his own publicity too much."

Yet Bulpitt offers an alternative view. "People like appreciation at times," he says. "People at the club think he should come back and give them a few signed shirts, get involved with the kids and say how great Cannock is. But as a club, Cannock should think, 'It's great that we gave an England captain his first chance to play in England.' In life, people say, 'Why should we celebrate someone who doesn't celebrate us?' KP is not good at looking back. That's not what he does. He just looks at what he has to do next to get to where he wants."

And next for Kevin was one final stab at establishing himself in Natal. He had slammed one door shut behind him and now it was time to prize open another back in his homeland.

ON THE MOVE

KEVIN PIETERSEN HAD NEVER been much interested in politics. He was a sportsman, after all. And politics and sport are completely unrelated, right? Wrong. A thousand times, wrong. They are intertwined as readily as rhythm and blues, the music genre that Pietersen prefers to listen to on his ipod. Just ask Mike Proctor, Graeme Pollock, Barry Richards, Clive Rice, Vincent van der Bijl, Jimmy Cook or any of the what-might-have-been generation of South African cricket. Or, indeed, the great coloured (as black people were called in South Africa) cricketers of that era who most of us are completely unaware of as they were never given the opportunity to display their skills by virue of the colour of their skin. For every Proctor or Pollock, there were thousands far less fortunate of darker hue that weren't even allowed near a cricket stadium in the old days. The forefathers of Makhaya Ntini, Ashwell Prince, Hashim Amla, JP Duminy and Herschelle Gibbs were forced to play out their cricket dreams on the Cape Flats and other urban ghettoes into which they were dumped by the brutal apartheid regime. White South Africans were fanatical about sport and it was this fanaticism that persuaded the rest of the world that sporting boycotts were the only realistic way of forcing them to change.

Pietersen and Grant Rowley were growing up in a society aspiring to make right the wrongs of the past. A new era was dawning. As schoolboys attending fee paying schools and living in the affluent suburbs of Pietermaritzburg, initially, they were not greatly affected by the rapid changes happening in their country. Non-white faces began to appear at Maritzburg College and public transport and toilets were no longer racially segregated, but in terms of their daily lives little had changed. They were too busy dealing with adolescence.

When I visited Maritzburg College, Mike Bechet handed me a photograph of the 1997 College first team, captained by a seated Rowley and with Pietersen standing proudly in the background. In it, the young men beaming in their blazers and striped caps are all white, as they had been for decades. But shortly before the turn of the century, the ruling ANC government imposed directives on the United Cricket Board of South Africa that changed the whole landscape of South African cricket and set in motion a chain of events that would have massive repercussions for Pietersen, Rowley and hundreds of other white cricketers in the rainbow nation.

Quotas (targets, affirmative action, positive discrimination – call it what you will) have been the means by which South African cricket has tried to rebalance decades of injustice. In 1998, it was decreed that provincial sides should include three 'non-white' players. The last all-white South African team took the field in November 1999 against the West Indies. "Ali Bacher was in charge and after the first match of the series he promised there would never be an all-white team again," recalls Jonty Rhodes. "His nephew, Adam Bacher, got dropped in the next game for Herschelle [Gibbs]."

At Natal in early 2000 the quota system was providing a few headaches for the province's five-man selection committee. "At the time we had to pick three players of colour," recalls the coach Phil Russell. "That was mandatory. Ahmed Amla, the elder brother of Hashim, was one, Imran Khan, an opening batsman who still plays now, was another. Gulam Bodi was the third."

The problem for Pietersen was that he found himself in direct opposition with Bodi, another young spinner who could contribute useful runs in the lower middle order. Bodi was born in India, but emigrated to South Africa as a teenager and had come up through the ranks, representing South Africa at Under-17s, Under-18s and Under-19s level, and playing in the Under-19 World Cup. After Pietersen's sterling performance against England in late 1999 he was given an extended run in Natal's first-team in the four-day game, but Kevin couldn't nail down a place in Natal's one-day side. His performances were patchy and he was overlooked in favour of Bodi on a few occasions.

Conscious of needing to seize any opportunity presented to him, Pietersen had left Cannock shortly before they won the Birmingham League to take his place in a Natal squad that toured Western Australia for a fortnight in September 2000. He performed impressively there, playing in all five matches and taking his maiden five-wicket haul in a three-day game against a Western Australia X1 captained by Mike Hussey. But Kevin returned to South Africa to be told he had been dropped for a one-day game against Northerns at Kingsmead so that Bodi could play. The frustration that had been simmering for many months finally boiled over. "I flew into a rage, flinging a water bottle across the Natal dressing room and shouting, 'I'm leaving here'," he admitted. "Perhaps not the wisest move, but I was so angry at the time because I knew Gulam wasn't as good as me. I had nothing against him, but I didn't think it was right that he replaced me. I remember ringing my Dad and crying down the phone to him when it happened."

Dennis Carlstein was in the dressing room at the time. "Kevin was upset and moaned [about being dropped] a lot. He was never one for hiding his feelings. In that way, he was quite immature as an 18 or 19-year-old."

Pietersen insists that he had been axed for political reasons. "I was dropped because of the quota system that had been brought into South African cricket to positively discriminate in favour of 'players of colour' and to fast-track the racial integration of cricket in the country," he said. "To me, every single person in this world needs to be treated exactly the same and that should have included me, as a promising 20-year-old cricketer. If you do well you should play on merit. That goes for any person of any colour. It was heartbreaking. I don't blame the player for what happened, of course I don't. It's the system. It's bullshit."

Despite Pietersen's accusations, few players or administrators thought it strange that Bodi was preferred to Kevin at the time. Russell says: "Gulam was an outstanding bowler at that stage. He bowled left-arm chinamen, he was an unusual talent. He could get hit around if he didn't get it right, but he could also be a threat. Graham Ford and I also thought he had the potential to bat. He won us a few games."

Carlstein agrees that Bodi was the better prospect. "Their batting was on a par – Kevin might have been a little bit better – but Bodi was the more accomplished bowler."

However Rowley sympathised with his old pal. "Gulam Bodi might have been a better spinner than Kevin, but he certainly wasn't a better batter. Everyone could see what was happening, even Bodi himself, who was under pressure and knew he wasn't performing or delivering the goods. The writing was on the wall. That's where Kevin got frustrated. He came from an Afrikaans family who believed that was unfair. Throughout South Africa, a lot of cricketers felt like that."

Yet the national selectors felt that Bodi had a lot to offer and tried to fast-track him into the South Africa team. At the end of the 2000/01 season he was summoned to the West Indies as a replacement for Nicky Boje in the one-day squad, but had to pull out after breaking a finger playing league cricket in Manchester and then slipped from the international radar. In an ironic parallel of Pietersen, he got fed up at Natal, joined the Titans franchise and, as his bowling skills waned and his batting flowered, reinvented himself as an explosive hitter. He has proved particularly successful as an opening batsman in the one-day game and won his first international caps in 2007 and was included in the South Africa squad for the inaugural Twenty20 World Cup. During the tournament the pair met and, Pietersen being Pietersen, had some heated exchanges. "We had a couple of issues, but we resolved everything afterwards," explains Bodi. "Just a couple of misunderstandings. There's no problem now. Back in Durban we were both spinners who could bat a bit, but there was only one place available in the team. The quota issue, in my view, was misrep-resented."

And what of his old rival's rise and rise? "The 10 years since then have definitely panned out a bit differently for us," says Bodi with a laugh. "He deserves all the accolades he receives. There's no doubting what he has done and achieved and he's become a world-class player, the best batsman in the world on current form."

No matter what he might maintain, there was more to Pietersen being dropped by Natal than just the quota system. "It was a combination of three things," explains Russell. "You've got the transformation, but there was also the strength of the team and the performances. We picked Kevin when we could. His one outstanding game was against England. Apart from that his performances were not great, although that has never stopped me looking at potential."

Russell's claim is only partly backed up by statistics. In 10 first-class games for the two Natal teams over three seasons Pietersen scored 253 runs in 13 innings at 23 and took 22 wickets at 31 apiece, not outstanding figures but decent ones, especially for a young player labelled as a bowling all-rounder, who frequently batted down the order, where he had to make quick, risky runs for the team, and was also widely regarded as an outstanding fielder.

"The quota system negatively impacted on Kevin, he was always competing against it," says Pietersen's mentor, Errol Stewart. "He had to perform in one or two games rather than four or five and was always playing under pressure. He was batting at four or five in club cricket, but his role in the [Natal] side was to take wickets. I don't think he got a fair chance. It comes down to opportunities. It also has to be remembered that Natal had good batsmen at the time and a really strong side. They had Jonty Rhodes, Dale Benkenstein, Neil Johnson, Andrew Hudson and Shaun Pollock and then Lance Klusener to come in at seven and eight. It was an embarrassment of riches. Those guys weren't always available because they were playing for South Africa, but when they weren't it was hard for the likes of Kevin to get a game."

Doug Watson, Natal's established opening batsman, was another of the old guard keeping the new broom, which included the likes of Pietersen and Rowley, on the sidelines, but he did Kevin a favour by recommending him to Cannock and helping him get a foot in the door in the English set-up. Watson has a great deal of sympathy for Pietersen and the other aspiring white cricketers in the province. He says: "We were winning trophies and it was a hell of a strong Natal team to try and break into at that stage. When you saw a youngster putting it in you always think, 'Cream will rise to the top'. The opportunity to go to England came about and that's where he rose to the top. But after school I didn't know how he was going to get into the team, what with all the rules and regulations we have in this country. He had the potential, it was just getting the opportunities."

The landscape in South African cricket was changing almost daily. Teams were no longer being selected on merit, at provincial or national level. Livelihoods were being ruined and the rug was pulled from under the feet of many fine careers. "The picture was pretty bleak long term," recalls Graham Ford. "There was a lot of fear among cricketers. They didn't know what was going to happen. This quota system had suddenly been thrust upon them. They didn't know if it was going to get worse or there was going to be a period when quotas wouldn't happen anymore." The white colonials could now understand how generations of disadvantaged black and coloured cricketers had felt when their dreams had been shattered by forces beyond their control. It was a completely different climate to the one that Rhodes had grown up in during the isolation days. He says: "I never experienced what guys like Kevin had to go through. We didn't have the quota system then. There was no South Africa to play for. I played hockey in the winter and cricket in the summer and my ambition was to play for my state, not my country. But I was picked for the 1992 World Cup soon after readmission even though there were much better players than me. The timing for me was perfect. I feel for guys like Kevin, who have to deal with the transformation. But how do you balance 30-40 years of inequality? There is no easy solution."

Pietersen, however, had a get-out clause, courtesy of his English-born mother, Penny – his British passport. This allowed him to play for an English county as a non-overseas player, which immediately made him a more attractive proposition for clubs keen to reserve the two overseas slots that each county had at the time for the proven stars. During the previous summer at Cannock Kevin had become increasingly conscious of the money he could make carving out a professional career in England. Guy Bulpitt recalls: "We had quite a few senior players who talked to him about the benefits of doing well in the Birmingham League and about how it could be a shop window for his career. At 19 he was well aware of what he wanted and how he was going to get it. He was very aware of the financial benefits of playing county cricket. Whatever the value of the rand was at the time he had worked out that it would be more beneficial playing in England."

In South Africa, only a small elite – the players centrally contracted to the national side – earn high salaries, although each of the six franchises hands out contracts to around a dozen players on a semi-professional basis. In England, with its huge base of professional players, there are far more opportunities to earn a comfortable living.

In between playing weekend games for Cannock and doing bar work in the clubhouse and other odd jobs, Pietersen spent the summer of 2000 trying to attract the interest of the counties. He was invited for nets at Derbyshire, Warwickshire and Worcestershire and even played in a three-day game for

Warwickshire seconds against Surrey, top-scoring with 92 (the next highest score was 26) against an attack that included Ben Hollioake and Carl Greenidge.

But it was Clive Rice who showed the greatest interest in Kevin. The South Africa legend, who had first spotted Kevin's potential when he was 17 at a schools cricket festival, was now the coach of Nottinghamshire, the county that he had led with such distinction during their glory years in the 1980s. He says: "I got wind that he was the leading run scorer in the Birmingham League. I had also heard that he had a British mother and a British passport, so I phoned him up and said, 'KP, I want you to come and play for me at Notts. I'm not asking you to come on trial. I'm offering you a contract. You're good enough to play international cricket. In four years time I'll have you playing for England'."

Pietersen didn't accept Rice's verbal offer immediately. He wanted time to assess his options and ascertain whether he had a future in South Africa. Pietersen claimed in his autobiography that his hand was forced when he was omitted to make way for Bodi a few months later. "The fact was, when Natal dropped me they knew I had been in England, had talked to Clive and that Notts were interested in me," he said. "It was something I was curious to talk about, but it is a move that may well have not happened had Natal not forced the issue. When they left me out they proved to me they couldn't have thought an awful lot of me. They must have known that there was a big danger I would be lost to South African cricket, but they did nothing about it, merely blamed the system."

Phil Russell, who Pietersen dismissed as a "yes man who did what the hierarchy wanted him to do", offers a slightly different view. He says: "At the end of the 1999/2000 season we offered Kevin a junior contract. It was only his second year out of school, so would have been around 50-60,000 rand (£3,350-£4,000). Even the senior cricketers had jobs apart from playing for Natal. They would be employed for six months and paid over the year. In South Africa it was really a game for students. There are not many professionals. We wouldn't have offered him a contract if we didn't see the potential in his cricket. He was a fine athlete, very quick in the field, worked hard, never missed a practice, got stuck in with the nets and got stuck in with his fitness. The problem was trying to get him in the team."

Pietersen knew he could make far more money starting at the bottom rung of the ladder in England than in his homeland. Nottinghamshire were offering to pay him £15,000 for the following 2001 season, four times the contract that Natal had put on the table. Kevin needed advice following Rice's call and dashed back to South Africa for a few days in the middle of the 2000 summer to speak to his family and Natal top brass about his future. "Kevin said he needed to go back to South Africa to find out what Natal's position would be if he was going to spend longer in the UK and if he could still play for Natal if he came and qualified for England," says Jamie Fleet, the Cannock chairman. "I guess that was on his agenda at the time, so he could play in England in the summer and South Africa in the close season." Pietersen was told that to qualify as a non-overseas player in county cricket he would have to pull out of the Natal squad and would no longer be able to play top level cricket in South Africa.

Large cracks had begun to appear in Pietersen's relationship with South African cricket and they only increased when he was axed by Natal after that encouraging tour of Western Australia. For Kevin, it was the final straw, but, before making up his mind for good, he decided to canvas the opinions of some influential figures who he had great respect for, including Ford and Shaun Pollock, the then coach and captain of South Africa, who he knew well from Natal. Pollock says: "There are no guarantees in sport, but I said to Kevin, 'You must try and stick around. We will try and do what we can for you.' I was captain of South Africa at the time and had a big interest in his future. I honestly believed in his ability and always thought he had the game to go all the way. The cupboard was pretty bare in terms of spin bowlers and anyone who showed promise at provincial level had a pretty good chance."

Ford remembers a number of meetings with Kevin and his father at Jannie's office in Pinetown, on the outskirts of Durban. "You could tell this kid was as frustrated as could be and I knew the family felt the same," says Ford. "Jannie was pretty firm on wanting him to go. He was a young kid and Natal had a pretty powerful side. What frustrated him more was that he quite often struggled to make the B side because he felt there the quotas had kicked in. There were some good cricketers in the province, there's no doubt about that, and it was going to be hard for him to break into the side. At the time Kevin was a highly competitive guy with an awesome work ethic. He knew where he wanted to get to, wouldn't take a step backwards for anyone, so that may not have helped and with some players he may not have been their favourite cup of tea."

As a final resort, Ford and Pollock arranged for Kevin and Jannie to meet Ali Bacher, the godfather of South African cricket, in an attempt to appeal for more opportunities at provincial level. Pollock had the ear of Bacher and recalls: "I said to Ali, 'I think Kevin can play a part for South Africa' and tried to get Ali to reassure him that he would have an opportunity."

Father and son were encouraged that Bacher flew them over from Durban to his office in Johannesburg at the board's expense, but any hopes of a resolution to the problem soon disappeared. According to Kevin, the supremo of South African cricket set a hostile tone from the outset. He said: "Bacher was rude to me in that meeting, and rude to my Dad. There were no pleasantries, no hellos or how are yous. We simply sat down and Dr Bacher said to my Dad: 'What do you do?' Not a hello Mr Pietersen, hello Kevin, welcome, or anything like that. As far as I was concerned, the least he could do was be polite." Moreover, he claimed Bacher did not give him the reassurance that he was looking for that his future would best be served in the new South Africa. "Dr Bacher said that the quota system would stop and that selection would go back to being on merit. So I said, 'Dr Bacher, does that mean that, say next year, if the black and coloured players are not good enough, will Natal field an all-white side?' He said, 'No, they will be good enough and they will play.' That was the big moment for me. I looked at my Dad and tapped his leg. We both sort of nodded each other. As soon as we walked out of the meeting Dad said to me, 'You're going, the quota system will never finish.'"

Bacher, the arch politician and a figure who commanded great respect in world cricket, made few miscalculations in two decades at the helm of the South African game, but he underestimated both Pietersen's frustration at the quota system and the advice about his cricketing potential. Ford says: "I don't think Ali had an idea of what a good player Kevin was. He wasn't asking for a place in the Natal team. What he was asking for was a place in any team, anywhere that plays first-class cricket. He was kind of asking for a guarantee, which cricket selectors, coaches and administrators are scared to give. Ali thought, 'I can't force this guy on to another province and say, "You must play this guy."' He just felt he couldn't do that."

Ford, Jannie and Kevin met up again in Pinetown and came to a unanimous decision. "The three of us decided that the contract that he had on the table from Notts was a sure way of having a cricketing career," explains Ford. "Over here, nobody knows whether he would have come through or not. He may well have played club cricket for a couple of years, become disillusioned and jacked it in. He knew he had a guaranteed contract there and with his ability you would have thought he would have played for at least 10 years in county cricket. Obviously, the pound's a lot better than the rand, so, in the end, it was a no-brainer. He wanted to play cricket and earn a living out of cricket and he wasn't going to manage to do it here."

History will remember Pietersen as a pioneer. He had not been the first southern African to cross continents and pitch his tent in the England camp. Basil D'Olivera, Tony Greig, Allan Lamb, the Smith brothers, Robin and Chris, and Graeme Hick (albeit from Zimbabwe) had all undertaken similar journeys. But all of those men did not have the opportunity to play Test cricket for the countries of their birth. Pietersen was the first since readmission to do so, thrusting himself into uncharted territory and placing himself in danger of becoming a pariah in his homeland. Admitting that it was a "life-changing" decision, Kevin weighed up the pros and cons extensively with those he trusted. "I wouldn't call it an agonising decision," he said. "It was a well thought-out decision. We'd talked about this a lot as a family and I'd canvassed a lot of opinions. My family were fantastic, so supportive. Man, did they back me – and now not one member of my family will ever support a South African team at any time. They are English all the way."

It was this convenient switch of allegiances that would later antagonise so many people in Pietersen's sports-obsessed homeland. While Kevin, partly motivated by his mother's nationality and partly as a game of one-upmanship with younger brother Bryan, had supported England at rugby as a child and his idol had been Rob Andrew, he has admitted to being a fervent South African fan at cricket, hero-worshipping Allan Donald and Hansie Cronje. Pietersen claimed it was a "huge thing to turn my back on any hope I had of becoming like them" and insists that, had the England option not been available to him, he would have been "frozen out by the system" and eventually "gone off and done something else".

Rice is even more forthright about what could have happened to Kevin had he not moved overseas. He says: "If he had stayed in South Africa he would have been a surfer on Durban beach." Interestingly, Rice believes Pietersen's personality played a part in his failure to establish himself at Natal, which, in a roundabout way, echoes Russell's belief that the quota system was only one factor in the rift between player and province. "The administration down in Natal was mediocre," continues Rice. "When you have mediocre management the team performs moderately. If someone upsets the applecart it is something for them to handle. When he is something to handle they won't pick him. Because Kevin was a super-confident young man they couldn't handle him."

Carlstein admits there is some truth to this. "I got used to him after a while," he says. "I always used to give him a hard time, to keep his feet on the ground. But he wasn't a problem guy to manage. He was just confident – and a trier."

Pietersen's talent for splitting opinion is no recent phenomenon. His decision to leave South Africa in favour of England was praised as brave and completely understandable in some quarters and condemned as hasty and disloyal in others. There are plenty of experts I spoke to, like Pollock, who echoed the stances of Ford and Rice. "Sportsmen have to make a living," says Pollock. "Kevin was guaranteed a four-year contract. A young guy has to make a business decision. I was disappointed we would lose him from South African cricket, but people make decisions in life. It's about how you back them up."

Conversely, Russell believes Pietersen was guilty of impatience. "He always struck me as a man in a hurry," he says. "He wanted to go places very quickly. If he had stayed here he would have taken longer to reach his peak. He would have had to wait a few years to make an impression. In South Africa they don't play as many games as they play in England."

Was he wrong not to give Pietersen more chances in his late teens? "Hindsight is a great thing. Nobody knew that Derek Underwood would become a great bowler when he signed as a batsman for Kent. I could see the ability [but] he has done brilliantly. To leave one country and go and play for another country is a fine achievement."

It promises to be even harder for the Pietersens of the future to break through in South African cricket. In 2007 Cricket South Africa's transformation review committee (it is not just English cricket that loves a committee) recommended even more stringent targets, including a minimum of four black players in the national team and seven black players in a squad of 15. In domestic representative cricket, for sides such as the South Africa colts team that Pietersen had played for a decade previously, the target is 50 per cent black players in the team. Like many senior figures in South African cricket Rice remains as exasperated by the quota system as he was a decade ago. "I don't care what colour they are – as long as they are the best. You could see there was going to be inequality then and if you ask me right now about some young players I would say, 'Don't waste your time here, don't waste your time for one second', because inequality still exists and people get selected on the basis of colour."

It is a message that has been fully digested by disheartened cricketers in the republic. Where Pietersen led, many others have followed. There were 28 South Africans plying their trade in county cricket last year, the vast majority as 'Kolpaks' (players from a country which has an 'Association Agreement' with the European Union and so must be regarded as if they are a citizen of an EU country), who had either retired from international cricket or had given up on ever playing for their native land.

It is not just white South Africans who are frustrated by the quota system. Ashwell Prince was among the players from the national team who sent a letter to Cricket South Africa in 2007 demanding an end to artificial selection policies. Furthermore, Charl Langeveldt pulled out of South Africa's tour to India last year after being picked ahead of Andre Nel, saying the controversy over his selection had put him in the wrong frame of mind, and consequently threw in his lot with Derbyshire. Jacques Rudolph, still comfortably the right side of 30, is so disillusioned by the quota system that he has declared he doesn't want to add to his 35 Test caps for South Africa and hopes to represent England, qualifying by residency, after deciding to buy a house and live permanently in Yorkshire. If those who turn their back on their country are judged to be traitors, then there are an awful lot of renegades fleeing the South Africa nest.

Pietersen was fortunate that his parentage gave him the option of playing for England, as was Jonathan Trott, the Warwickshire batsman who was also born and raised in South Africa and followed in Kevin's footsteps by playing international cricket for his adopted country in 2007. Yet, what of those, like Rowley, who did not have dual nationality to fall back upon? Rowley, the schoolboy prodigy seemingly destined for the top, has played just 13 first-class matches in 11 years despite scoring three centuries in his opening eight games and averaging in the late 30s. His opportunities were limited not just by the quota system but by the introduction of the franchise system in 2004, which reduced the number of professional teams from 11 to six. Rowley says: "What happened was 80 to 100 cricketers lost their jobs. You can take that into consideration and you can also take into consideration the fact that the quota system increased from three to four players of colour out of 11. Add in two or three others in the squad and it made the competition hellish tough. I lost out on a contract while guys who averaged mid-20s were given contracts. People ask me, 'Why didn't you make it?' I don't blame it solely on the quota system. Maybe I could have been hungrier, more disciplined in certain areas, which I do acknowledge, but I do think it certainly played a part."

Rowley is now working for a South Africa brewery as a salesman and is contracted to play Twenty20 for the Dolphins franchise. Like those black cricketers of the apartheid years, he is a victim of his country's political machinations, a sportsman who found to his cost that politics and sport are inextricably interwoven.

Rowley says he feels no envy towards Pietersen. "What Kevin has done has opened a lot of people's eyes. Everyone admires what he has done for turning his back on South Africa and saying, 'I don't want to be part of this quota system.' It's sending a message to a lot of boys in South Africa that they can play international cricket in spite of it. If they have a British passport and any interest in playing at a higher level they have seen there are other avenues to explore."

Rowley concedes there is a sizeable element in South Africa who will never forgive Pietersen for leaving and for being so outspoken about the quota system. "There's a lot of people in South Africa who think he's a prick for what he's said, but what is wrong with being driven, what is wrong with being confident, what is wrong with backing your ability? If you believe you are good enough to play international cricket, as he always did when he was at Natal, why not go overseas? What's stopping him? He took that step to go and left a lot behind. To be honest I did not see him as a potential Test player when I last played with him in 2000. I can only imagine what the drive and motivation must have been like for him over the last eight years."

South Africa had allowed Pietersen to slip the net and he was hell-bent on making the country of his birth, its coaches and administrators regret its failure to spot his talent, one that the player himself had never, not for a single second, stopped believing in. Others were not so sure. "I took a bet with Dennis Carlstein, who had a love-hate relationship with Kevin," smiles Ford. "When Kevin was leaving, he was saying, 'Let him go, he'll never do anything'. I said, 'He'll play for England'. I knew he was going to do well."

THE SPECIAL ONE

KEVIN PIETERSEN ARRIVED IN Nottingham two months before his 21st birthday as a cricketer of minimal achievement at senior level and with everything to prove. He had sacrificed the bosom of family life, his close friends, his home in Durban, even his country, for a shot at life as a professional cricketer. It had been his goal since he was 17 to make cricket his living and the contract with Nottinghamshire was the black and white proof that he had earned the stage to consistently display the skills that had been mostly unappreciated in South Africa.

The young Kevin was not especially worldly – he had spent too much time at home with his close-knit family for that – but the season spent at Cannock had hardened him up and proved that he could cope with being uprooted and on his own 6,000 miles from home. Cannock had been crucial on two other fronts. It gave Pietersen experience of how to play on the slower, seaming English wickets and had convinced him that his batting, and not his gentle off spin, was now the principal weapon in his armoury.

You don't have to be earning a handsome salary in the Sky commentary box to offer the observation that the 2009 Pietersen vintage can wield a cricket bat like few others on the planet. Back in the day, or April 2001 to be more precise, there were few experts willing to go out on a limb for Kevin. Graham Ford and Shaun Pollock had been part of a minority – albeit an influential one – in South Africa who thought Pietersen had the X factor, but even they were unable to fast-track him to the top. The man to whom English cricket should offer a prayer of thanks is Clive Rice, the coach who faxed Kevin a three-year county contract without even bothering with the niceties of a trial. Rice could offer Kevin only the slow track to international cricket as Pietersen had to serve a four-year qualification period, making him available for England in September 2004, and had to sever his links with Natal and first-class cricket in South Africa in order to be registered as a non-overseas player for Nottinghamshire. He could continue to play club cricket in the land of his birth, as he occasionally would for his old team Berea Rovers over the next few English winters.

Pietersen was not short of motivation to succeed. In the far distance there was the carrot of international cricket and the potential glory and riches on offer. In the short term, he wanted to fulfil his destiny as a professional cricketer and the material rewards that came with that, gain acceptance in the country of his mother's birth and prove wrong the many doubters in South Africa – the 'I'll show you what for' mentality that was scorched into his psyche even at junior school. Another big motivating factor was Rice himself. Kevin was desperate to shine in front of Rice and prove the Nottinghamshire coach right. "Kevin didn't come to England to play for Notts or for England at that time. He came to play for Clive Rice," says Mick Newell, the long time Nottinghamshire coach who was Rice's assistant at the turn of the decade. "There was a huge respect from him towards Clive and he definitely wanted Clive to be impressed with what he did."

Pietersen's first engagement with his new county was not too far from home – a two-week pre-season tour of Johannesburg. This proved to be an invaluable experience for Kevin, not only in getting to know his new team-mates, but also because it was the last occasion his technique underwent a major nip and tuck. Newell remembers Rice spending hours tinkering with Kevin in the nets at the Wanderers ground. Newell says: "Kevin used to plant his front foot down the pitch and play around his front pad a bit more than he does now. Clive said, 'You can't bat like that, you've got to do this' and changed his foot movements. That was quite a common thing with Clive at that time. He wanted everyone to have a pretty similar base. You always had to move your back foot first, then your front foot, whereas Kevin would just slide his front foot forward. He had played a little bit of first-class cricket, but a lot of it had been school and club cricket so he hadn't had a lot of experience of short-pitched bowling and he didn't have a lot of experience of the ball moving around, which it does over here compared to South Africa. It was probably the last time anyone has made any serious adjustment to his technique." The identity of the messenger helped. "Kevin took anything Clive said on board. If Clive had said 'bat left-handed' he would have done," Newell adds.

Something clearly clicked for Pietersen in the Wanderers nets. Newell had seen him for the first time in the Trent Bridge nets the previous summer and admits that Pietersen did not strike him then as an outstanding talent and was surprised when Rice told him at the start of the tour that Kevin would bat at six in the first team that summer. "It was quite a big call for an unproven 20 to 21-year-old. Then it became fairly obvious in Johannesburg that he was a good player," Newell says.

Injury restricted Jason Gallian, the Notts captain from 2000-2004, to just one county championship game in 2001, but he had been part of the club's think-tank in early season. "Clive found the talent. He saw what was going on," recalls Gallian. "The plan was to bat Kevin at six initially, then get him up the order to three to learn to defend the ball and then put him in his rightful place at four or five." The Notts dressing room, a typical mix of seasoned pros, hired hands and promising sprogs, was immediately impressed by the new boy. "In terms of his style and the way he went about things, we knew he was special from day one," says Gallian. "He was very athletic, had time to play and had such an advantage being very tall because you are always hitting the ball on top of the bounce. We knew we had a very good cricketer on our hands."

Pietersen had been pigeonholed as a bowling all-rounder at Natal, but, given the security of a middle-order berth, the results were instant. He hit the ground running with two centuries in pre-season, made a string of useful contributions in the limited overs arena, including 171 runs without being dismissed and some economical overs in the 50-over Benson & Hedges Cup, and quickly settled into the four-day team. Kevin scored a half-century in his second game, but his breakthrough innings came in his fourth County Championship appearance at the end of May. The venue? Lord's, naturally. It was an early sign of his sense of timing and occasion.

Batting at No. 6, Pietersen helped Notts recover from 191-6 to 467 with his maiden first-class hundred, an unbeaten 165 off 218 balls. Pietersen always appeared as massively confident and, indeed, mostly was genuinely confident. But even he required the reassurance that his debut ton brought him. "After that, I thought I could play," Pietersen told the *Guardian* in 2007. "That's when I thought, 'I could make a proper job of this' and started to take it seriously." Kevin's former Notts team-mate and good friend Richard Logan remembers that game well. He says: "In early season at Lord's you play on the outer pitches at the end of the square so on one side there is a short boundary. In that game he kept hitting Phil Tufnell into the stands with reverse sweeps and pulls. Everyone was talking about the audacity of it."

For good measure, Pietersen howitzed a hurricane half-century in the second innings. Tufnell had run through the middle order, taking five cheap wickets, but Pietersen refused to be tied down and hit four sixes in his unbeaten 47-ball 65. He had scored 230 runs without being dismissed and in both knocks had surpassed his previous highest first-class score, the unbeaten 61 for Natal against the England touring side 18 months previously. A star was born.

"Everything I saw in him was confirmed. I hadn't made the wrong decision," says Rice.

It was not just Pietersen's batting that excited the man who brought him to England on little more than a hunch. Rice explains: "He was an athlete and his co-ordination was better than the others. When he was in the slips he was brilliant.

When he was in the outfield he was brilliant." He was tough, too. "There are plenty of players that you see that can go out there and score runs against a mediocre attack. When the chips are down can he be the guy with the big match temperament? Does he back himself in difficult situations? When Mark Boucher was 13, you could see he had that inner steel, that confidence to perform when it mattered. When I first saw Kevin, I thought he had it too."

Pietersen began to reel off some brilliant innings. A 92-ball 103 not out as Notts were dismissed for just 160 at New Road; a 255-ball unbeaten 218, including nine sixes, at Derby; 150 off 164 balls, including six sixes, in the return match against Derbyshire at Trent Bridge. In his first season as a professional, he ended up topping the Notts first-class batting averages with 1,275 runs at 57.95, scored at an electric rate of 82 runs every 100 balls, quite an achievement for someone who was a complete unknown at the start of the season. They were starting to sit up and take notice, too, back in South Africa. Jonty Rhodes says: "I remember reading the newspapers when he joined Notts and he kept getting hundred after hundred, as well as double hundreds. That was not how I pictured him performing. I pictured Kevin as someone who bowled spin and was a lower order batsman who hit the ball really hard."

By now, Pietersen's bowling had taken not so much a back seat as a position somewhere hanging on to the exhaust pipe. Although he spent most of his first season batting at No. 6 and in the fifth or sixth bowler role, there was little substance to his claims to be an all-rounder. Newell says: "He always thought that he could bowl and he can bowl [but] it's not a front-line skill that he's got, really." Pietersen's nine Championship wickets cost 85 apiece and, although he was more effective in the one-day arena, his spinning skills plotted a downward graph while his batting lurched inexorably upwards. Batting had become his means of making a living. Rice felt Kevin was "possibly a bit lazy in his bowling" and should have practised it more in the nets. Newell believes off-spin does not suit his temperament. "Bowling was a bit boring for him, spin bowling anyway," he says. "He needed more patience and more control . . . he didn't have those things because he was quite excitable, a high energy sort of fellow, he wanted to be doing different things all the time. He wanted to bowl an arm ball, a quicker ball, a slower ball, a big spinner, a little spinner . . . that sort of thing. Therefore you are always experimenting and you are never too far away from a bad ball. He didn't have the mentality of a bowler. He's got much more the mentality of a batsman."

Being the new boy in his early days at the club brought out the more mellow side of Pietersen's character. It would be some time before the flamboyant extrovert came to the fore. Newell, who had roomed with Kevin for two weeks in Johannesburg, says: "He was very quiet for that initial period. We all thought, 'nice lad, quiet lad, respectful to his elders' and he fitted in okay. He asked a lot of questions, wanted to know a lot about England, English cricket, the set-up at Notts." Gallian adds: "He was very polite and very respectful, which was nice." Gallian likened Kevin's attitude to his own a decade before, when he had made a similar decision to cut all ties with the land where he had learned his cricket. "I came from Australia and had to prove myself," he says. "When you come from a different country you want acceptance and you want respect. He wanted it there and then and was getting it because of what he could do."

After his sometimes troubled experience at Cannock, Pietersen found it easier to settle in Nottingham. The club found him a flat in the city centre, which he rented from the girlfriend of former Notts captain Tim Robinson, and he much preferred the bright lights of Nottingham to the more prosaic delights of Cannock. He formed close and lasting friendships with Logan and Matt Whiley, who had just left Notts for Leicestershire but still lived in the city. "We got on really well together straight away and the three of us used to hang out all the time," says Logan, who, ironically, was born and bred in Cannock and had played all his junior cricket for the club before turning professional. "A lot of the players were married or had girlfriends. We were all single at the time – although Kev had a girlfriend in South Africa – and we fell into spending a lot of time together. I had just bought a house and he spent a lot of time at my home in Nottingham, in Netherfield. We hit it off and became good mates. We socialised a lot together."

The three amigos settled into an active social routine. They had similar music tastes and would loaf around at Logan's house watching TV and listening to R&B before hitting the town. They would go out for dinner – Kevin, a self-confessed meat lover, would usually opt for steak – and then on to a bar or a nightclub. Their usual haunts were Faces and the Living Room, rowdy venues where you could be guaranteed a late drink and the chance to eye up attractive young women. Not that Pietersen would over indulge on the alcohol front. "Kev is not a massive drinker," says Logan. "When we went out we used to drink nothing but Jack Daniel's and coke."

As he became more comfortable off the pitch and more successful on it, Pietersen began to assert himself in the dressing room. Daily rubbing shoulders with the great men around the counties did not humble Kevin. He played with hardened pros on level terms right from the start. The old guard desperately need to scratch together their quota of runs or wickets to keep their place or win a new contract. Anything to postpone the dreaded day of retirement. But the unheralded and unknown Pietersen strolled in, belted out thousands of runs at a fearsome lick, played shots that were beyond mere mortals and became increasingly aware that he was operating on a different plane to most of those he shared a dressing room with. Moreover, he didn't care for sensibilities or reputations, and spoke his mind – which began to grate on his colleagues.

Newell, sitting in his ground floor office at Trent Bridge, adds: "Almost in a correlation between how well he did, his success went that way (pointing upwards) and his popularity went a little that way (pointing downwards). His confidence and brashness would grow as he became a better and better player."

There was a clear division between the old – an established core of players which included Gallian, Chris Read, Paul Franks, Andrew Harris, Paul Johnson and Darren Bicknell – and the new. It particularly irritated the senior players that Pietersen and Usman Afzaal, a gifted left-hander who could dazzle one minute and be unspeakably dozy the next, appeared to be cut a little more slack by Rice. Newell recalls: "A lot of people were scared of Ricey and wouldn't say boo to him. He was considered a bit of a disciplinarian, a bit of a God. Kevin and Usman got quite pally and had more of a jokey relationship with him. They might be five or ten minutes late for training or their attitude towards training might not be spot-on because they were confident they would go out and score runs – and they did. That started to grate a bit. There was a perception that they got away with things under Ricey that other people didn't get away with. Being a bit late, being a bit slack with their kit. They would take the p*** out of his bald head. As the summer went on they were getting a higher opinion of their abilities. More so Afzaal than KP. Afzaal played for England that year and got under the skins of the Aussies, but they countered that with their ability and their run scoring. Ricey was fine about it. As players, he loved them both."

Rice actively encouraged Pietersen's individuality. "He was an out and out matchwinner from day one," he explains. "They were jealous of him at Notts. Kevin upset the locals because of his confidence and self-belief. I just wanted a bit of his attitude to rub off on the other guys. With regard to a lot of the English players he believed in himself miles more. They can be playing county cricket in a huge comfort zone. They are good enough to keep a county [job] but they don't set their targets to play for England." The 2001 season had been a poor one for Notts. They were also-rans in the one-day arena and failed to achieve their goal of championship promotion, finishing seventh out of nine in the second division. Rice says: "I will never forget one day when I got all the players together and asked them, 'What is your confidence out of ten?' They were each coming up with three or four. When I got round to Kevin he said his confidence was 20 out of ten. I knew then that I could steer him down the right road. It is much easier than steering a guy whose confidence is four out of ten."

Nottinghamshire's two South Africans developed an excellent working relationship founded on mutual regard and trust. "I would speak to him all the time," says Rice. "I would try to guide him and give him the benefit of my experience. 'Try this, try that. What about that?' We worked a bit on his technique.

My job was to give him some input and make it work for him. He tried hard to improve and certainly listened. He listens well. Even today I text him about ideas and trying different things." Rice knew how to get the best out of Pietersen. He would set him realistic targets and Kevin would move heaven and earth to try and achieve them. Gallian says: "Clive saw him as a surrogate son and understood him really well. That was what Kevin was buying into. Clive was very much a target-orientated manager. He set Kevin targets and Kevin would try to beat them. I remember quite early on he beat Clive's highest first-class score and that meant a lot to him."

At the end of a hugely satisfying first season of professional cricket, sadly there was no tour in which Pietersen could maintain the profile of an excellent young cricketer in form. But there was financial recompense. He was offered – and accepted – a year's extension to his contract and a big pay increase, which doubled his salary to £30,000-a-year. Kevin eagerly returned to his homeland at the end of the summer to catch up with his family and friends and play some club cricket for Berea Rovers. His old mentor Errol Stewart remembers: "He got business cards with the words 'Kevin Pietersen, professional cricketer' printed on. He rented a BMW and the signage on the side of the car said, 'Kevin Pietersen, Nottinghamshire professional cricketer'." Stewart chuckles to himself as he tells this story, but some saw this as evidence of a head that had swelled too much. He adds: "His detractors would say, 'How arrogant is that?' He had the confidence and was proud to tell the world what he was about. The best sportsmen in the world border the confident-arrogant level. He is passionate about what he does. He is very goal-orientated."

THERE WERE SOME at Nottinghamshire who were not too devastated when Pietersen began the 2002 season in something of a trough. He couldn't buy a run in April, May and early June. Sophomore syndrome; the county bowlers had worked out the new gun; that'll bring him down a peg or two, went the whispers. In 16 innings in all competitions up until mid-June Pietersen did not muster a single half-century. Kevin's struggles reflected that of his county. After Notts were dumped out of the principal one-day competition, the Cheltenham & Gloucester Trophy, Rice ended up paying with his job. He was sacked and Newell was appointed to replace him. "I bitterly disagreed with Notts' decision," said Pietersen. "I had lost my father figure, the man who had brought me to England and Notts, and the man I believed in 100 per cent. His methods were my methods and I thought he was a top-notch coach and manager too. Clive had done so much to make the county more professional. I thought, 'Is this really the type of club I want to be part of? Is this the sort of environment in which I want to play my cricket?'"

There was more bad news to come. The day after Rice was axed Pietersen was dropped to the second team. Newell called him to his home on a Sunday and told Kevin that he would not be playing in the four-day game starting the following Tuesday. "I decided to leave KP out because he hadn't made a half-century at that point in the season," he says. There were no water bottle tantrums like the last time Pietersen had been demoted, at Natal two years before. "As far as I remember that conversation it was reasonable, it was okay. I didn't expect him to be particularly happy about it, but he wasn't aggressive towards me at that point." At Notts, the coach shared selection duties with captain Gallian, who rang Pietersen to explain that it was a decision that had preceded Newell. He says: "Clive and I selected the team and we had already decided that we were going to put Kevin in the second team, and as soon as he got some runs put him back in the side. I told him it was a form issue."

Pietersen didn't agree with the decision and, in a foretaste of what was to come with Peter Moores, simply felt that Newell was not up to the job; his opinion no doubt influenced by Newell dropping him so early in the throes of their relationship. "Newell told me that I was below par and I wasn't going to play in his team on my name and reputation alone and on what I'd achieved in the past," Pietersen said. "I didn't accept his explanation and I didn't care how he attempted to justify his selection. I felt that he was just trying to push his weight around. He wanted to put me on some sort of trial."

Newell denies this but admits he was expecting trouble from a particular section of the dressing room. "When I took over I knew the three people that would cause me trouble were Pietersen, Afzaal and Greg Smith, the South African bowler we had at the time who had been brought over by Clive Rice," he says. "Now, Greg Smith didn't give me any trouble at all. He said, 'Look, it's fine. I'm going to get on with it. I just want to play for Notts. I like Ricey, but I didn't come to play for him. I wanted to make a living for my family.' He just got on with it. But I knew Pietersen and Afzaal would be difficult because of their relationship with Ricey. They were big Clive fans. They were very upset. They didn't understand why he had left and thought it was a harsh decision by the club."

Pietersen only spent a couple of weeks in the seconds. His replacement in the first team, Bilal Shafayat, got a pair in the one Championship game Kevin missed and, after scoring 70 against a Durham attack led by Steve Harmison and 113 in the only senior game he ever captained before leading England, Pietersen was recalled to the first team. He cranked up the demonic intensity a notch or two and showed Notts what they had been missing in his best 'I'll show you what for' fashion. Over the five weeks in the height of midsummer he embarked on a golden run of form, scoring 907 runs in all competitions at 113.75, including four hundreds in 10 days in one patch of the deepest purple.

Newell detected a greater maturity in Kevin's batting, particularly in a career best 254 not out as Notts walloped Middlesex by an innings in the county championship. "They bowled at him with five, six men on the boundary, they tried to frustrate him and bore him out, but he never got frustrated," he recalls. "He batted for a long time, hit his singles and set the whole game up for us against a pretty decent attack. He batted absolutely brilliantly."

The game was Stuart MacGill's second for Notts in a two-month locum spell as overseas player at the end of the season. The Australia leg-spinner took a career-best 14 wickets, but recalls: "It was Kevin who got the man of the match, not me. The innings that he played was mind blowing. Early on, Middlesex put out a long-on, long-off, a deep mid-wicket and deep extra cover. Kevin came off at tea and said, 'They've put all the fielders out, that is ridiculous. Don't they want to win the game?' But he was still hitting them for four. It wasn't his big power hitting that was memorable as the majority of his shots were on the ground. It was insane. He was hitting on the ground on the up past the bowler with a long-on and long-off. I'll never forget it."

Pietersen was equally destructive in the limited-overs game. Logan picks out two one-day innings against Somerset in consecutive days in mid-August. "On the Sunday at Trent Bridge he scored an amazing 122 and then we went to Taunton on the Monday and he hit an even more incredible 147," he says. "All I remember was him whacking sixes off the same bowlers for two days. That sticks in your head."

Newell was now convinced that Pietersen had what it took to become a Test batsman. "The fact he was 22, the ability he was now starting to show was quite amazing, quite breathtaking, really. He played fantastically well in the second half of that season. For whatever reason, he turned it on. Perhaps he was aware that other counties were now starting to show an interest, but he was on a long contract here." Logan adds: "The way he played was similar to now – very attacking, very unorthodox, especially the way he played through the leg side. He is obviously a big man and was quite intimidating for bowlers." It wasn't just cricket skills that set the big African apart from his peers. Gallian saw a flint-eyed inner steel and a desire for self-improvement that set him apart from other cricketers. "He was totally different. What you did notice was a certain drive and determination. The bigger the challenge you set him, the better he played."

A fractured leg sustained at Colwyn Bay when diving for a ball in the field brought Pietersen's Bradman-esque run to a halt, keeping him on the sidelines for the last month of the season in what he remembered as a "very unhappy time". Yet Pietersen had responded magnificently to the twin traumas of losing Rice and his first team spot in a draining 24 hours by topping the Notts first-class batting averages with 871 runs at 62.21 and helping the club achieve its aim of promotion from the Second Division. For good measure he also weighed in with 515 runs at 64.37 in the 50-over league, an average twice as good as any of his team-mates.

The departure of Rice had left a big hole in Pietersen's world, but it was partly offset by the arrival of MacGill. With their southern hemisphere backgrounds, outspoken natures and reputations as mavericks, the pair had much in common and hit it off immediately. So much so that MacGill arranged for Pietersen to spend the winter playing grade cricket in Sydney for Sydney University, the club captained by Australian cult hero and former Test all-rounder Greg Matthews.

It was Pietersen's second spell of club cricket away from South Africa, but he found it a completely different experience to Cannock. He loved the Australian lifestyle – the club found him an apartment in the city only five minutes from the university – of barbecues and beaches and found the uncompromising nature of the cricket a rewarding experience, even if it was below first-class level. MacGill helped to test out his friend. HHe explains: "Every night before he played a game I would phone the other team and say, 'He gets bored easily. Have a long-on out and a long-off out, a deep square leg and deep point and see what happens.' I remember him coming to me and saying, 'Mate, they put this field out, I got s****y with it and got out.' I said, 'I know, I told them to do that.' He said, 'Why did you do that?' I told him that when I was playing with him at Notts the only weakness that I could see was if somebody set a deep-set field, he would get bored before the bowler got bored. I thought, 'Let's see what he's got' and he had it. He had it plus some." Pietersen finished the season as the club's top run scorer and helped them to their first grade title.

This was one adopted pom who had won over his demanding hosts.

"When English county players go to Australia, they generally feel they are better than us – they are professionals and get paid and are used to being successful – and because of that you could generally wipe the floor with them," adds MacGill. "When I consider the players who have played in first grade cricket in Australia who have not even been a blot on the landscape. The pressure on them to perform is immense. Kevin didn't appear to feel the pressure. He scored 800 runs in 12 games and would have beaten the records if he had played every game. He had an amazing season. He destroyed Sydney grade cricket."

It was an invaluable winter for Pietersen. "What Australia taught me was to value my wicket," he said. "In grade cricket you can go a month without batting. Your side bats one week and fields the next and all it needs is for bad weather to intervene and you are going a long stretch without any time at the crease." This helped keep him hungry for runs. Even now, as he spends so much time on the international treadmill, a schedule that has been squeezed even further by the arrival of the Indian Premier League, Pietersen says he occasionally likes to think back to what it was like at grade level, when he would sell his wicket dearly and every visit to the crease mattered. "Kevin can switch it on in a heartbeat and he learned that in Australia," explains MacGill. "He realised what he had to do in terms of specific preparation for an innings and that suited him. He needs to feel good about himself and alert when he goes out to bat."

By his own admission Pietersen has more in common with the straight-talking Australians than the more reserved English. "I've always got on well with Australians. They are my favourite people," he once said. "I like working with them and I like socialising with them, and they seem more similar to me in terms of their outlook on life than anyone else I've known."

Had he been equipped with the benefit of foresight and known what tribulations were in store in the 2003 English season, Pietersen might have felt he was better off staying put down under.

ROWS AND RUNS

KEVIN PIETERSEN'S FOUR YEARS at Nottinghamshire can neatly be split into two distinct phases: Before Clive and After Clive.

Phase one was Pietersen the pupil striving to impress his teacher, Clive Rice, and attain the targets that his mentor set him within the parameters of a team environment. Phase two was Pietersen the master batsman striving to become even more masterful. There was no Rice to impress (not directly anyway, although the pair continued to keep in close contact and Rice kept setting Kevin targets) and his goals became more self-oriented rather than team-oriented. "Once Clive had gone, I'm not really sure he cared that heavily whether we won or lost," claims Mick Newell. "But then he would train hard and practise hard and make sure his performance was good."

In 2003, Pietersen operated in a sphere of excellence that was far removed from the territory inhabited by most of his team-mates. Nottinghamshire had an annus horribilis. Pietersen, naturally, had another annus mirabilis. Notts won just two first-class games all year – the first and the last – and got relegated from Division One of the championship. They were equally dismal in limited-overs cricket. Yet Pietersen had his most prolific season to date, scoring bucketfuls of runs – 1,546 of them in the championship at 51.53 and a club-record 776 in the one-day league. In the two main competitions this was nearly 1,000 runs more than the next best batsman in the team.

The antagonism that grew between player and club over the course of the season stemmed from the disparity in contributions between Pietersen and his team-mates. Notts employed four overseas players that year – Chris Cairns for most of the campaign and Stuart MacGill, Steve Elworthy and Daniel Vettori for smaller chunks of it – and yet the club's outstanding player was clearly one with a British passport. The problem was he knew it all too well.

"The pitches here weren't great, the matches were quite low scoring, but KP still stood out as the best player by scoring a lot of runs," recalls Newell. "His frustration grew with the other players. As he continued to score runs and other people didn't he became more vocal in his criticism of the other players, really. He was mainly critical in the dressing room, but he also went public in the local paper about the state of the pitches and the state of the nets, which he wasn't impressed with. He was trying to play for England and felt that he shouldn't be playing on pitches of that quality." This didn't especially endear him to his colleagues. Nor did some of his outspoken comments behind closed doors. Jason Gallian says: "We would be sat on the balcony during our innings and Kevin would be saying, 'He should have pulled that ball' or 'He should have driven that ball.' It would frustrate him and he would be more than happy to tell you what the batsman should be doing. He expected other people to be able to do what he could do, which is sometimes impossible."

Pietersen had operated on level terms with county cricketers from day one. His rapid elevation to the elite left him with mixed feelings. It gave him great satisfaction, of course, but it also enraged him. Pietersen was no longer playing with equals – he was the best cricketer by miles. He pursued and achieved excellence as a matter of course and could not stomach the fact that his team-mates' standards were so far below his own. "That was one of his problems with county cricket," says Newell. "He couldn't understand why the gap was so wide between him and some of the other players. It was massive because he was so much better than them. By the middle of 2003 it was clear that he was going to be an international star. I said to him a couple of times, 'You could be as good a player as you want to be.' We weren't coaching him. You just try and manage him, make sure he is as happy as he can be and make sure he can go out there and perform, which he did."

Yet MacGill insists that Pietersen's actions were not malicious or even conceited. "The way Kevin looks at the world is different to everybody else. When a team set really defensive fields for him, he didn't understand it was because he was seriously good. He thought everybody should be able to drive on the up like he did. I said, 'Kevin, no-one else I have played with can drive on the up through mid-wicket and extra cover.' For him, it is normal. He gets bored of straight driving for four – especially if they put out a long-on and long-off –so he starts hitting across the line. He would invent things to keep himself interested."

Pietersen lacked the maturity to see that his Notts team-mates were doing their best and that, while they were not as good as he was, he was stuck with them.

The problem was that Kevin had not grown into his talent. His spiky nature made it a serious problem, at least for his colleagues. A man reared in the southern hemisphere who calls a springbok a springbok, Pietersen saw it as completely normal to offer his frequently withering opinions on his team-mates. Tact and diplomacy were never his style. He would have made a useless hostage negotiator. "In the dressing room he was brash and a big character," says Jason Gallian. "He would say something and that rubbed people up the wrong way. He was always really raucous and opinionated. He was very controversial."

Many of Pietersen's Notts team-mates lacked the charity to understand he was a one-off who sometimes played by his own rules. MacGill offers an interesting insider view: "They knew that he was different to them," he explains. "They knew he was better than lots of people they have played with and would go a lot further. When you are slightly different to your team-mates you do get treated badly sometimes. Many at the club were simply waiting for him to fail. A lot of people I have played with who have come across him judge him on the criteria that everybody should be warm and fuzzy on a cricket field. For a long time in England and in Australia people have believed everybody has to be exactly the same all of the time and everybody has to be living in one another's pockets to be part of a successful team. People look at Kevin Pietersen and go, 'He is different to us, he is going to be a problem for me.' Why on earth would you care whether he shares the same hobbies or speaks the same as you? People say to me if I had done this and that differently I might have played more Tests. I say, 'If I had done it differently I might not have played at all.' Kevin is very much the same."

Pietersen, being Pietersen, didn't always help himself. His inability at hiding his feelings was crystallised in a major bust-up with Newell and Cairns on the first day of a championship game against Kent in the middle of August. Notts had won the toss and elected to bat on a tricky Trent Bridge pitch. Pietersen came to the crease at 17-2 and played a lone hand in another poor batting performance from Notts, scoring an even 100 off 99 balls as the home side were bundled out for 177 soon after lunch. Furious that he had to throw his wicket away when left with only MacGill and Charlie Shreck for company, two of the biggest batting rabbits on the circuit, he stormed into the dressing room to confront his coach. "He came off and said to me, 'I won't be fielding,'" says Newell, still shaking his head six years later at the memory. "I said, 'Sorry?' He said, 'I'm not fielding.' I said, 'Why are you not fielding?' He said, 'This lot are s***. I'm not fielding with this lot.' I said, 'Oh, okay, right' and we sort of sat there for a bit. Chris Cairns was there in the dressing room. He got up and just took Kevin into my little office and held him up against the wall by the throat and gave him a bit of a verbal tongue-lashing in regards to his commitment to the rest of the team. It was just words, no punches were thrown. There wasn't a huge amount said from KP."

The sight of a 6ft 4in seething South African being pinned to the wall by an equally seething New Zealand powerhouse is something most of us would pay good money to witness. Newell believes, ironically, that Pietersen's outburst was partly prompted by his growing contempt for Cairns, who, as the club's principal overseas player and one of its top earners, was expected to produce the goods, but rarely did that year. Newell says: "Kevin had seen our overseas player not have a great season and therefore he became more vocal in his criticisms of the players, the club and me throughout the year. Probably his respect for me wasn't great at this point and I was a mate of Cairns who had brought him back into the team." Yet Cairns was no foreign mercenary. Trent Bridge was his adopted home. He played for the county from 1989 to 1996, before returning in 2003. "He was totally committed to the club," says Newell. "He played overseas cricket for us and didn't really want to play for anyone else. He's a club man, a Notts man, even though he is not from here. And he just couldn't believe what he was hearing. Everybody knew that Kevin was a fantastic player, but then the better he got, the more vocal he got. He was getting frustrated. It's a little bit understandable. Other people couldn't get a run, we were losing matches, he was still scoring runs, the team were struggling, his favourite coach had left, things were probably not all that happy for him at that point."

It would be wrong to say that Pietersen became a loner in his penultimate season at Notts or withdrew into himself. He was no Geoff Boycott. Kevin had close allies in Richard Logan and MacGill and remained on good terms with Usman Afzaal and bowlers Greg Smith and David Lucas. But Pietersen thought it was only right to tell Gallian that he didn't think much of his captaincy, only proper to tell established first-teamers that they were letting the side down. Speak out and hang the consequences, could have been his motto. "I always believe in speaking my mind and telling people what I think and I had no hesitation in saying publicly that I felt I was carrying the team," said Pietersen. "It got so bad that I would sometimes warm up on my own rather than be with certain team-mates. It was awful that it had come to this, but I was determined to stand up for what I believed in, and if that saw me as a man apart so be it."

Newell admits that Pietersen and MacGill were particularly difficult to manage. "Stuart's wife didn't like living in England so if she was p***** off, he'd come to work p***** off. He could explode. He exploded at Jason, he exploded at several players for slack standards, but he was totally committed to the team. To a certain extent, he would stoke Kevin up on occasions. Kevin didn't explode in quite as verbal a way at the team or in front of the team but could be a bit more undermining, perhaps. For example, if I was talking, he would be looking the other way. He was more dismissive of me and of Jason."

Pietersen didn't see it as his duty to be politically smart. "All progress has resulted from people who took unpopular decisions," said the 19th century US vice-president Adlai E Stevenson and this was undoubtedly how Pietersen viewed it. He didn't doubt himself for a second. "Kevin didn't necessarily set out to win friends and influence people," observes MacGill, another who was frequently portrayed as a misfit during his career. "The other players lost sight of what was important and what wasn't, to be honest. From time to time he was disrespectful. He was dismissive to people that he felt were disrespectful to him. But I can't disagree with him. Kevin got a whole lot of grief there. He got treated a lot more badly there than people will ever admit. I find the people in English county cricket very protective of their status as a first-class cricketer and a professional sportsman. They value it very highly. Somebody who comes in and does things their own way, only better, can be really, really unsettling. I'm not suggesting for one moment that all parties were innocent. [But] at the end of the day who is setting the world on fire for England?"

Rice also leaps to Pietersen's defence. "There is no doubt he upsets mediocrity. They think he is too confident or cocky, and full of it. That wouldn't bother me one little bit. The people that know him realise 'Bugger that, let's go with him because the shooting star is going places'. People might call it confidence or arrogance, but a good player walks out seriously confident. If the opposition have only seven out of ten confidence in their game he is dominating them right from the start. He walks out to bat and everybody around him wilts. He has an aura. It was the same with Viv Richards and Graeme Pollock – the opposition were negative from the word go."

As anyone who has played in a professional sports team will know, the side where everyone is bosom buddies is a fictional one. "A team full of clones is one that doesn't win many games," is how MacGill neatly puts it.

Yet there is only so much any sportsman can take, even one with a skin as thick as Pietersen's. Towards the end of that turbulent summer of 2003 he decided too much water had gone under the bridge and it was time to move on. Kevin still had 12 months to run on a contract that was now worth nearly £50,000 a year, but admitted he had "started to look seriously at the possibility of taking legal action to release myself from the final year of my Trent Bridge contract". Like most successful athletes he was aware of his market value. "Kevin talked openly about other clubs being interested," recalls Gallian. "He shared an agent, Adam Wheatley, with Ian Botham, who was a consultant for Somerset at the time and we knew there was interest from Somerset and there were negotiations going on between the agent, Kevin and the club."

Pietersen made his intentions official two days before a championship game against Essex in early September. Newell says: "He came to me and said, 'I won't be here next year, I'm off.' I said, 'Right, okay, but you've got a contract.' He said, 'Well, I'm off.' We went down to Essex and before the game he told the rest of the players in the dressing room that he was resigning from the club, which wasn't great before a match we had to win. He played two terrible innings, slogged two balls up in the air, watched the Test match in the dressing room the whole game, didn't watch a ball of our game apart from when he batted. He carried on like a pain in the a***."

The rift between player and club was becoming painfully obvious for all to see. "He started to go through this period at the end of 2003 where he wouldn't acknowledge the dressing room," explains Newell. "If he made 50 or 100, he would just look for his girlfriend in the crowd. He had turned his back on us, he wanted to leave us, our applause or congratulations wouldn't mean anything. You know, like he does at the Test matches when he looks for his missus and then might go to the changing room. Well, he stopped looking for the changing room. We were not existing. Of his friends, Logan wasn't playing and Afzaal wasn't around much. At that time Kevin didn't really care whether we won or lost, to a large extent."

Yet Pietersen's increasing rebelliousness did not manifest itself in his cricket. Apart from those slogs in the Essex game, he was the epitome of professionalism. "You could never say he didn't try and apart from the first six weeks of the 2002 season there is no spell of him being out of form. We used him at slip a lot and he was good at slip. The only problem was Afzaal used to stand next to him and he was hopeless. KP was a pretty good second slip and in one-day cricket was very athletic. His fielding was always very good."

The mutual dissatisfaction culminated in an incident that is regurgitated ad nauseum whenever a stick is required with which to beat Pietersen. It is used as evidence of his capacity for abrasiveness, yet it was Kevin who was actually on the receiving end. Notts had ended a long, difficult season with a consolation championship win against Middlesex at Trent Bridge. In what he thought was his final match for the club, Pietersen scored 52 and 37. The club hosted an end-of-season party at the ground for the players to let off steam, but Kevin wasn't much interested in socialising with those he was certain he would be leaving behind and left early. "Kevin shook hands with everyone in the dressing room and said, 'I'm off, I'm not going to be here anymore'," recalls Gallian. Pietersen did, though, leave his kit behind. Fortified by drink and the rancour of the season, the Notts captain spotted an opportunity and seized it in a manner which embarrasses him to this day. Legend has it that the entire bag was flung over the dressing room balcony and ended up 20 rows back in the members area. This is not entirely true. "I had a few beers and when the dressing room had emptied I saw his bats nicely lined up alongside his kitbag," Gallian grimaces. "I picked up one of his bats, smashed it up in the dressing room and chucked it over the balcony. I also put his kitbag in the away dressing room, although I came in next morning and put it back."

Youngster Bilal Shafayat rang Pietersen to tell him his kit had been thrown out of the dressing room. Shafayat didn't know who had committed the offence, so Kevin contacted the top man. Gallian recalls: "Kevin rang me, saying, 'I hear someone was messing with my kit.' I told him, 'I'm sorry, it was me. I'm happy to meet up with you and talk about it.' He didn't want to." Understandably, Pietersen was furious with Gallian. "I don't think he would have had the guts to do something like that in front of me, and if he had attempted to do so I would have thumped him, no question," Kevin said.

Gallian, who comes across as inoffensive and measured as we chat in a coffee bar in the City opposite to where he now works as a banker in the winter, is reluctant to state his case or rationalise his state of mind at the time. "I was angry and disappointed with him," he says by way of explanation. "I understood he wanted to go. That's fine. But I'm a believer that you fulfil contracts. Nottinghamshire had looked after him and helped him to qualify for England and in his quest to be an international cricketer. I was captain and party to what was going on. Mick and I had a plan and Kevin featured highly in that. You don't want to lose your star player and he was our trump card. As a captain it does become personal. He had lost respect for Mick and myself and it was just the sight of him trying to get out of his contract." To his credit, Pietersen has admitted that he "probably said a few things I shouldn't have said". Newell believes the constant chirping from Pietersen had finally got to the captain. He says: "Jason had taken a lot of personal criticism from Kevin. He had had a difficult year with the bat. Jason likes a drink and it was at the end of a long, hard season." Gallian was fined by Notts, given a verbal dressing down and a written warning as to his future conduct. "It was massively out of character, just the frustration of the season. He cared, he was passionate," adds Newell.

BACK IN JULY Pietersen had been selected for the England Academy for the forthcoming winter, recognition that he was being groomed for the full international side as the countdown began to his qualification in September 2004. As he prepared to spend his first winter in England, training with the Academy at their Loughborough base before Christmas and then embarking on a six-week 'A' team tour of India and Mayalsia in the new year, Pietersen found himself in limbo with his county employers. He wanted to leave and felt he had a good case for constructive dismissal after his captain tossed his bat over the balcony; Notts wanted him to see out the year remaining on his contract and remain the ace in their pack. Both sides were unwilling to budge an inch. When Gallian tried to hold out the olive branch by ringing Pietersen at the Academy to thrash out their differences he was met with more than just the cold shoulder. "I left a message for him and the next thing I know I had a message from the club not to contact

Kevin because he had taken a restraining order out against me. I was not to contact him or go within a certain distance of him," says Gallian. "That was very petty," adds Newell.

It was the beginning of a long campaign by Pietersen and his advisers to extricate him from his county contract. Legal letters poured in to Newell and David Collier, who was Notts chief executive at the time, claiming that Kevin would be leaving and not fulfilling his contract. There was also a hostile meeting involving Pietersen, Wheatley, Newell and Notts chairman Stewart Foster. Newell says: "Kevin basically told me that I was not up to the job of being coach, that I was lucky. It wasn't a surprise because that was how he felt. He was looking to leave and he was going to make it as difficult as he could."

Notts' stance was equally intransigent. There was a feeling at the club that the Gallian row was merely a convenient pretext for Pietersen's desire to leave. "I have a strong suspicion that he had signed something with Somerset," says Newell. "I was as convinced as I could be that he had come to some certain of agreement, if not written then verbal, that he would sign for Somerset. I have no evidence. Again, he had a car all that winter which we hadn't provided for him and which I'm confident and had heard on the grapevine that Somerset had provided. Somerset had it all lined up and they were expecting him to join them."

Despite the deluge of water that had gushed under the bridge, Pietersen was a player that Notts felt they couldn't lose. "It was a point of principle as much as anything," says Newell. "He was basically suing for constructive dismissal, but in our opinion we weren't making his life so unbearable that he had to leave. I felt we had done pretty well by Kevin and were trying to look after him as best we could and we were being treated pretty shabbily and it was very public at this time." There was also much cricketing logic to holding on to one of county cricket's brightest stars. "At the end of the season David Collier asked me what we should do, so I produced a two-three page strategy for what we needed to do to get back on track. The pitches needed to be better, we needed to get rid of Afzaal and keep Pietersen and bring in some good, home-grown players. So we went out and signed Anurag Singh, David Alleyne, Mark Ealham and Ryan Sidebottom."

Following their bitter meeting at Trent Bridge, Newell and Pietersen did not see one another again that winter until February, when they both happened to be in Chennai, where Kevin was playing a four-day game for the England Academy. The pair had a ten-minute chat by the pavilion, but failed to thrash out a solution. Notts then received a letter detailing an industrial tribunal scheduled to take place a month into the 2004 county season. "I thought, 'What's he going to do until May?'" says Newell. Shortly after that conversation, Rod Marsh, the hugely respected Academy director with whom Kevin had established a good working relationship, had a word in Kevin's ear and said, 'You should just get your head down and play for Notts'. His advice had the desired effect, as, at the end of the Academy tour, Pietersen's agent wrote to Notts notifying the club that his headstrong client would see out the final year of his contract. "We had a meeting – me, him and Jason – just before pre-season started in the Long Room down here and then went upstairs and told the players that Kevin would be staying and we would just be getting on with it," says Newell. The legal thunderclaps off the pitch had finally abated.

The England Academy and the carrot of international cricket rescued Pietersen from what, he has admitted, was a "horrible situation" at Notts and it was this, coupled with the "hardly enticing prospect of a long drawn-out legal saga", that persuaded him to down wig and gown. County cricket, as Pietersen has pointed out in more forthright terms than most, is an insular world and word soon gets around the circuit about anyone who plays or behaves in a manner that is different to the norm. Kevin, with a CV pock-marked by runs and rows, was pinpointed as talented but a trouble-maker. Former chairman of selectors David Graveney had told Pietersen of England's interest in him back in 2001, but when Geoff Miller, another England selector, spoke to Kevin two years later, it was with a degree of concern. Miller said: "What's this we're hearing? Why are you causing trouble? Why are you saying things about people? Why don't you let your cricket do the talking?" When Pietersen joined the Academy, Marsh and his assistants Nigel Laughton and Richard Smith sat him down and said they had heard a few negative stories about him but would judge him on merit and solely how he behaved under their roof. The criticism did not wash over Kevin, but nor did it floor him. He took stock, had a long look at himself in the mirror, concluded that he hadn't done anything wrong at Notts and vowed to prove his doubters wrong.

Pietersen was afforded some leeway by the Marsh regime, which put some noses out of joint. The idea of the Academy is that all the players muck in together and live on the university campus at Loughborough, but Marsh made an exception for Kevin and allowed him to commute from his flat in Nottingham 12 miles away. The Academy students, regarded as the cream of young English cricketing talent, were pushed hard by Marsh. They worked 13-hour days, six days a week and were given a thorough grounding in what was required to be an international cricketer. Simon Jones, who became such good friends with Pietersen at the Academy that he asked Kevin to be godfather to his eldest son, Harvey, says: "It was a harsh regime and it broke a few people, it really did. For Rod, that was his aim. Mornings you do your gym work and cricket in the afternoon. They would set the bowling machine at 95mph and fire taped tennis balls at us. They would hurt if you got hit. I didn't even see it. Kev did. He just took it on. It was relentless all day, every day. We had Christmas off, but you knew if you didn't keep your fitness up, you would be found out when you got back. Rod would cane you."

Apart from Jones, Pietersen's intake included future internationals Matt Prior, Kabir Ali and Sajid Mahmood, some who have carved out solid county careers like Scott Newman, James Tredwell, Graham Napier, Alex Gidman, Bilal Shafayat and Michael Lumb, and others who have disappeared without trace, such as Shaftab Khalid and Simon Francis. Some found the Academy too much, but Pietersen breezed through with flying colours and believed he "matured a lot as a person" and "definitely turned a corner that winter in terms of how the selectors viewed me". As a grizzled veteran of the sport, Marsh is not one to chuck around compliments but he was struck by Pietersen's dedication. "He didn't leave any stone unturned in his preparation. You expect that. If you commit your life to the game, you have to. The ones who work hardest generally do the best. We gave Kevin every opportunity and every bit of support. I would hope the time he spent at the Academy was beneficial to his cricket. I had no trouble with him. When you are hungry for knowledge, there is no better place to be. We had such a wide variety of classes and programmes. He was smart enough to get the best out of it."

The serious examination came in the new year, Pietersen's first representative tour. The 15-strong party spent a week acclimatising in Malaysia before flying on to India for the main part of the tour. It did not start well for Pietersen. He scored 10 and 30 in two routine one-day wins in Kuala Lumpar and began equally inauspiciously during the first leg of the India tour in Bangalore, scoring 17, 16 and 4. This proved to be a turning point. Marsh recalls: "Kevin got out to a leg-spinner twice early in the tour. He was obviously a bit worried. I said to him, 'If you want to improve your play against leg-spin, go and watch Graham Napier bat in the nets.' He stood side on to Napier with his pads on – he was next in to bat - and had a look at what he was doing. Ten minutes later, he said to me, 'I understand what to do now.' From that moment he didn't have a problem against spin. It was freakish. It was just footwork. You have to move all the way forward or all the way back – that's what Graham Napier did. Kevin learned that in 10 minutes. That's highly unusual. The English player's policy generally is to get the coach to tell them. I'm never a big believer in that. My attitude on coaching is that if you learn something yourself, you never forget it. He took his own advice on board. He understood what Napier was doing." Pietersen's willingness to watch and learn from one of his peers (one who has become a county stalwart who made his name in Twenty20) shows not only a degree of humility, but also simple common sense.

From then on, Pietersen was unstoppable. He was promoted to open in the second of the three one-dayers against India A and responded with a 122-ball 131 out of England A's total of 228. Marsh's team had been invited to compete in the Duleep Trophy, India's premier first-class competition, and in the three four-day games against quality opposition, Kevin was superlative. He scored 147 off 169 balls, before retiring hurt with a knee injury, and 31 against Tamil Nadu. He followed that up with twin hundreds, 104 and 115, against South Zone and finished with 32 and 94 against East Zone. In a losing side, Pietersen shone like a 100-watt bulb in a room full of candles. His total of 523 first-class runs at 104.60 was nearly double the output of Prior, the next most prolific batsman in the team.

"He is the second most talented batsman that I have worked with, after Ricky Ponting," says Marsh, who ran the academies of Australia (eleven years) and England (four years) for 15 years. Explaining why Pietersen performed better in the heat and humidity of the sub-continent than his fellow students, Marsh adds: "He had more talent, simple as that. He adapted to conditions quicker. He has a very good mind for batting. He realised early on what was required. The other players didn't have the knowledge or awareness."

Jones left that tour early after proving his fitness to link up with the full England squad in the West Indies, but Pietersen left an indelible impression. "He was totally different to anything I had seen – in terms of his approach and the way he bats," says Jones. "He just oozed belief. I can't remember what it was but he had an argument with someone and he said, 'I've got more talent in my little finger than you've got in your entire body.' I thought, 'Geez, does this boy *believe* in himself a lot.' The first time I met Kev was at Colwyn Bay in 2002. Glamorgan were playing Notts and I had just done a rib muscle and he had just had a stress fracture in his shin. I came off after the third ball of the game and he said he was looking forward to facing me. I thought, 'Who's this cheeky little whatever . . .' But on the tour he was the only one of the boys – and there was a lot of talent – who succeeded in India. He was the only one. As a batsman, he was just different. He was better, it was simple as that. He has more talent than any other batsman I have seen. I'm not saying that because he is a good friend of mine. It was just something that I had never seen before. He's a big guy, he's got a presence about him and an absolute nightmare to bowl to."

At the end of trip Marsh told the 23-year-old Pietersen that he was ready for international cricket and reported this back to the England selectors. Kevin had been given his chance and, in trying conditions, had responded in a fashion that was to become extraordinarily familiar. What was even more impressive was that he had done so with the huge complication of his county employment shrouded in great doubt. During the tour Pietersen told one journalist that this was "most definitely a distraction", so it says a great deal about his inner steel that he was able to ignore it and excel. Many top players of former and current vintage would have been unable to do so.

There was, however, the small matter of Pietersen's final season at Notts. By his own admission, Kevin's goals were more self than team-orientated. "The team had stuffed me around, so I was a little less motivated to do well for them, for the first time in my life." To his credit, Pietersen got his head down and played a big part in a side that got promoted to the first division of the county championship. The runs did not flow quite as quickly as in the previous three seasons, but his 1027 first-class runs in 14 matches at 54.05 was a commendable effort. For once, Kevin was not the main run-getter. He was outscored by the burly Australian David Hussey, whose 1,208 runs came at 63.57.

Pietersen believes it was easier to forget the ghosts of the past because the team was winning, a view supported by Newell and Gallian. "In 2004, he had been easier to manage than he had in 2003, or even 2002," says Newell, revealingly. "He didn't cause me any strife. His attitude was okay. He scored runs and fielded pretty well. We knew he would score a lot of runs because he was going to qualify for England in September. There was no doubt. He helped us win the Second Division, he helped us get promotion in the Pro40. Hussey and Kevin had a bit of a competition going, which was good for us. All of a sudden Pietersen wasn't the best player by so far. He got on well with Ealham, which was good for us as well. He had been on the Academy tour and had been the standout player by a million miles. I saw them play Chennai and the rest of them were hopeless. Rod Marsh was telling Fletcher and Vaughan, 'this boy will play first out of this lot'."

Gallian, whose offer to stand down as captain had been rejected by the club during the winter, also has no complaints about Pietersen's attitude that season. Gallian says: "He had to toe the line because he wanted to play for England, so both sides got on with it and we had a working relationship. He did things his own way, scored his runs."

The bat-throwing saga had also been put to one side, evidence of Pietersen's ability to forgive, if not forget. "He doesn't dwell on things like that. He is a 'live-for-the-moment' kind of guy," explains MacGill. Gallian and Pietersen shared many important stands that season but there was little outward friction. "It was okay," says Gallian. "We batted together a lot. We would get together at the end of the over and talk tactics, which hasn't always happened with other players in the past. He was always professional. Selectors and officials would say to me, 'We hear he is hard to handle' so he had to toe the line."

Newell recounts one telling story, which suggests that Pietersen's loyalties had lay elsewhere before the start of the summer of 2004. "To back up my Somerset theory, he did not play in either of the four-day games against Somerset," he says. "He dropped out with injury on both occasions. We played Somerset at Bath in a four-day game and he dropped out on the morning with a knee or calf injury. He was fit to play against Middlesex at Lord's on the Sunday. We played Somerset down here in September, by which time we were almost there in terms of promotion, and he said he was in no fit state to play mentally. He said 'mental turmoil'. I think he was having a bit of girlfriend trouble."

Nevertheless, such was the new-found mutual regard that, during the course of the season, Pietersen's agent had been discussing with Newell the possibility of a new contract, a considerable u-turn from the discord of the previous winter. In September, Pietersen was offered a contract with a salary of £70,000, which he was told would make him the highest paid player at the club. Kevin thought he deserved more and, when Newell told him that MacGill and Logan, his two best friends at the club, were being released, he made up his mind to leave. The air was far less heavy with acrimony than it had been 12 months previously, but it was time for a new broom to sweep away Pietersen's cobwebs. He had bigger fish to fry.

HARDCORE HITTER

AFTER FOUR SEASONS SLAYING county attacks and a golden Academy tour, Kevin Pietersen had established a reputation in English cricket as a brutal striker of the ball. Standing at 6ft 4in with a well-muscled physique, he was a far cry from the puny 17-year-old who had to have two stints on Creatine to build up his strength. The 24-year-old Pietersen was a highly toned athlete who possessed withering power and the skills and nous to utilise it. He was no village slogger. Kevin had learned that there was more than one way to crack a nut – he could calmly prise it open with the precision of a surgeon and he could sledgehammer it with the force of a lumberjack.

Pietersen also had the defensive technique and concentration to build an innings to go alongside those weapons in his armoury which could destroy any attack. Bowlers on the county circuit began to fear him. "Psychologically, a lot of bowlers are done before they bowl to him," explains Simon Jones. "There's his presence. He's a massive, massive man. You see him standing at the other end, you see this massive bat in his hand. Then you see the way he plays. You always know he's going to come at you. You always know that. It's something he does. He tries to impose himself on people. You know you are in for a massive fight because if you can tie him down, you can tie anyone down."

Jones remembers on one occasion bowling to Pietersen at Swansea and cursing his luck when an induced edge failed to carry to first slip because of the slowness of the pitch. The following delivery was quicker, straighter and delivered at rib height. The result? "He hit me for a flat six straight over my head," Jones laughs. This is what the most destructive batsmen are capable of. They destroy hearts and minds. Any tail-ender can biff a few sixes (remember Devon Malcolm's assault on Shane Warne in the Sydney Ashes Test of 1994-5?), but it takes a special player to consistently blitz attacks in a blaze of aerial boundaries.

Pietersen's relaxed, sportive approach stood out in county cricket, where dour seriousness and caution reigned. Word got around that he was 'box office'. It was not just the amount of runs that he was scoring, it was the way he was scoring them. During his first four years as a professional cricketer his strike-rate was as impressive as his 50-plus batting average. In 2001, his first-class runs for Nottinghamshire came at the scorching rate of 82.20 per 100 balls; In 2002, it was 78.04; in 2003, 81.71; in 2004, 69.95 when he was promoted to the pivotal No. 4 position and had to play with greater care.

There is something magical about a six. It is a joyous pronouncement of a batsman's self-expression and willingness to back his talent and ignore the consequences. Get out and you look a mug. Clear the boundary and you're a hero. It is what essentially makes Twenty20 so popular. Young men are willing to drop their plastic glasses of beer for the chance to catch a ball arcing into the stands. Watching a Pietersen six climb for the heavens like a startled starling had become a regular experience for Trent Bridge members. He had developed a formidable range of power shots; big, booming straight drives, inside-out heaves, leg-side pick-ups, sweeps, slog-sweeps, pulls, hooks and mid-wicket clouts. He loved the appreciative roars from the watching public, he loved the alpha-male thrill of clearing the ropes and he loved the satisfaction of demonstrating his mastery over the bowler in the most emphatic manner.

In 2001 he hit 39 sixes for Notts (30 in the first-class game). In an injury-interrupted 2002 Pietersen hit 18 sixes (only six in first-class competitions). In 2003 he hit 48 sixes (24 in first-class cricket). In 2004, it was 25 sixes. Pietersen was bringing joy to Nottinghamshire's cricket with his mutineer's sense of adventure. He was similarly uninhibited during the Academy tour of India, weighing in with 17 sixes (13 in three first-class games). These figures were a long way off the record 80 first-class sixes that Ian Botham hit in 1985 (he also added a further 25 in the one-day competitions for good measure), but it was, nonetheless, thunderous striking for a front-line batsman. It is instructive that of the eight biggest hitters in Test history, four (Adam Gilchrist, Chris Cairns, Andrew Flintoff and Ian Botham) are all-rounders. Only Brian Lara, Viv Richards, Matthew Hayden and Clive Lloyd relied solely on their sublime batting skills.

It was Pietersen's ability to change a game in an instant that England were buying into when he was called up at the first available opportunity in the autumn of 2004. Although Kevin's first-class stats shaded his only slightly less impressive one-day performances, England's selectors, with the innate caution with which they are renowned, initially picked him only as a one-day specialist. Pietersen was on holiday in Majorca when chairman David Graveney called him with the news that he had been waiting the best part of four years for. He had been selected for a short one-day tour of Zimbabwe – news he regarded as "one of the best moments of my life" and celebrated by drinking a bottle of champagne. However, he had not made the cut for the main leg of the winter to South Africa, for either the Tests or one-dayers. This was not merely fickleness by the selectors. Andrew Flintoff and Marcus Trescothick had been rested for Zimbabwe, while Steve Harmison pulled out of the trip on moral grounds. All three were reinstated for the one-day games in Pietersen's homeland. It also should be remembered that life was fun for England in 2004. They were winning Tests with unprecedented regularity – a magnificent seven out of seven at home, a first series triumph in the Caribbean for 36 years – and were even a force in the one-day game as they showed the world how to play cricket in thermal underwear during the late September Champions Trophy, coming a close second to Brian Lara's inspired West Indians.

The Zimbabwe trip was inconsequential in a way, given the weakness of a home team decimated by a race row over the white players, but it proved to be one of the most controversial and politically-charged tours in cricket history. On many occasions in the build-up to the series it appeared as if it would not go ahead – and Pietersen would be denied his debut – because of safety issues and moral concerns about Robert Mugabe's abhorrent regime. But the ECB were threatened with huge fines by the International Cricket Council if they pulled out and had little choice but to send a team once it became clear that there was little possibility of physical violence befalling what was a high-profile international touring team. A last-minute row involving members of the travelling press corps being denied entry to Zimbabwe to cover the series added to the farce and Pietersen spent nervous hours holed up at a Johannesburg hotel waiting to hear England's fate. "This was a big worry to me," Kevin said. "I'd already experienced enough politics in my career over what happened at Natal and I didn't want politics to interfere now I was so close to where I wanted to be." It was a huge relief to Kevin, although perhaps less so to other players, when the management confirmed the tour would go ahead, although the original schedule of five one-day internationals had been cut to four.

After Pietersen disowned South Africa, England had provided the golden road for his colossal and undeniable talent. Now here was his chance to make his mark, but would he prove a 'flat-track bully', the negative label bestowed by John Bracewell on Graeme Hick, another African who had to bide his time in the shires carving out one hundred after another while qualifiying for England? Pietersen was not quite thrown in at the deep end as Hick had been against the mighty West Indies in 1991. His debut was, by comparison, unimaginably low key and the antithesis of what was to come over the next 12 months. For the first time since the Nehru Cup in the autumn of 1989, there were no satellite television pictures from an England overseas assignment beamed back home.

Pietersen arrived in a successful, close-knit England dressing room with something of a reputation, a by-product of his frequently turbulent spell at Notts. The England players were not prepared to tolerate any big-time behaviour. Simon Jones was one who could speak highly of Kevin after they had got to know each other well at the Academy the previous winter, but there were few other friendly faces. "I always get annoyed when people go on someone else's say-so," says Jones. "You judge someone when you meet them. You make your mind up and not believe what someone else has said. I got along really well with him. I couldn't see what the fuss was about."

Others were more wary. Ashley Giles, an earthy member of the England dressing room who had rejected coach Duncan Fletcher's offer to rest from the Zimbabwe tour, adds: "I think it's fair to say that a lot of us were ready for him. We thought, if he wants to be big time around us then he's in for a shock. We had heard a lot about him, much of it negative. Some had said he was a destructive influence, others that he wasn't a team man. I wanted to make my own mind up."

Given his South African connections, there were also question marks about Pietersen's commitment to his adopted land. He passed all these examinations. "I found him to be completely different to what I had been expecting," says Giles. "Kevin was great in the dressing room, he was a team player and he was a great influence on those around him. Also he played with such passion and determination that no-one could be left in any doubt as to how much it means to him to play for England. In county cricket you can get dragged down by those who are jealous. Kevin can put some noses out of joint, people who have been around a long time and maybe don't share his depth of ambition, but in the England dressing room we all want to be the best we can and he fitted in with us straight away. He became a good friend of mine from the start."

Pietersen's settling-in process was made easier by the 'buddy' system that operated on that trip in order to bed in a number of inexperienced young players (Ian Bell, Matt Prior and Alex Wharf were also on their first England overseas tour). Kevin's buddy was Giles.

On 28 November 2004, Pietersen made his long-awaited international bow, not that many folk saw it. You will have to search long and hard to see footage of his first England appearance, but suffice to say he made a good first impression. Coming to the crease at 146-3 in pursuit of Zimbabwe's inadequate 195, Pietersen ensured there were no embarrassing hiccups with a cautious, unbeaten 27, blighted only by a few nervy singles. It occupied 47 balls and included just a single boundary, but he had shown he was not completely out of place, even if the atmosphere and size of the crowd at the Harare Sports Club was more akin to a county, rather than an international, match.

Ordinary schoolboy: It was a long time in coming, but Pietersen finally nailed down a spot in the Maritzburg College first XI late in his final year of school in 1997. He is pictured on the back row (fourth from left) alongside team-mates Butch James (fifth from left), Grant Rowley (front row, second from left) and coach Mike Bechet (front row, centre).

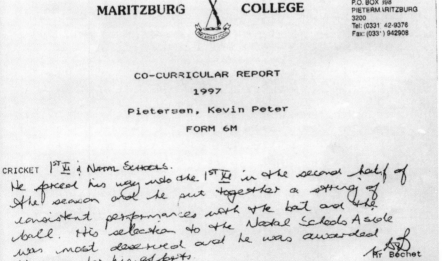

MARITZBURG ✕ COLLEGE

P.O. BOX 398
PIETERMARITZBURG
3200
Tel: (0331) 42-9376
Fax: (033') 942908

CO-CURRICULAR REPORT

1997

Pietersen, Kevin Peter

FORM 6M

CRICKET 1ST XI & Natal Schools.
He forced his way into the 1ST XI in the second half of the season and he put together a string of consistent performances with the bat and the ball. His selection to the Natal Schools A side was most deserved and he was awarded Honours for his efforts.

Mr Bechet

RUGBY
Third XV
A very adept fly half who excelled at ensuring his forwards played ahead of the gain line. His goal & line kicking was of great benefit to the team. A very valuable member of the side.

Mr Whitear

High-flying sportsman: Pietersen's 1997 College sports report.

MARITZBURG COLLEGE

P.O. BOX 398
PIETERMARITZBURG
3200
☎ (0331) 42-9376
FAX (0331) 94-2908

Pietersen, Kevin Peter

FORM 6M

013915

REPORT: JUNE EXAMINATIONS – 20 JUNE 1997

SUBJECT	GRADE	PUPILS MARK	SYMBOL	MAXIMUM	FORM AVERAGE	SUBJECT TEACHER'S COMMENT
ENGH	H	195	E	400	221	Kevin does not have natural ability in this subject. He needs to realize that more effort is required along with a more serious attitude if he wants to improve his mark. *Ms Clerk*
AFRS	H	178	D	300	170	A satisfactory result although he is capable of achieving a 'C' symbol. *Mr Morgan*
MATH	S	202	C	300	136	A good result. He is obviously more comfortable at standard grade. *Mr Guides-Brown*
PHSC	H	186	E	400	252	I have no complaint with his effort. He will improve on this result. *Mr Miller*
TECD	H	208	D	400	256	Kevin has the ability to improve on this result with greater effort. *Mr Bennetts*
GEOG	H	189	E	400	227	He worked well and produced sound work this term. I look forward to a much improved result from his trials next term. *Mr Sutherland*

AGGREGATE: 1158 D   RESULT: MEETS THE REQUIREMENTS FOR AN EXEMPTION PASS
NUMBER OF DAYS ABSENT: 1

A SEPARATE CO-CURRICULAR REPORT IS ISSUED AT THE END OF THE YEAR

REGISTRAR'S COMMENT: He is a hard-working, dedicated pupil who is highly motivated to succeed. I have no doubt his grades will improve in the weeks ahead

HEADMASTER/HEAD OF DEPARTMENT COMMENT: He needs to make every *Mr Miller* effort next term so that he can achieve the results of which he is capable. The areas of weakness require special attention.

School re-opens on Monday 21 July 1997.   Boarders return by 7.30 a.m. on 21 July.

Hard-working pupil: Pietersen's June 1997 report for academic subjects six months before he matriculated.

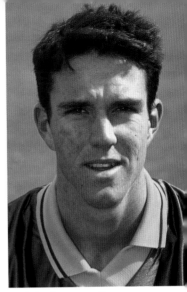

Old boy: Mike Bechet with Pietersen's signed 2005 Ashes shirt and headline from the Natal Witness paper in the 'hearth' memorabilia room at Maritzburg College.

Fresh-faced youngster: Pietersen at Nottinghamshire in 2001.

Lone stand: Pietersen walks off 78 not out in a B&H Cup semi-final versus Surrey after the rest of the Notts side collapsed around him to lose by 174 runs. Was this the first sign of frustration that KP was playing at a different level to his team-mates?

Visionary coach: Clive Rice at Notts.

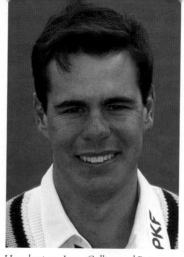

Huge bust-up: Jason Gallian and Pietersen fell out spectacularly.

Tough guy: Chris Cairns gave Pietersen the dressing-down of his life.

A-grade student: A magnificent first representative tour with ECB Academy under Rod Marsh in 2003/04 earned Pietersen a full call-up the following winter once he had qualified.

Hardcore hitter: Pietersen made his mark on the international scene in sensational style. From left, scoring 77 not out in his second ODI v Zimbabwe, celebrating his first international century against his home country of South Africa and, right, with his man-of-the-match and series awards after scoring 454 runs and three centuries in six innings in his first major series.

Speed freak: Left, celebrating a wicket in flamboyant fashion with best mate Simon Jones and (right) the motor racing fanatic visits the Ferrari garage at the British Grand Prix with Jones.

Dead skunk: Who can forget the hairstyle that guaranteed Pietersen even more attention? Here he is making his debut at Hampshire's Rose Bowl for his new county.

True Brit: Pietersen wears a Union Jack Flag after victory against Bangladesh in May 2005.

Hours of dedicated training, much of it alone, made KP physically superbly fit for Test cricket, and proved he had the winning mentality.

Ashes hopefuls: England players on pre-series photo shoot. From left, Pietersen, Matthew Hoggard, Simon Jones and Ian Bell.

Freak debut: 50 at Lord's. Pietersen top-scored both innings of his Test debut against Australia Lord's, with splendid knocks of 57 and 64 not c

Running-mates: Pietersen's rivalry with friend Shane Warne was one of the highlights of the 2005 Ashes. Here Warne has an lbw appeal rejected at Lord's.

Great innovator: Pietersen displaying his unorthodox style in the second Test at Edgbaston during his rousing first innings 71.

Lion roars: Celebrating the tense series-levelling victory at Edgbaston.

Fielding woes: Dropping Warne at Old Trafford. Pietersen had a poor series in the field, dropping six catches and acquiring the uncomplimentary nickname of 'Cymbals' from the Australia team.

Happy hooker: Pietersen's sense of adventure occasionally led to his downfall in 2005 but here he hooks for 4 at Edgbaston.

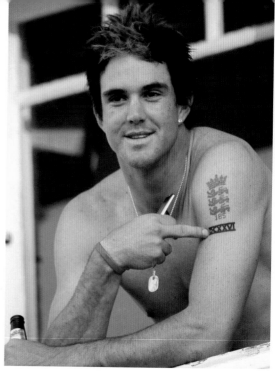

Straight bat: Pietersen's game is based upon sound principles. Here he straight drives for 4 at Trent Bridge in his first innings 45.

Two tattoos: Showing off his new acquisitions on the Trent Bridge balcony after England's victory. Pietersen took on Darren Gough's dare and went under the needle to get tattoos of the Three Lions and his England number in Roman numerals. But his father wasn't too happy.

Serial winner: Celebrating Hampshire's C&G Trophy victory over Warwickshire by 18 runs at Lord's. KP failed with the bat, scoring only 5.

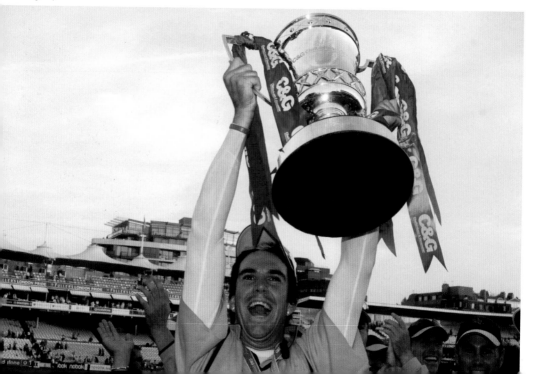

Nervous times: Watching on pensively from the Oval balcony during the start of England's second innings with coach Duncan Fletcher.

Legend begins: A full house at the Oval join a grateful nation in rising to acclaim Pietersen's astonishing Ashes-sealing 158.

Ashes winner: Celebrating with the urn and a bottle of champagne in the Oval dressing room.

Party time: The two public faces of the Ashes celebrations. Left, with Andrew Flintoff the morning after the night before, although Pietersen at least managed two hours' sleep before visiting 10 Downing Street. And right, with parents Jannie and Penny and the Queen receiving the MBE.

Quiet times: Pietersen struggled to adapt to the low-key atmosphere in Pakistan but scored his second Test century at Faisalabad.

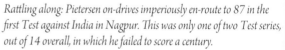

Hanging on: Catching Mohammad Yousuf in the third Test against Pakistan. After his Ashes fumbles, this was only his second Test catch in his eighth Test.

Rattling along: Pietersen on-drives imperiously en-route to 87 in the first Test against India in Nagpur. This was only one of two Test series, out of 14 overall, in which he failed to score a century.

The birth of the switch-hit; KP hits Sri Lankan spinner Muttiah Muralitharan for on way to 142 out of an England total of 95 at Edgbaston in May 2006.

In demand: Pietersen signs autographs in a clamour in May 2006.

Marketing dream: npower are one of many blue-chip brands who have used Pietersen's image to market their companies. Left, giant projection onto a building in Manchester as the hype builds up to the Ashes in November 2006. Right, Inzamam-ul-Haq fields in front of a huge Pietersen hoarding at the Oval in August 2006.

Fired-up Aussies: Not so friendly now. Warne launches the ball at Pietersen in the first Test at the Gabba as Australia demonstrate their desperation to reclaim the Ashes in 2006/07.

Thumping defeat: Out for 92 in the first over of the fifth day at the Gabba as England's Ashes campaign Down Under begins with a humiliating loss.

All over: The Ashes are back in Australia's hands after England limp to defeat in the third Test at Perth but Pietersen is there until the end. He walks off 60 not out and puts a consoling arm around Monty Panesar's shoulder.

Wise words: Two outspoken individuals from different eras. Geoff Boycott has a friendly word in Pietersen's ear.

Friends again: Pietersen embraces with Warne and Nic Pothas as Hampshire stroll through to the Friends Provident final with a semi-final victory over Warwickshire.

Girl power: Pietersen's fiancée Jessica Taylor, who he later married in December 2007, shows him how it's done as they promote npower's Urban Cricket programme.

Modern icon: Pietersen is very much a 21st century cricketer. Left, the blue rinse is unveiled before the 2005 Old Trafford Test and centre, the skinhead takes a bow in 2008. Right, his third tattoo, of wife Jessica, is revealed to the world.

Crowd puller: Even putting a box in can draw an audience. During a World Cup warm-up at Gros Islet in March 2007.

Lone stand: Crunching cover-drive in the World Cup Super Eight stage versus Sri Lanka. Pietersen top-scored with 58 but England limped out of the tournament in embarrassing fashion.

Media favourite: Pietersen's quotability and frankness makes him a hit with the media.

Hitting out: On the way to a match-winning 129 against New Zealand at Napier in March 2008.

Switch-hitting genius: Pietersen stuns the cricket world with his two brilliant left-handed sixes off Scott Styris against New Zealand at Chester-le-Street in June 2008.

Special meaning: Celebrating scoring a masterful century against the country of his birth South Africa at Lord's in 2008, an innings that drew such a huge ovation Pietersen claimed he had "never felt so loved" by his adopted country.

In command: Appointed captain after Michael Vaughan's resignation.

Captaincy demands: The job brought even greater scrutiny for England's star player. Left, answering questions from the press in India, centre, directing his fielders and right, celebrating a 4-0 ODI whitewash against South Africa in September 2008.

Statesmanlike leadership: Pietersen led from the front in persuading all of England's players to return to India after the Mumbai atrocities seemed certain to curtail the tour.

In crisis: With coach Peter Moores. Despite the thumbs-up from Pietersen, all was not well behind the scenes. Long meetings involving the pair and senior ECB officials failed to heal the rift that had developed.

Media storm: Pietersen returned from holiday in South Africa in January 2009 to learn of the decision to strip him of the England captaincy, announced by, right, ECB chairman Hugh Morris.

Disastrous collapse: Bowled by Jerome Taylor as England were shot out for 51 in the first Test in Jamaica in February 2009.

Testing times: After a rocky six-month period, Pietersen openly admits he struggles to cope without Jessica, who he spent 11 weeks apart from during the 2009 West Indies tour.

In the second game, Pietersen's innings had the air of a statement. He showed some of the exuberant destructiveness that he regularly displayed for Notts, hitting three sixes in an unbeaten 77 off 76 balls and adding 120 for the sixth-wicket with Geraint Jones in a comfortable 161-run victory. It earned him the man-of-the-match award and, more importantly, the approval of his coach. "He had played just two games in Zimbabwe when I said to Michael Vaughan, 'We've got to get this guy to South Africa'," wrote Fletcher in his autobiography. "It was glaringly obvious that he had to be part of the one-day side we were attempting to build. People always ask me what I saw in him, but it's almost impossible to describe. There are lots of little signs – the body language, how he played a shot, that control. He just had it. With some people you can just tell. It was wrongly thought that Pietersen replaced Flintoff in South Africa. He did not. He was coming anyway."

Pietersen did little of note when the tour moved on to Bulawayo. He did not bat in the third match and was dismissed first ball in the final game when a casual flick to square-leg brought a withering stare from his captain. Fletcher, though, had seen enough to be convinced that Pietersen had the mental strength to cope with the travails of international sport. "I had noticed that immediately," he later wrote. "He had scored a duck and then dropped a sitter of a catch in Bulawayo and was still clapping and encouraging his team-mates for the rest of the match. Weaker characters would have sulked and retreated into their shell."

True to Fletcher's word, Pietersen got a call from David Graveney in January 2005 that he had been added to the party for the one-day leg of the South Africa tour as a reward for the promise he had shown in Zimbabwe. Returning to the homeland that he had shunned did not daunt Pietersen. It inspired him. In Pietersen's mind his country had let him down. Of course, it was an oversimplification, but it was a powerful motivating force. It was a golden opportunity to, in his own words, "show everyone in South Africa what they were missing".

Ever since he was a schoolboy struggling to make the school or college first team, Kevin's sporting raison d'etre had been to prove the doubters wrong. At the elite level of sport it is not just talent that separates the good from the very good. "He was always hardcore," says Mike Bechet. "Maybe 100 guys in England have the talent to play Test cricket. But only a handful have the toughness to face down [Glenn] McGrath calling your mother a bitch. KP can look McGrath in the eye with the attitude that says if you want to get me out, you'd better get a gun."

Pietersen expected a baptism of fire in the land of his birth following his change of allegiance and the senior South Africa players did their best to stoke up the patriotic feelings of the home crowds ahead of the seven match one-day series that followed England's 2-1 Test triumph. National captain Graeme Smith was Kevin's most vociferous critic: "He ran out when things got tough," Smith told the press. "If he didn't want to be here then we don't want him here now." This naked hostility spread to the supporters. Pietersen was given an idea of what to expect during a 50-over warm-up game in Kimberley against South Africa A. Arriving at the crease with England 57-3, he was greeted by a chorus of boos when he came out to bat and a hostile crowd continued to shower him with abuse during the course of his innings. Remarkably, Pietersen, showing the attributes which Fletcher had spotted, remained unfazed and played the dominant role in a 169-run stand with Ian Bell that took England to the cusp of a handsome victory before he was dismissed for an 84-ball 97 attempting to hit his fourth six and bring up his century. It was an impressive riposte to the abuse of the crowd, but his mentor was seething. "He played a silly shot and got out," says Clive Rice. "I phoned him up and said, 'The difference between me and you is I would have got three singles, another ten and walked off 110 not out.' He said, 'You're right, but I will show you'."

Few international cricketers, if any, have faced the vitriol that Pietersen endured at the Wanderers in Johannesburg on 27 January 2005 in what was only his fifth one-day international. From the frying pan – or make that the refrigerator – of Harare and Bulawayo into the fire of the famous Bullring, a stadium that had gained a reputation as the most hostile in world cricket. Pietersen was warned by Rice about the sort of ferocious verbals he could expect from a public who mostly despised him for rejecting their country. Rice says: "Before the first one-day international, I said to him, 'The crowd will try and boo you. Just turn it around to your advantage. When they do boo, tell yourself, "The harder you boo, the better I play." Make them suffer.' He did just that. The more they booed him, the better he played."

The night before the game, for the first time in his career, Pietersen consulted a sports psychologist, Steve Bull. He was concerned about his voyage into the unknown. Bull's advice was simple. Pietersen recalled: "He said to me, 'What do you do in county cricket? What do you do when you bat? What's the process? Do you watch the ball at the start of the bowler's run?' I told him I never stopped watching the ball until I had either played it or left it and he said, 'Well, just do that tomorrow. Watch the ball. Don't worry about the crowd. Shut them out. Don't worry about anything.'" This was one of the few signs of mortality, or insecurity, that Pietersen showed over the following three weeks.

It is commonplace in team sports such as football and rugby for players to stand in a line and belt out the national anthems before the start of an international. This public display of national pride is something that has never caught on in cricket, but, unusually, that is what the England and South Africa teams had to do ahead of the day-night floodlit game at the Wanderers. All eyes were on Pietersen and he didn't disappoint. Without a hint of self-consciousness, he belted out the words to *God Save The Queen* with word-perfect gusto as if his life depended upon it. It was at that point that his father Jannie, who was sat in the stands with wife Penny and youngest son Bryan, was convinced Kevin had made the right decision to change his allegiance.

One Pietersen story that has done the rounds is that his Notts team-mates would often make him stand in the corner of the dressing room and sing the national anthem. This is disputed by Richard Logan. "That story is only half true," he says. "At Notts, we used to have fines meetings at different times. There was one jokey meeting which Chris Cairns and Stuart MacGill were heavily involved in and Kev had to stand in the corner and sing *God Save The Queen*. He did it okay. He was always well prepared."

Pietersen had stirred up feelings of great national pride in many South Africans. In a smart piece of captaincy, Vaughan drew all the England players together in a huddle before they went out to field and said, "If KP gets any abuse out here today we must all stand behind him. If they give him stick they are giving us all stick. If they say anything to him or us we must abuse them back." The new boy was immediately made to feel part of the England team and that he was not on his own. He took an early catch in the inner ring to dismiss Herschelle Gibbs, but was then sent to field on the boundary in front of the noisiest section of a capacity 32,000 crowd already baying for his blood. "All the proper Afrikaners were there, drinking beer," said Pietersen in an interview with the *Independent* in 2005. "I was there for about 25 overs, with stuff being thrown at me. It was frightening. People were going hysterical."

Worse was to come when Pietersen came out to bat with England struggling at 44-3 chasing the home side's unimposing total of 175. The lynch mobs were out for England's new middle-order jackhammer. He emerged from the dressing room, through the pitch-side tunnel and into the Bullring's pit of mass hate to be greeted by an extraordinary cacophony of noise and abuse. The infamously partisan stadium had morphed into a seething cauldron of Pietersen-baiting. Swear words littered the air like confetti at a wedding. His former countrymen screamed at him that he was a traitor and a racist. It was cut-throat stuff, like a Roman gladiator taking on wild animals, purely for the entertainment of spectators.

The din was so loud Kevin could not hear what Vaughan was saying when he finally joined his skipper at the crease. Out on the pitch he was ceaselessly sledged and his moral character questioned by the South Africans, led by Smith from first slip. It was perhaps fitting that his first ball was delivered by the feisty Andre Nel, a pantomime villain who knows how to play to a crowd and a moment. It made for great theatre. Nel was vociferously clapped to the wicket and a nervous Pietersen was within a hair's breadth of nicking a pearler. Vaughan marched down the wicket to gently remind his junior partner to keep his eyes fixed on the white ball. Kevin managed a shapeless inside edge to his third delivery and attempted some over-ambitious swipes in a desperate attempt to get off the mark. The atmosphere was raw and electric. The crowd continued to simmer with passion. Pietersen's mother was in tears. She couldn't understand why there was such antipathy towards her son. "I honestly think those people wanted to take out their frustration with the system in South Africa," she said. "I don't think it was anything personal." Kevin finally got off the mark to his 12th ball, followed up by striking Nel for a boundary through backward point and was off and running. He had contributed an unbeaten 22 to a partnership of 59 off 78 balls with Vaughan when a monsoon swept over the ground and brought play to a premature end.

England won by the Duckworth/Lewis system and Pietersen had survived a fierce test of his character and temperament. He was completely shattered by the time he caught up with his family at the team hotel later that night. "People who were there told me afterwards that they had never heard anything like it on a cricket field," said Pietersen. "Yet the reception when I walked out to bat was two minutes of the biggest character-building of my life. To me, getting through that was a big indicator I could do well at international level." Fletcher was impressed with Pietersen's ability to compartmentalise. "Believe me, some of the abuse from the crowd wasn't normal: it was personal, vicious stuff," he observed. "I chose not to draw any attention to the crowd. I'm a believer in the old golfing psychology: if you say 'Don't hit it in the water', you'll probably hit it in the water. You forget the 'don't' bit. I didn't want to bring the crowd to the fore in his mind. Instead I tried to emphasise what he had to do as a batter, which was to stay positive."

Before the second one-day international in Bloemfontein, a place in the heart of Afrikaner country with none of the big-city sophistication of Johannesburg, Rice phoned his former protégé to give him another target. "I said, 'Show what you can do. Get a hundred. It is important to get a hundred quickly because it will prove that the crowds can't faze you'," he explains. As a big believer in fate, Pietersen will appreciate that it seemed written in the stars that he would score his first international century that day. He rode his luck – with four sharp chances either falling short or going to ground – and the inevitable boos to rehabilitate England from a sticky position (67-3) to a dominant one (270-5 off 50 overs) with an unbeaten 108 off 96 balls.

This innings proved not only that he could dominate against a high-calibre international attack (Shaun Pollock, Makhaya Ntini, Nel, Jacques Kallis and Andrew Hall) but that he was more than just a power-hitting substitute for Flintoff at No. 5. Pietersen calmly played himself in with almost exaggerated care and worked the ball around in the middle overs before slamming down the accelerator in the final quarter of the innings. On a day of few boundaries, he hit only six fours, but displayed his awesome strength, extraordinary hand-eye co-ordination and eye for the spectacular with two memorable sixes. The first came off Kevin's boyhood hero Pollock when a slightly over-pitched delivery that would have up-rooted off-stump was lofted high on the leg side and into the stands with a vigorous snap of his bottom hand. The light Bloemfontein air, which, at an altitude of 1,400ft above sea level, allows the ball to travel further, added to the majesty of the shot. Pietersen later claimed that this was the moment when he felt he had truly arrived in international cricket. "You could even say it was the moment that changed my life," he said.

Hammering the great Pollock for six acted like an injection of confidence into Pietersen's veins. He followed it up with an even more outrageous shot against Nel. Shuffling outside his stumps as the ball was delivered he planted his left foot down and hammered a full toss over mid-wicket with his right leg in the air and all three stumps in full view. "There aren't many batsmen who could have played those shots," says Pollock. "I knew Kevin was good when he was at Natal, but I didn't think he was that good. With his leg-side dominance and power you could understand the comparisons with Viv Richards."

However, Pietersen's century celebrations were a far cry from Sir Viv's. Rather than given the Three Lions badge on his helmet an obligatory peck, Pietersen slobbered all over it like a lovesick teenager. Not that the 20,000 spectators crammed into Goodyear Park saw it. In an almost unprecedented display of public indifference they refused to acknowledge him with applause and many in the stands turned their back on England's new star. Pietersen's display was not quite enough to win his team the game, which produced a thrilling finale ending in only the 20th tie in one-day internationals.

Pietersen met up with Rice for a chat on the morning of the third one-dayer in Port Elizabeth. Kevin had not been dismissed in the first two games and Rice's advice was: "Don't get out. Stay unbeaten," to maintain his superiority over the South Africans. For once, Pietersen did not heed his mentor's words. He threw his wicket away with 43 deliveries of England's innings left after hitting a sprightly 37-ball 33 and their final score of 267 proved insufficient as Smith's century inspired the home side to a last-over victory.

The Port Elizabeth leg of the tour is more memorable in the Pietersen story for being the place where the seeds were sown for the hairstyle that was to become his signature. At the time he had fashionably rumpled hair, but it was getting too long for his liking so he mentioned to Darren Gough on the flight to Cape Town for the next one-dayer that he fancied a change of style. Gough's response was, "Why don't you do something stupid with it?" With their desire to be the centre of attention and extrovert personalities, it was only natural that Gough and Pietersen would fall into step as bosom buddies and it was a challenge that the younger man could not resist. Gough insisted on accompanying Pietersen to the salon at the Cullinan Hotel in Cape Town, where the team were staying, and dared Kevin to put a line through his hair. Thus, the 'dead skunk' look was born. The skunk took on many colours in 2005, from blonde to blue, but the original was a peculiar orangey red and, although Pietersen wasn't best pleased with the stylist's efforts, he was convinced he could pull it off.

"When he got those haircuts done, the message was, 'Notice me, look at me, I need approval here'," says Mike Bechet. "He was different and wanted to be different," observes Jason Gallian. "He had an interesting dress sense when he was at Notts. He turned up in these ridiculous trousers once, which he said were Vivienne Westwood. They were like a pair of curtains drawn tight around his legs and meant he couldn't walk properly. He liked to be different and was confident that he could pull it off." Playing for his adopted country in his homeland, Pietersen was already under the spotlight's gaze. With a simple squeeze of hair dye, Pietersen guaranteed that even more attention would be fixed upon him. If it hadn't already become obvious this was no shy and retiring character.

His nearest and dearest were uncomfortable. When asked about her son's radical new look, Kevin's mother replied, "A mother will always love her son no matter what he does". His father didn't even recognise him when he came out to bat the following day. "I said to Penny, 'That's not Kevin, is it? What's happened to his hair?'" said Jannie. It didn't go down too well at Berea Rovers, either. "Everyone here, Grant, me, we all slated him," says Scott, shaking his head in the neat clubhouse. "I was flabbergasted. To this day, we still speak about it. What was the reason behind it? I don't think there was a reason, he just wanted to be different. From the time he left school he has always had that confidence about him. Whatever he wants to do, he will do anyway."

The dead skunk left Pietersen wide open to cutting dressing room banter, although Richard Logan is in no doubt the comments would have slid like water off a duck's back: "I gave him my opinion once and it was not complimentary. He just laughs about it. He is not one to get down about people's opinions. You need that when you are in the public eye. If you walk around worrying what people talk about all the time you wouldn't want to leave your front door." The skunk even had its advantages. "At the time it was a good marketing tool for him," Logan adds. "It made him very noticeable. It was his calling card."

Not that a daft haircut was going to affect Pietersen's single-minded drive to show the Rainbow Nation that he was far better than they remembered. His Dad couldn't recognise him, but Kevin's fluent batting was unmistakeable in a shoddy England display under the gaze of Table Mountain. England's hopes of chasing a distant 291 rested solely on Pietersen after the top order were obliterated by Pollock and Ntini in the opening half-hour and he made a good fist if it, blasting 75 off 85 balls before succumbing attempting to hit a third successive six, and fourth in all, against Nicky Boje. The next highest score by an Englishman was 20.

Playing the comic-book baddie to partisan crowds was becoming a familiar role for Pietersen and it inspired him to produce his most breathtaking performance yet when the one-day circus moved on to East London. England's bowlers had once again been savaged by the home side, with captain Smith (115 not out) carrying his bat, although even he played second fiddle to Justin Kemp, who hammered an astonishing seven sixes, mostly on the leg side, in his 80 off 50 balls. England were well behind the required run rate when Pietersen joined Vaughan, who was making snail-like progress, at the crease halfway through the 27th over. Rice had urged him to score another hundred to show his Bloemfontein ton was not a flash-in-the-pan. Again, Pietersen did not disappoint. Given a licence to attack from the start he almost engineered an incredible victory, racing to a 38-ball 50 and marshalling the lower order brilliantly in pursuit of South Africa's 311. Nel and Ntini exercised just enough control in the final overs to win the match, if not to stop Kevin's personal triumph. With one ball of the innings remaining, he was on 94. His batting partner Gough told him to go for the hundred. Nel delivered a low full toss and, with a magnificent sense of occasion, Pietersen duly dispatched it over the rope for his fourth leg-side six. In the process, he completed the fastest hundred by an England player in a one-day international, off 69 balls. This, it should be remembered, was only his eighth such match. "He was becoming a really hard man to contain," says Pollock. "He had all the shots. Anything straight and he whipped you through leg side, give him some width and he clattered you through the off side. The thing is he is so powerful with it and has such a good eye. In the one-day game, that is a pretty awesome combination."

Heavy showers denied Pietersen the opportunity to bat in the sixth and penultimate match of the series on his 'home' ground at Kingsmead in Durban, the venue where he had taken the first tentative steps towards a professional career. It was the only game on the trip in which he wasn't booed in the field, and, at one point, even had a laugh down on the boundary with some former college mates, but he never found out what the reaction would have been when he walked out to bat. He was the next man in when rain brought play to a halt, with England precariously placed on 7-2 in reply to South Africa's 211. The abandoned match condemned the visitors to a series defeat with a game still to play.

Like all great performers, Pietersen saved the best for last. His *pièce de résistance* came with a sensational century in the final one match of the series in Pretoria when he single-handedly salvaged England's innings from disaster. Rice says: "Before the final match, I told him to get a hundred and become man of the series and show that he was now the main man. I wanted him to emphasise to the South Africans that they had got a hiding from a South African whom they rejected. And he did it." The circumstances were the least auspicious of an inauspicious series for the visitors. A tired England had limped to 32-3 and then 68-6, but were rescued once again by Pietersen, who had earlier been abused relentlessly during the warm-ups by groups of locals sat drinking on the grass embankments.

In company with Giles he bided his time before launching the now familiar ferocious late assault. Kevin reached 50 in 80 balls, careful to eschew undue risk, and with 10 overs of the innings left England were still precariously poised at 129-6. What followed was carnage as Pietersen destroyed all the bowlers with booming, bottom-handed drives and effortless leg-side pick-ups that, exaggerated by the elevated altitude, soared high into the packed stands. He cleared the leg-side rope six times, mostly quite comfortably, and his second fifty took a mere 24 balls. Kevin's last 37 balls yielded 82 runs. When he was bowled trying to launch another huge six, he left to a gracious standing ovation from a capacity crowd impressed by Pietersen's pluck and grateful for having seen a contest, not a capitulation.

Pietersen recalled the gesture of acceptance as "one of the most emotional moments of my life", adding: "I don't think there is anything else in life that can take you to the place where that innings took me. I thought about the decision I had taken to leave the country, everything that had been said and written about it, the sacrifices, and I was just dumbstruck, hearing the people." He was not the only one who had been through the emotional wringer. Jannie said: "I was sitting with my family in the stand and at one point Gregg turned to me and said, 'The palms of my hand are soaking wet, Dad. I'm so nervous.' And when Kevin got to a hundred I just got off my chair and went over to Penny and hugged her. It was an unbelievable feeling because, right at the last, the crowds accepted Kevin and stood to him, recognising what he had achieved." Pietersen had turned the jeers to cheers, but he was unable to save his side from a three-wicket defeat with an over left.

England lost the seven-match series 4-1, with one tie and one abandonment, but the consolation was that they had discovered not just a remarkable talent, but a man clearly made of different stuff from ordinary mortals. How else to explain the way he had blocked out the relentless abuse of vast, hostile crowds to consistently destroy a world-class attack? By any yardstick, his performances were jawdropping. Six innings in the series, three hundreds, dismissed only once under 75. A total of 454 runs from 430 balls at an average of 151.33 – more than the combined aggregates of Vaughan, Marcus Trescothick, Andrew Strauss and Paul

Collingwood. He had also hit 15 sixes, the second most in any one-day international series (the record of 18 was compiled by Matthew Hayden at the 2007 World Cup – from 10 innings); Bradmanesque and Bothamesque all at once. "That was the fortnight that changed his life," says Logan. "It was going to happen anyway because he was a class player, but that was the factor in making it all happen for him. You can't imagine the pressure he was under and the treatment he got in that first game, but he won the crowd over during the series. It was like being booed at the start of a boxing match and then everyone in the crowd calling, 'Rocky, Rocky' at the end."

The English camp were amazed by the new boy's skill and phenomenal self-belief. Fletcher would frequently caution the press that it takes 50 matches to learn international one-day cricket properly. Pietersen had played 11 games. "He has come in and set the world alight, playing innings at unbelievable tempo in pressure situations. You've got to be a very good player to do what he has done," said Vaughan after Pietersen had been named man of the series. Giles adds: "He added something to our team that we just didn't have to the point where people were saying, 'Where has this guy been?' I had heard that he could hit the ball even cleaner than Andrew Flintoff and my reaction to that was, 'B******s, that's a huge thing to say'. Then, after those one-day internationals in South Africa I was saying the same thing myself. I couldn't believe how hard he could hit the ball."

The entire cricket world was sitting up and taking notice of this extraordinary interloper, but Pietersen wasn't entirely satisfied he had dispelled suspicion of his 'mercenary' motives. He wanted to provide further proof of his commitment to the England cause. Once again, Gough was on hand to coax the daredevil out of him. Kevin had told the press at the start of the one-day leg of the South Africa tour that he was thinking about copying England's veteran fast bowler and having a Three Lions tattoo, but put it off after Jannie expressed his displeasure. Even aged 24 Pietersen did not want to upset his parents, especially his disciplinarian father, but at the end-of-tour party after half-a-dozen glasses of champagne he promised Gough that he would go under the needle. He couldn't resist the dare and admitted he "was getting more and more into the idea of displaying my commitment to my country in a very visual way". The following morning, after just two hours sleep, Kevin went to the Sandton mall in Johannesburg and had a Three Lions tattoo imprinted on his left bicep, even ringing Gough mid-tattoo to come and see it if he didn't believe him. Pietersen was happy to show his team-mates but couldn't pluck up the courage to tell his parents and vowed to keep it hidden from them for as long as possible.

It wasn't until four months later that the world found out about Pietersen's body art, when a camera picked up on him sat in a vest on the England dressing room balcony during a one-day international against Bangladesh. "Thank goodness I was in England and [my parents] were in South Africa," said Pietersen. For Jannie, the arch-conservative, it was hard to come to terms with his son's self-styled 'rapper-chic' image. He recalled: "When I heard Kevin might be getting a tattoo, I said to him, 'There's no way you're doing that'. I blamed Darren Gough for influencing Kevin. It's not something I would have had done, but I have to accept it."

For Pietersen, the tattoo was proof of his individuality and devotion to England. "No-one can take it away from me and say I'm not English," he said. It rested less easily with others, however, who merely saw an impressionable outsider aching for approval. Behind the strut and confident exterior was a man who, according to Giles, "can be as fragile and insecure as the rest of us deep down, perhaps even more than the rest of us". No Three Lions tattoo, however well intentioned, could hide the fact that the first 20 years of Pietersen's life had been spent living in another country. Errol Stewart sensed a deeper cultural confusion. He observes: "Kevin went overboard in this fierce passion for England – while denying South Africa. He was desperate to prove his commitment to England, but I know how much he was missing the Durban beaches and South Africa itself. As he matures he'll hopefully reconcile these two sides of his identity." Jannie adds, pointedly, "When he gets to 40, Kevin might have a good old laugh about hairdos and tattoos and other things like that."

KP: MBE

IT WAS SHANE WARNE who lured Kevin Pietersen to Hampshire. The money was considerable by the standards of county cricket – a salary of £85,000-a-year was £15,000 more than Nottinghamshire had offered – and the club had emerged as the most glamorous and ambitious in the country. In Hampshire's employ were lots of Africans, men such as Nic Pothas, Sean Ervine and Greg Lamb, who shared Pietersen's background and experiences. But it was the opportunity to rub shoulders with the Australian champion that was the clinching factor. Pietersen had agreed to join Somerset in 2003 when Warne was in the middle of a 12-month drug ban, but, a year later, the leg-spinner was back on the scene and keen to sweet-talk one of the hottest properties in the county game into a move to the south coast.

Once again, Ian Botham was a key figure in greasing the wheels of a move and put his friend Warne in touch with Kevin. Warne's first impression of Pietersen when they had been on opposing sides in 2004 was: "Who the hell is this cocky little upstart?" But he warmed to the idea of captaining such a swashbuckling talent and finding out what made him tick. Warne's powers of persuasion are legendary – as the England selectors coerced into picking Hampshire players can testify – and Pietersen was seduced.

Seeking greatness, he decided to surround himself with it. Who wouldn't be flattered if one of the best players of all time invited you for a pub lunch, as Warne did in Southampton, and promised that you would become a better player if you joined his club? "We hit it off straight away," said Warne in 2006. "KP was an impressive guy. He knew what he wanted, which I liked straight away. There were a few counties chasing him at the time so we chatted about life, Hampshire and where I thought the club was going. I told Kevin that I thought Hampshire would be a good learning place for him, both on and off the field."

There was one tricky issue, though. The Rose Bowl was a swish new stadium, but the square was not totally bedded in at that time and had a reputation for producing challenging pitches that were not particularly conducive to selector-nudging scores. Warne, however, had the answer already worked out. What better way to prod the powers-that-be than to churn out hundreds on one of the sportiest wickets in the country? "I believed his technique would improve playing at the Rose Bowl and he would enjoy himself at the club. We have created a wonderful environment for players to become the best they possibly can," said Warne. Shaun Udal, who was vice-captain of Hampshire at the time, adds: "He had the pick of numerous counties, so there was enormous excitement that he had joined us. He got a hundred against us around 2002 in which he hit a reverse sweep for six and I remember thinking, 'Oh my god.' It was clear he was outstandingly gifted. I met him for a drink the night before he signed, to get to know him. I was immediately struck by how personable he was. He was a confident person and what came across was that he had total faith in his ability."

Hampshire couldn't believe their luck after Pietersen's astonishing batting in South Africa had showed the world what he always knew – that he was exceptional. They had signed the most talked about cricketer in England ahead of the most anticipated international summer for years. Talk about a marketing coup. Recruiting Kevin the previous October, before he became the talk of dinner parties, was a masterstroke. "Hampshire started saying to me, in good humour, 'Will we be seeing much of you this summer after all?' and 'We got you on the cheap signing you up before South Africa'," Pietersen recalled.

When Hampshire hosted their pre-season press day in mid-April they had not just one figure guaranteed to get Fleet Street cricket correspondents zooming down the M3, but two. Attendance at these events can often be in single figures, certainly at the smaller counties, but I was one of around 50 journalists crammed into a hospitality suite at the Rose Bowl to hear Warne's views on the upcoming Ashes series. As usual, he did not disappoint. Warne has been accused of much, but he rarely fails to provide interesting copy. We were disappointed to be told that Pietersen would not be available to speak to the media, but a few of us grabbed him after training anyway and he was more than happy to oblige. This was the first time I had seen Pietersen close up in the flesh. He is taller and leaner than you might imagine and if his considerable height and athletic movements were to leave any doubt that this is a gilded, 21st century sportsman, then the diamond twinkling from each earlobe confirms it. Pietersen talks like he bats, at 100 miles per hour. He cut a confident figure, taking the Mick out of a few of the reporters he knew from England's tour to South Africa and talking in the mezzo-soprano tone that would become familiar in the years to come. In clipped, African vowel sounds he revealed his respect for Warne and desire to plunder county attacks in the opening month of the season and then leave it to the selectors to decide whether he had done enough to press his claims for a Test spot. The self-assurance and certainty almost oozed out of him, but he was engaging and open rather than arrogant.

Yet Pietersen was slow out of the starting blocks that season and it almost certainly cost him the chance of a Test debut in the two-match rubber against minnows Bangladesh that served as a gentle warm-up to the Ashes. A foot injury sustained running on the beach during a week's holiday in Australia kept him out of Hampshire's Championship opener against Gloucestershire and it took him some time to re-adjust from the hard wickets of South Africa to the slower English tracks. Batting at No. 4 he scored 5, 9 and 3 in three matches in the 45-over one-day league and his opening Championship matches were equally inauspicious. In three four-day games before the England squad was selected for the first Test against Bangladesh he scored a first-ball 0 and 61 (which included three sixes off Mushtaq Ahmed and spanned just 51 balls) against Sussex, 0 and 28 against Middlesex and 1 and 125 off just 111 balls against Kent.

Despite Pietersen's instant one-day heroics under immense pressure in South Africa, England's selectors were not convinced that he had done enough to deserve promotion to the five-day team despite a growing clamour for his inclusion. They did shake up the batting order and changed a winning side by dropping Robert Key, but it was Ian Bell who got the nod rather than Kevin. Bell was regarded as the next cab off the rank after scoring an assured 70 on his Test debut the previous summer against a weak West Indies attack. On his return to Warwickshire after being summoned to join the Test squad in January as injury cover and captaining the England A team in Sri Lanka, he broke the record for first-class runs in April, creaming 480 in four matches. Perhaps oddly, this seemed to count for more than Pietersen's big-match brilliance and Graham Thorpe's doughty excellence (four Test centuries in 2004) since scoring a career-saving century on his recall to the Test side at the Oval in 2003.

Duncan Fletcher explains the selectors' muddled thinking. "Mark Butcher, our established number three, had injured himself in South Africa and his replacement Robert Key had not shown enough form to warrant a place," he said. "So we were looking for a number three. The problem was that we did not have one. We wanted to play Bell, who had made a sparkling start in county cricket that season, but three was too high for him. As it was for Thorpe, who was obviously nearing the end of his career and was struggling against the moving ball. And also as it was for Pietersen, whose technique we felt was only suitable for number five at that stage." Vaughan volunteered to move up to three, allowing Bell to slot in at number four. "That left a straight shoot-out between Thorpe and Pietersen for the number five spot. Crucially, Pietersen had made a poor start for

Hampshire and was also batting at five for them – too low in county cricket for an England aspirant."

Not everyone in the England set-up agreed with Fletcher. Simon Jones felt the selectors had erred by not fast-tracking Pietersen to the Test side the previous winter. Jones says: "When Kev qualified. I thought to myself, 'They've got to pick him.' So did a few others in the team. Yes, I was good friends with Thorpey and Butch, but when you've got someone like him, he's got to come into the top order." Udal was similarly surprised at Pietersen's omission. "He was unlucky not to play in the Bangladesh games. When I saw those hundreds [in South Africa] I thought he was definitely going to be involved in the summer. England came back from a successful tour that winter and didn't quite know what to do and how to get him in the team."

While England's top order predictably dipped their bread in two routs of Bangladesh – Bell's two unbeaten innings yielded 65 and 162 and Thorpe weighed in with unbeaten knocks of 42 and 66 – Pietersen's time was arguably spent more usefully finding his feet at Hampshire. He was beginning to find his explosive range in the one-day game with consecutive innings of 76 off 49 balls, including six sixes, against Shropshire; 80 off 50 balls, including six sixes, against Middlesex; and 69 not out off 64 balls, including four sixes, against Glamorgan. In three more Championship games fixtures before the one-day internationals began, Pietersen continued a trend of mixing mountainous scores with low ones. He scored 126 against Glamorgan (particularly significant because it was his first ton – in only three attempts – on his home strip in Southampton), 42 and 0 against Warwickshire and 0 and 41 against Nottinghamshire. Steve Harmison once said of Michael Vaughan that he was a "brilliant liar", meaning that he had the capacity to hide his feelings, and in particular, his doubts. Udal detected a similar outward nonchalance in Pietersen. He explains: "One of the virtues of Kev is whether he gets 0 or 100, he is the same. He gets into the dressing room, takes off his gear, sits on the balcony and is as chatty as he always is. You wouldn't know with his demeanour whether he has got runs or not. His demeanour was the same. It's a good trait to have. A lot of players are up and down. They either rant and rave or throw their toys out of the cot. He wasn't just like that at Hampshire. The two winter tours I went on with England, he was no different. He got a 100 against Shoaib [Akhtar] on a quick wicket in Pakistan and was exactly the same as when he got nothing. He has a very strong mind and never gets too down with failure."

Nevertheless, eleven Championship knocks for his new county had produced four ducks, enough for Pietersen to consider some remedial work to his technique. Many ex-players and commentators shared Fletcher's concern that it was too loose for Test cricket. "I decided to have a close look at my technique on DVD to see whether the doubters had a point," he said. Kevin recognised that his footwork had been minimal, but other than that reckoned he had little to worry about. "I thought, after I had carefully considered the matter, that it was a bit simplistic of people who had not seen too much of my batting to assume that I played the same way in first-class cricket as I did in the one-day game. I concluded that I didn't have to change my technique just because some people didn't think it looked totally orthodox. Mark Waugh came to mind. He scored the bulk of his runs through square leg and midwicket. Why couldn't I if that was a strength of my game?"

Those two months champing at the bit on the south coast did more than just make Pietersen ache for his Test debut. Spending eight weeks in close company with Warne helped to demystify the great leg-spinner. The apartment Pietersen shared with Richard Logan at the exclusive Ocean Village Marina on Southampton's waterfront was a short walk from Warne's house and soon the pair were inseparable. Warne had a reputation as lively, sometimes hazardous companion but that didn't bother Pietersen. He saw a soulmate and was eager to learn from a master of the genre. "We spoke lots and talked about so much stuff and became very close," said Warne. "I think I understood him, and as captain I think he enjoyed that and it made a change from where he had come from. Throughout the 2005 season we talked about the temptations and pitfalls of being successful and how to handle expectations, both his and other people's."

Pietersen was a good pupil. He picked Warne's cricket brain and listened to how he dealt with the sometimes harsh media spotlight. "Kev wanted to see what made Warney tick and follow how he approached things," recalls Udal. "He saw how Warney handled the limelight so well and that how Warney is perceived by the press doesn't bother him so much. Kev picked up on that."

Stuart MacGill offers a telling insight into why Pietersen struck up such a good relationship with Warne, the incorrigible roisterer. He says: "People make comparisons between Kevin and Shane Warne all the time. The most accurate and appropriate comparison is to do with the fact that what you see is what you get. Neither of them are pretending to be anything else. Shane and I always got on like a house on fire because he is what he is. If you expect anything different, you are an idiot."

There might have been doubts about Pietersen's Test credentials, but he was one of the first picks for a month-long one-day programme that formed an interminable but fascinating build-up to the most eagerly anticipated Ashes series in modern times. The curtain-raiser was a Twenty20 match, the first ever involving England and Australia, played at a sun-drenched Rose Bowl in front of 15,000 patriotic spectators. A heady evening set the tone for a summer of unforgettable drama as England irrefutably indicated they were bursting for the challenge ahead. Pietersen's buccaneering first encounter with Australia again got him noticed. He was entirely nerveless, striking 34 from 18 balls and epitomised England's greater youthfulness and athleticism by pouching three catches in a thumping 100-run victory. Yet even he had a milli-second of doubt beforehand. "It was my first game against Australia and I stood there at practice looking at the likes of Ricky Ponting, Brett Lee and Glenn McGrath," he said. "I wouldn't say I was in awe of them. I was just looking at them and thinking, 'How can we beat these blokes?'"

Pietersen had showed he belonged in elite company at the Rose Bowl. His stunning performance at Bristol six days later went much further. With one of the greatest one-day innings ever played by an England batsman he demonstrated that he was operating at a rarefied level. In the first of seven 50-over games against Australia during the height of midsummer his controlled explosion of strokeplay singlehandedly won England a dramatic game they looked certain to lose. But the facts do not do justice to the majesty of Pietersen's batting and the delirium it created in a nation high with pre-Ashes excitement.

The heat was on – metaphorically and literally – when Pietersen, perversely demoted to No. 6 to make room for Flintoff's return to the 50-over team, arrived with England faltering and requiring 134 to overhaul Australia's imposing total of 252. The County Ground was bathed in sunshine and the atmosphere in the middle was as crackling as in the stands. "You can do it in Twenty20 cricket, let's see if you can do it now in the big stuff," shouted Damien Martyn from the inner circle. The taunt concentrated Pietersen's mind. He bided his time and knocked it around for a while, aware that the small boundaries encouraged big hitting in the final overs. When Geraint Jones was the sixth man to be dismissed with 93 needed, the asking rate had climbed to eight an over. Pietersen pressed down the accelerator, swung Brad Hogg high over square-leg for six and, with ruthless efficiency, began to pulverise Australia's bowling into submission. High on attitude and latitude he identified Jason Gillespie as a weak link, set himself up in a wide stance and blasted the once-great bowler into oblivion. Pietersen struck three further sixes of immense power over long-on and the assault was so devastating that his unbeaten 91 spanned just 65 balls, spurring England to the finishing line with a full 15 balls to spare. Vikram Solanki and Jon Lewis provided canny support, but they were merely bit-part roles next to the headline act. The Australians were coming to terms with the outrageous hitting of England's new cavalier. Lee observed: "He hits a very long ball and at Bristol I don't think any plan would have stopped him."

Even before he made his Test debut Pietersen was already halfway to being a superstar. He had captured the public imagination like no player in recent memory and the question of whether he should play in the Ashes was burning with the ferocity of a bush fire. Pietersen was, though, kept on a tighter leash during the middle of the one-day series. Unlike some of his England colleagues he didn't get much opportunity to flay Bangladesh, scoring 23 in his only innings in three games against the minnows and this somewhat halted his momentum. Scores of 19, 6, and 15 against Australia had followed his Bristol spectacular and he arrived at The Oval for the final one-day game of the summer with the clamour for him to make his Test debut having abated a little. After England were inserted on a typical Oval belter on a beautiful day in south London and faltered, first to 44-2 and then, more seriously, to 93-6, England's new No. 4 saw his innings as make-or-break. So did the men in green and gold. "I put a lot of pressure on myself at The Oval," said Pietersen. "We were up against it and I said to myself, 'This is the innings that could get you into the team for Lord's.' It seemed to me the Aussies were trying to target me. During that game they were saying, 'This is what Test cricket is like. Can you handle it?'"

The response was emphatic. Pietersen batted with a mixture of caution and flamboyance for an 84-ball 74 that included one extraordinary flat-batted six back over the head of Gillespie, who could only shake his mullet in disbelief. England were thrashed by eight wickets, but Pietersen was convinced he had passed the test of his readiness for the five-day game. He told the media so that evening. "When I was asked the question in the press conference, I told everyone that I had no doubt for the first time I was ready for Test cricket. Why lie or deal in platitudes? I don't like to beat about the bush and I like to speak what I believe to be the truth."

There was much debate along the lines of Thorpe v Pietersen, but surely each would have benefitted from the other. Every short, crabby left-hander with a bad back should have a dazzling young right-handed giant to bat with. The England selectors, in their wisdom, had boxed themselves into a corner after deciding early in the summer that Bell would bat at No. 4 and only the No. 5 position was up for grabs. "I never had an issue with the selection of Kevin," says Thorpe. "I saw it made sense to pick someone like that, who was young, in great form and flamboyant, exactly what you need to take on the Aussies. I only queried to the selectors about whether it was Ian Bell or myself. That was the only thing I ever spoke to them about."

Warne had kept a relatively low profile by continuing to captain Hampshire during the one-day series and added his considerable voice to the pro-Pietersen lobby. He said: "The more I saw KP play, the more I thought, 'Wow, this guy could be something special.' It is no secret that's how I felt, as I am on record as saying at that time that England would be crazy not to select him." Pietersen even orchestrated a little campaign in the media for his selection. He was a man in demand by the press and nudged the selectors with the various interviews he gave. In one there was a none-too-subtle put-down of his rival. "Warney says that he thinks the best way for England to beat them is by blooding some young players who aren't brainwashed," said Pietersen to the *Independent*. "He says he'll knock Graham Thorpe over, for instance, and that maybe England should choose some batters who aren't used to being dominated by Australia."

There were signs that England's best batsman of the previous decade was ready to collect his cricket pension. During the first Test against Bangladesh, Thorpe revealed in a statement that he had accepted an offer to coach New South Wales that winter, thereby signalling an end to his international career at the end of the 2005 summer. Early in the season, he granted the *Evening Standard* an interview and told me his back was causing him such pain it required frequent injections and he would "not be fraught with massive disappointment" if he was overlooked.

Nevertheless, Pietersen was expecting the England selectors to opt for Thorpe's battle-hardened experience and was surprised when David Graveney rang him at his apartment with the good news. Thorpe recalls: "Physically I was getting towards the end. I had announced I was going to take a job out in Australia. I sort of half expected it, really. I could sense a feeling of change from people around the team. Duncan knew I was starting to struggle more. If I had been in better physical shape there wouldn't have been the whispers going around. That was a big thing counting against me. My fitness wasn't great. The people inside the camp knew that." Fletcher later revealed: "It was a truly 50-50 decision, one of the hardest I had to make in my time with England. Two things swung it Pietersen's way – if Thorpe's coaching revelation had not already done so because that did irritate me a little. First, that I was worried about Thorpe's lack of batting because I knew he needed time in the middle and, secondly, that I honestly thought a right-hander would be better at five because of the problems Shane Warne creates when bowling into the rough for left-handers. We also wanted our number five to be positive. That was the only way we were going to beat Australia. And Pietersen did that and so much more."

As the hype ended and the cricket finally began, Pietersen was not overcome by tension at the prospect of a debut in the most highly charged circumstances. Excitement was his primary emotion. He felt part of the England 'bubble' after playing 21 one-day internationals and a month spent in nose-to-nose limited-overs combat with the Australians had debunked the myth of Baggy Green immortality. And Pietersen being Pietersen, he wouldn't bow down to anyone. "Pietersen has got this ability to fear nobody," says Mike Bechet. "He has got a bull terrier attitude. He waited for four years to get into the England changing room. He was scoring hundreds and double hundreds in the County Championship. He would have gone into the changing room and said, 'F*** Glenn McGrath, f*** Shane Warne, f*** Australia. They are no better than us.' He would have said, 'Who is this McGrath? I'm going to belt him back over his head. I don't give a s*** who he is. I don't care how many wickets he has taken, what his reputation is. All I'm seeing is a human being running in to bowl at me and I'm going to show him no respect.'"

Few who were at a Lord's packed to the rafters on 21 July 2005 will forget a day of dramatic events packed together with relentless intensity. A Steve Harmison-led attack bowled Australia out for 190 with ferment growing in the stands as the wickets fell, but Glenn McGrath reminded England's new order of times past by dismantling their line-up with surgical precision as the hosts staggered to the close on 92-7. In between, a fresh round of bomb plots only a fortnight after the 7 July London bombings, which had killed 56 people, had led to high-level talks about the match, and, indeed, whole tour being abandoned. The Australian players' wives had been caught up in the terror alert while shopping in London and captain Ricky Ponting marched into the MCC offices to demand the game be stopped when news of the bomb threats began to emerge via the dressing room television. The MCC did not want to call a halt to the Test, fearful of the mass panic that might take hold if it did. Instead, they sat Ponting down with a cup of tea and calmed him with promises to round up the wives and bring them to Lord's. It did not emerge that the 21 July bombings had mercifully failed until the end of Australia's first innings. Nevertheless, there had been frenetic scenes inside the pavilion. The ECB, under pressure from Cricket Australia, gave serious consideration to calling a halt to the entire series and it was only averted when chief executive David Collier convinced his Australian counterpart James Sutherland that cricket needed to be strong in uncertain times. The great summer of cricket that was 2005 had nearly been ended before it had truly begun.

To the backdrop of jangling nerves in the boardroom Pietersen strode out to bat with England perilously placed on 18-3. They were soon 21-5, with all five batsmen victims of an unforgettable spell by McGrath from the Pavilion End. "Before I went into bat I felt apprehension," said Pietersen. "There was the feeling of the unknown. I wondered what was in store for me, but once I got into the middle I was fine." In partnership with Geraint Jones, Kevin began to rebuild England's innings against McGrath and the ferocious pace of Lee in the biggest test of technique and temperament he could ever face. Jones and Ashley Giles were mopped up shortly before the close but Pietersen displayed great calm to survive for a painstaking unbeaten 28. Next morning, his treatment of McGrath warmed the soul. In three balls he cross-batted him to the pavilion railings, lofted a slower ball into the second tier of the members area and cover drove a four. He cracked Warne into the second tier of the Grandstand and next ball almost did it again, but didn't strike it quite as cleanly and Damien Martyn took a breathtaking catch inside the boundary rope. "I wasn't surprised at how quickly Kevin made himself at home at Test level because of what I'd seen him do in South Africa," said Geraint Jones. "What did surprise me was how he scored his runs. He is an amazing front-foot player, but in the first innings at Lord's he played the short stuff so well, too. I could see he was really up for it. At one stage, when Brett Lee was flying in at him, we came together in mid-pitch for a chat at the end of the over and he just said, 'Sorry, china. Can't talk now. Too pumped.' For a debutant, Kevin had some match."

Pietersen had helped to narrow the deficit to a manageable 35, but England failed to take their chances in Australia's second innings – Kevin was the biggest culprit, fluffing his third catch of the game when he dropped Michael Clarke on 21 – and the hallucinatory winning target turned out to be 420. The hosts went meekly, apart from Pietersen, who became the first England batsman since Tony Greig in 1972 to top-score in both innings on debut. He struck an unbeaten 64 off 79 balls studded with two sixes off Warne and scored all but 12 runs gathered by the team while he was at the crease. Batting-wise, he had virtually taken on Australia on his own. Having Warne in the opposition side helped him to settle. Pietersen studied Warne closely in Hampshire games – although he reckoned that if the spinmeister bowled the same for county as he did for country he would take "120 or 130 wickets every season" – and his presence eased any anxiety. "It helped that we were mates," said Pietersen. "It relaxed me out there and helped me to be positive against him. We did talk quite a bit in the middle. Warney would bowl to me, go back to the non-striker's end, rubs his hands in the dirt, look up to me and say something. I could see they were showing my face up on the big screen and I was desperately trying not to laugh. Sometimes I had to turn my back on Shane to make sure I didn't giggle."

Pietersen's game is based on confrontation and the relentless unmissability of the second Test at Edgbaston, widely acclaimed as the greatest of all time, suited his gung-ho style perfectly. The final margin was a two-run victory to England, the closest in Tests between the countries, which levelled the series and lit the blue touchpaper for the summer. Pietersen's display at Lord's had shown his bamboozled colleagues that the best approach against these Australian bowlers was to be fearless. The home side shed their inhibitions and vulnerability, and hurtled to 407 inside 80 overs against a McGrath-less attack. Pietersen came into bat in the 33rd over, but, astonishingly, England already had 170 on the board. When Vaughan skied a hook England's middle order giants were brought into harness. While Flintoff dominated the strike and flailed his way out of form, Pietersen intelligently held back before taking over to score his third half-century in his first three Test innings. He wafted a forthright 71 off 76 balls, including one mighty six off Brett Lee and a couple of jaw-dropping, whipped forehands through mid-wicket that were more Sampras than Sobers. "Kev's a clever batsman," says Simon Jones, who became the sixth England batsman to strike a six in England's high octane innings. "He doesn't just go out and bash it. He can throttle back and weigh up a situation as well as anyone. That's what makes him extra special. You could see the Aussies were beginning to fear him. They were putting a lot of the fielders on the boundary and hoping he would get himself out. The thing is, Kev always backs himself. It can work against him sometimes but he loves to take on a challenge." Boring Pieteresen into submission was a logical strategy and one that had frequently been adopted in county cricket. It was remarkable, and a great compliment, that the all-conquering Australians had resorted to it in only his second Test.

England secured a handy 99-run lead, but had slumped to 31-4 on the third day and on the verge of surrendering the series, when Pietersen arrived. He faced up to Warne, who was inevitably beginning to commandeer the series, and went chop-chop: two sixes soared over mid-wicket. Kevin can hardly be said to have saved the Test because he was given out sweeping soon afterwards for 20, but the symbolic value of this mini-confrontation was far greater than its literal output of 12 runs. It told Warne that Pietersen, unlike a generation of subservient England batsmen, was not going to be hypnotised into a scoreless trance by the enduring magician. Pietersen puts his natural insouciance down to the fact that he doesn't "blow things out of proportion". "Maybe that's why I do so well when the pressure's on – I keep things on a level platform all the time and just play the game," he added.

After victory was secured on a passionate final morning at Edgbaston, the third and fourth chapters of the remarkable 2005 Ashes story were not statistically successful ones for Pietersen. In the drawn Test at Old Trafford he was suckered into hooking Lee down the throat of a deep mid-wicket stationed on the boundary rope exactly for that indiscretion after looking well set on 21. It came minutes before the end of the first day and by Pietersen's admission, "This was one occasion where perhaps I hadn't played the situation properly". It was the fourth time Kevin had been dismissed in Test cricket and on three of those occasions he had been caught on the boundary. In the second innings he registered his first golden duck in Tests when he was deceived by a brilliant McGrath slower ball that he claimed not to even see.

At Trent Bridge there was again personal frustration for Pietersen in what was another nail-shredding victory for England. He played with admirable restraint in the first innings before edging a pitched-up delivery from Lee to Adam Gilchrist for 45 off 108 balls, his slowest Test knock to date. After England had forced Australia to follow on for the first time in 17 years and given themselves a supposedly simple fourth innings victory target of 129, Warne created huge problems bowling into the rough and reduced the hosts to 57-4. There were few alarms in a sprightly stand between Pietersen and Flintoff before Kevin threw the kitchen sink at a wide half-volley from Lee and, for the second time in the game, edged to the wicket-keeper. He was furious with himself for not taking England over the finishing line, even though his 23 had been in a winning cause.

English cricket was now teetering on the brink of its first Ashes victory for two decades. For Pietersen, the backdrop to the final Test at the Oval racheted up the pressure a notch or two, some of it self-inflicted, some not. Goodwill messages flooded in from, amongst others, Tony Blair and David Beckham as the nation fixed its gaze upon south London. Kevin was paid £55,000 by a London jeweller to wear a pair of diamond earrings during the game and was lent a £70,000 limousine, which were viewed as tacky adornments by some of the more traditional pundits. Some were tiring of the strut; it was time for substance.

Moreover, one of the themes of Pietersen's Ashes summer had been his surprisingly fallible catching. It was a surprise because he came into Test cricket with a reputation of being, in the words of the Australia coach John Buchanan, earlier in the summer, "a world-class fielder". A magnificent athlete, who was unusually agile for his height (compared, for instance, with colleagues Flintoff, Ashley Giles, Marcus Trescothick, Matthew Hoggard and Steve Harmison, who were nobody's idea of gazelles), he had a safe pair of hands and possessed a rocket-like arm.

At Nottinghamshire he had been a second slip of some renown and, although England had used him as a run-saving fielder in the midwicket or cover regions during limited-overs games, there were no suggestions he was a weak link. All of Pietersen's former team-mates and coaches agree that he was a reliable fielder and occasionally an excellent one. Yet he fumbled all six catches that came his way in the first four Tests – three at Lord's, two at Old Trafford and one at Trent Bridge. Fletcher espied a minute technical problem. "Eventually I picked up at Trent Bridge that, in his natural excitability, he was walking in so quickly that he was on one leg, and therefore totally unbalanced, when the ball was hit." The Aussies took to calling Pietersen 'cymbals' when they were in the field, a sledge he confessed he "hated". In restaurants people would throw pens at him to see if he would drop them. While his batting had caused many to look on in awe, his catching had become a national laughing stock, but Pietersen shrugged it off. "Thank goodness for two things: one, that he was sufficiently determined to listen and work hard to rectify the problem and two, that he possesses a strong enough character to put such misses behind him," added Fletcher.

The pressure intensified after Pietersen was dismissed in the first innings playing another aggressive shot, this time to Warne on 14. Four days of inclement weather and see-saw cricket that had been typical of what was universally acknowledged as the most exhilirating series of all time had brought the Ashes down to the wire. England had to bat out the final day to snuff out Australia's chances and achieve their holy grail. Not that Pietersen appeared to be overawed by the magnitude of the task. His agent Adam Wheatley recalled: "I was a little concerned that he didn't seem to be nervous at all. While to the outside world it was important to create the air of calm, he was giving me the distinct impression that this was just another innings. I sat down with him for a brief moment in the England team hotel reception and made it pretty clear how important tomorrow could be. As he started to walk off, I remember thinking to myself: I don't think much of that went in. He was so relaxed. I shook his hand and said, 'Make history.' He smiled back at me and said, 'Cool, china.'"

It took the most important of days to prompt Pietersen's best. True to form, Kevin slept like a baby the night before England's day of destiny, but he had butterflies while he watched from the dressing room balcony as Vaughan and Trescothick made steady progress in the first hour. His final innings of the summer began in a scrambled rush for pads and equipment as McGrath struck in consecutive deliveries, removing Vaughan and Bell. He had no time to think about nerves and felt at ease as he prepared to face the hat-trick ball. A brute of a lifter struck his shoulder and looped into the slips. Next over he was dropped by Matthew Hayden at slip off Warne. Eight overs before lunch Pietersen, on 15, drove at Lee and the ball flashed to Warne, normally the safest of first slips. He parried it and failed to grab the rebound. A nation half covered its eyes. Pietersen can be an unwatchable starter. Stuart MacGill, a member of the Australia touring party, says: "I was sure he was going to get out at any minute. I thought we had it in the bag."

Pietersen had been pushing and prodding to little effect. The advice of Greg Matthews, who had rung him before the game, came into his mind. "You're not playing your normal game. Go out there, be positive, be confident, be arrogant, stop messing about," Matthews had urged. With the match and series hanging by a thread, Pietersen walked down the wicket and said to Trescothick, "I'm going to whack it now." Warne had bowled to Kevin with a deep mid-wicket all series, a running joke between the pair in the build-up to the game. He had berated his friend for not taking him on. "Bring your cow corner up and I will hit you," Pietersen said. True to his word, he now took advantage of a more attacking field setting and mowed Warne for two huge sixes. The release of tension was short-lived. Warne snaffled Trescothick and Flintoff to give Australia the edge: at lunch, England were 133 behind with just five second innings wickets remaining and more than 70 overs left in the Test. During the interval, Vaughan told Kevin: "Stop messing about and go and express yourself".

Pietersen had the courage to take his captain at his word and persist with his attacking strategy after lunch, making for an epic contest between him and Lee, who was consistently operating at and above 95mph. Pietersen admits he would be a "liar" if he said he loved facing fast bowling, but the quicker Lee hurled the ball at him, the quicker he threw his bat at it. He took 35 off three Lee overs straight after the interval, sending two ferocious bouncers into the sunlit stands and another hooked from off his eyebrows was nearly scooped up by Shaun Tait on the fine leg boundary. Lee pummelled him on the body three times. MacGill says: "The impressive thing for me was, looking at Kevin, that was the first time he realised, 'This is actually tough', and played on. The state of the game and gravity of the situation was irrelevant. He knew the best means of approaching it was to do his thing."

Supported by Paul Collingwood and then Ashley Giles, Pietersen reeled off outrageous shots in any circumstances, unimaginable in these, breaking two Woodworm bats in the process. One straight drive against a length ball from Lee – an impossible tennis forehand – with the game still in the balance was unreal, symptomatic of a player reliant not solely on technique, but consumed by mood and surfing a monster wave of adrenaline. Giles said: "When Brett Lee came back all I could think about was surviving with my life intact, but Kev was flat-batting deliveries around 96mph back past Lee and straight to the boundary like a rocket. I was just standing at the other end in awe, saying to myself: 'How does he do that?' Kev made it look so simple."

By tea, Pietersen had smashed, bashed and dashed his way to a 124-ball maiden Test hundred, applauded by 23,000 ecstatic souls, Warne and the millions in their living rooms wrapt in the all-consuming action. While Giles consolidated his reputation for solidity, Pietersen continued to blaze away in boundary mode against the fast bowlers while playing Warne with greater circumspection.

Only when the Ashes were won and Warne brought in a second slip did Kevin play him adventurously and strike him for a couple of celebratory sixes, including his 50th and final one of an extraordinary season. McGrath brought an end to the fun, but it guaranteed Pietersen a sustained, standing ovation, which he later likened to an "out-of-body experience".

His 158 had occupied 187 deliveres of barely believable entertainment and included 15 fours and seven sixes, breaking Ian Botham's 1981 record for the most sixes in any Ashes innings.

Pietersen had absorbed the criticism and alchemised it into mastery of the biggest occasion of English cricket's recent history. MacGill adds: "People will have watched him and said, 'I can't believe you did that. If you had got out you would have lost the Ashes.' It was like a staring competition. Kevin just stared longer. I would suggest many, if not all, great batsmen don't consider the consequences. That is the difference. A sports psychologist would call it positive reinforcement. Kevin looks at what he wants to do. He doesn't consider what might happen."

In an insane four hours and 45 minutes of batting Pietersen had spun the roulette wheel and hit the jackpot. "Being at the other end when he played that innings will stay with me forever," said Giles. "Our partnership was special. He helped me through those three hours in a way I will never forget. It was real grandchildren stuff. Gather round and I'll tell you about the innings I played with Pietersen, with the white stripe and the earrings."

Against all the predictions of those who had learned the story of Pietersen the perpetual misfit, he became a central part of a champion team, captained by an understanding man, and playing alongside a tough bunch of players who respected him and who he respected in return. After four years learning the ropes on the county circuit and aching for international cricket, he had mastered the game's zenith in one season. The boy from Pietermaritzburg had brought home the Ashes and won the affection of a nation. Even the Queen offered a regal slap on the back. Five months after his demented century took England to the cricketing summit, Pietersen planted his pioneer's flag in Buckingham Palace and accepted the honour of an MBE from her majesty. Kevin Pietersen: Member of the British Empire. The journey had been worth it.

TABLOID STAR

KEVIN PIETERSEN IS A SPORTS editor's dream. He is also an editor's dream. Consider the evidence. Spectacular talent; outspoken personality; controversial background; and pop star wife. In the eyes of media executives with newspapers and airtime to fill that's most boxes ticked. Interesting to watch, interesting to hear, interesting story and interesting lifestyle. Job done. Hold the back page.

Ever since he launched his international career in a manner that had the air of an announcement Pietersen has grabbed attention like no Englishman in flannels since Ian Botham (although it is hard to imagine Pietersen getting fat and complacent in the second half of his career, as Botham did). He is, as the Americans say, pure box office. An entertainer and a sportswriter's dream. Even a post-skunk stripe, post-nuptial Pietersen is more newsworthy than the rest of the England batting order (bar Andrew Flintoff, and these day's that's more for his persistent injury problems than any of his ill-judged pedalo-related 'incidents') put together.

Whether Pietersen is winning the Ashes or dating models there is enough material to satisfy the most jaded sports editor's appetite. Even when he isn't stockpiling centuries and his extra-curricular activities have been curtailed he is one of those sportsmen who dominates the news agenda. Tabloids can concentrate on his marriage, jewellery, hairstyle or wealth. Broadsheets need to take a higher road to Pietersen overload, but there is rarely a shortage of material. KP, as he has become known thanks to sub editors in newspaper land, is endlessly fascinating. Be it the runs he scores, the ways he gets out, the friends and enemies he racks up, the endless debates about his ego and commitment, his clashes with authority – the talking points, especially in these days of the radio and TV phone-in programme, are seemingly neverending. Whether by accident or design, Pietersen the personality is scrapping with Pietersen the run machine for the back page lead. However, a problem with being a fixture of the press and lifestyle magazines is that you can become easily misunderstood. Invite *OK!* magazine into your front room, as Pietersen once did, and you invite criticism and envy. 'Who does he think he is?' goes the peculiarly British train of thought in classic build-them-up, knock-them-down style.

So how did it come to this? How did an Afrikaans-speaking boy from a religious background in Pietermaritzburg gravitate towards the spotlight like a moth to a flame and, in the process, become, in classic 21st century fashion, a *celebrity*? Is it right to bracket him with self-basting poster boys like David Beckham, Danny Cipriani and Gavin Henson? One accusation thrown at Pietersen is that he is the first cricketer who chose to be famous rather than merely a great sportsman. One prominent English sportswriter dubbed him 'cricket's first rock star', presumably ignoring the behaviour of Shoaib Akhtar for the last decade and Botham himself, who used to hang out with rock stars, or the lesser-known, but altogether more deserving of the title, Paul Smith of Warwickshire, whose drug-and-alcohol-fuelled antics, worthy of the most hell-raising of international playboys, were documented in his 2007 autobography *Wasted?*. Yet if greatness comes with the judgement of time, then so must other hypotheses.

The image of Pietersen the playboy simply does not stand up to scrutiny. It is a popular, even lazy, perception, but plain wrong. It is true that Pietersen has an exhibitionist streak and enjoyed the limelight when he scorched his name into the national consciousness in 2005 with some of the most staggering feats ever achieved by an England cricketer, but the hectic rounds of parties and premieres that year were the exception in his adult life not the norm. Kevin was a late developer in sporting terms and he was also slow off the mark when it came to the fairer sex. "My brothers say I was a nerd at school because I wasn't involved with girls until I was 19, 20 years-old," said Pietersen in an interview in the *Times* in 2006, rubbishing the Jack-the-lad myth. "I didn't go to nightclubs, hardly drank."

No, he was too dedicated to succeeding for that. At Berea Rovers, Kevin and his younger brother Bryan would have a few post-match beers and then head off home or to church. It was not until he left South Africa and had to fend for himself away from the gaze of his strict parents, first in Cannock in 2000, and then during four years in Nottingham, that Pietersen really got a taste for late-night possibilities. With his low threshold of boredom and inability to sit still for more than a few moments he preferred the noise and bright lights – and girls – of bars and clubs to session drinking in spit-and-sawdust pubs. He didn't care much for the taste of lager or ale so, armed with a few quid in his back pocket, he would opt for the more expensive and chic Jack Daniels and Coke. During their carefree, singleton days in Nottingham, Kevin, Richard Logan and Matt Whiley would drink nothing but. "Kevin was pretty busy on the social front," recalls Jason

Gallian. "Nottingham was a big city, he was living the life of a professional cricketer and getting paid for what he loved to do."

Yet, Pietersen was no George Best. Or even Botham. He wasn't remotely self-destructive. He didn't smoke or gamble and, although he admitted that "as a young guy I lived life to the full and I've definitely done things in nightclubs that I'm not too proud of", he was never a serial dater of women. He had a taste for attention rather than alcohol. "When I have a drink I have a good go at it, but I might not have a drink for two weeks." In recent years, he has developed a taste for New Zealand Sauvignon Blanc, but is no fine wine connoisseur.

When he first came to play county cricket, the drinking culture took him aback. "I'm still surprised by how much drink is a way of life here," said Pietersen. "People say, 'Let's go for a pint', but what for? Why go for a pint? It just puts weight on." With his bottomless self-confidence, Tigger-like hyperactivity and indifference to booze, it is easy to see why Pietersen might be viewed with suspicion in the blokey world of the pavilion. Even in the era of dieticians, nutritionists and ice baths, English players still view alcohol as an indispensable release from the pressures of cricket and spending day-in, day-out with a group of lads for whom the sport itself is often the only thing they have in common. For Kevin, alcohol merely jeopardises his six-pack. He is a big man, 15-stone plus, or "98 kay gees" and, though he says he trains hard enough to eat what he fancies, professes to watch his weight "all the time."

Not that Pietersen lived a monkish lifestyle while he bided his time for England qualification. In an interview in the *Daily Mail* 2008, he said: "There was one time when I was playing for Nottinghamshire against Surrey. I got hammered the night before and when I turned up the next day I was spewing all over the shop and I was next into bat – it was a nightmare. I think I scored 80 – but I could never do that now. The way I wake up now after a big night there's no way I could train, let alone play."

During Pietersen's first representative tour to India – after a week's acclimatisation in Malaysia – there were few carousing opportunities. "It was tough in India because there's not many places you can drink," explains Simon Jones. "You have to respect the culture and can't do what you can do back here [in Britain]. You can't go out and get smashed and p****d. You're in someone else's country."

It was in South Africa in early 2005 that the playboy reputation began to emerge. Duncan Fletcher encouraged the extrovert Darren Gough to keep an eye on the exuberant new boy. They had much in common and a great friendship soon blossomed. "We are very similar characters," explained Gough. "We both like being the centre of attention. We both like to enjoy ourselves off the field, when the time is right. We quickly became very close and started to go everywhere together." Pietersen was seduced by the magnetism of 'Dazzler' and the exciting possibilities that a high-profile tour with England provided. The tattoo and badger stripe were Gough's ideas and Kevin, eager to fit in and show his sense of adventure to his new mate, happily obliged. In county cricket, the raciest hairstyle Pietersen ever plumped for was the 'surf dude' look when he jazzed up his then flowing locks with blonde highlights.

Hitting the town with Gough got Pietersen in trouble with the England management before the serious cricket began in his homeland. A big night out in the upmarket Johannesburg suburb of Sandton had ended with the pair noisily returning to the Sandton Sun Hotel at 2am and waking up some of the other players. Although they were not under curfew and this was 10 days before the start of the one-day series, Pietersen and Gough had not considered the feelings of the players who were involved in the ongoing Test against South Africa in nearby Pretoria and were hoping to wrap up a series victory the following day. Assistant coach Matthew Maynard put the word out that Fletcher wasn't happy. Gough owned up and Pietersen followed suit when he was confronted by the England coach. "Duncan told me it wasn't on and that he had brought me over to South Africa as a reward for the promise I'd shown in Zimbabwe and that I should remember that," said Pietersen. "It was a rap over the knuckles and a good lesson in how to behave as an international cricketer."

The Pietersen phenomenon was soon seized upon by the British press. After shooting to fame through his incredible exploits in South Africa he became big news almost overnight. Pietersen was identified as the type of personality who could sell newspapers and swiftly leapfrogged the middle-ranking England cricketers such as Ashley Giles, Andrew Strauss and Geraint Jones to be placed at the top table of the news-setting agenda alongside Andrew Flintoff and Michael Vaughan, English cricket's two biggest names at the time. Some observers were suspicious of his brashness, others applauded his confidence. Journalists liked his candour. In a PR-sanitised sporting world of platitudes and mind-numbing cliches, Pietersen offered opinion and insight. It is hard to imagine the diplomatic David Beckham, for one, referring to a respected international captain as 'an absolute muppet', as Pietersen said of South Africa's Graeme Smith. The *Daily Mail* signed him up to write a ghosted column for the 2005 season, well aware that he promised to be a big story with the Ashes looming. Offers from sponsors began to flood in. Brand names wanted to be associated with cricket's sexy new star.

Pietersen began to enjoy the material rewards that came with his new status and wealth – the five-star hotels, flash cars, expensive restaurants, fashionable clothes, jewellery, endorsements, photo shoots and sponsored equipment. It was only a matter of time before the pull of the bright lights and expedience took him from Southampton to the cricket capital of London, where he took up residence at a bachelor's pad in Chelsea later that year. "KP has brought a bit of football-style glamour to cricket," said Gough in 2006. "He loves a night out, loves dressing in good clothes, and dating pop stars or models. I was the first person to bring a bit of individuality to the game and I love to see it now in people like KP and others like Simon Jones. They wear their hair the way they want, wear nice clothes and jewellery and generally be themselves rather than conforming to the traditional idea of what a cricketer should look and act like. Kids can relate to someone like Kevin much more than they could to players of the past."

Fame and its accessories bring its inevitable pitfalls. In the few months after hitting the back pages, Pietersen began to appear at the front of the paper, too. In his early 20s he had a two-year relationship with Cate, an Australian girl he met while playing grade cricket in Sydney, but his higher profile brought more prominent courtships. In 2005, he dated TV presenter Natalie Pinkham, the model Caprice, and his English cultural assimilation was complete when he was the victim of a kiss 'n' tell tale in *The People* from a Big Brother contestant. In the 'exposé' it was claimed that he liked his name to be called out during love-making. The cricketing establishment began grumbling into its microphone that he was too flash and prominent for his own good. "He was young, had just had a massive pay rise," explains Jones. "Are you telling me he's never going to spend the money? He was only enjoying himself. Leave him alone. Let him have some fun. Everyone makes mistakes. Just because you're in the public eye, people hammer you for it. I've been in the papers three or four times for kiss 'n' tells. I've lost a couple of girlfriends over it. One believed what she read and dumped me by text. She walked out and I never saw her again. She believed what was written in the paper and it wasn't true."

Pietersen celebrated as hard as anyone in the aftermath of England's 2005 Ashes success. He slept for just three hours (three hours longer than Flintoff!) on the night England brought home the urn and, for the first time in his life, downed beer for breakfast ahead of his vodka and wine-fuelled antics on the open-top bus ride around London and in Tony Blair's garden. Pietersen then became a fixture on the London party scene, so much so that Flintoff quipped he would turn up to the opening of an envelope. "In 2005 most of the lads in that side went through that stage," says Simon Jones. "More so for Kev because he was very recognisable and living in London. After winning the Ashes I was permanently drunk for a month, I reckon. I was out in Cardiff a hell of a lot. And that wasn't because I wanted to go out and get recognised – it was because I wanted to get rid of the stress. It was the longest, hardest summer of my life. Six months is a long time to live with that kind of expectation."

With the paparazzi beginning to plague his every step Pietersen suggested to Jones that they go on holiday to escape the chaos. Jones recalls: "Kev would have been getting it a lot more. With his hair, you could hardly have missed him. I get recognised more in England than in Wales. He said, 'We've got to go away, mate.' I said, 'Okay, what's the options?' He said, 'Cape Town, but it's not so hot in September, or LA.' I said, 'I've never been to America, so let's go.'" Not before they were snapped by the paparazzi at check-in and again when they touched down in Los Angeles. It was an eye-opener for the pair. Not that it ruined their holiday. Jones says: "We stayed in the Mondrian Hotel with the famous Sky bar where all the stars go. We had a whale of a time, just went out to all the big clubs. What was I? 26 and he was 24. We were hanging out with film stars out there, just relaxing, drinking and enjoying ourselves." The ostentatious extroverts were at the forefront of the Ashes-inspired movement that had made cricket cool again. When Mickey Rourke gets you into a club, you know you've arrived. "We were up there," adds Jones. "Everyone knows that but people misjudged us a little bit. They just thought we were playboys. We were young and had fun, we enjoyed ourselves. We were both single at the time so who gives a toss?"

In a revealing insight into the Mickey-taking and one-upmanship among the four Pietersen boys that would have been a constant theme of Kevin's childhood, younger brother Bryan said, with only a hint of envy: "He might have women throwing themselves at him now, but that is only due to who he is – because he's not the best looking bloke, is he?" Even now, Kevin admits that when he meets up with his brothers they "abuse each other constantly".

Fletcher had reason on only one other occasion to bring Pietersen to task and again Gough was involved. During the pre-Christmas tour of Pakistan in 2005, Kevin's tour came to a premature end after he sustained a rib injury during the second of the five one-day internationals that followed the Tests. "There was no way he could continue," said Fletcher. "But I did have a word with him before he left, telling him I did not want to hear stories of his swanning around, living it up in clubs while we were still batting away on a difficult trip. 'You don't hear of Vaughan doing things like that,' I said. To be fair, Kevin agreed and I did not expect to hear a peep from him when he went home. He had scarcely been home a minute when there was an article in the *News of the World* supporting the inclusion of Darren Gough in the one-day team. All of a sudden, he had become a selector. And then, even more gallingly, he was seen on television in the audience as Gough appeared on *Strictly Come Dancing*. I was straight on the phone. I was seething. Rarely did I give a player such a blast. Trescothick overheard the conversation and later said he had never heard anything like it. 'Who do you think you are?' I screamed. 'You have only been on the scene two minutes.' I do not swear very often, but I could not help myself here. He said he had not written the article – that old chestnut, blaming the ghostwriter. Take the money, take the rap, I told him. 'How can you look the likes of Liam Plunkett in the eye now?' I asked.

'You've basically said they're useless.' As for the television appearance, he said he was big mates with Gough. 'What? Have you not got any mates out here?' I bellowed before slamming down the phone. I think he got the message."

In 2005 the suit of celebrity was suddenly thrust upon Pietersen. It took some time for it to fit him properly. As Shane Warne, who took on the role of mentor to Pietersen during their early days at Hampshire, told him frequently during chats in the slips and on the dressing room balcony, the downsides of being a public figure can be as plentiful as the upsides. He began to find it harder to trust people and was occasionally graceless to autograph hunters and casual acquaintances. "I think he got sick of the limelight after a while," says Stuart MacGill. "He found it tiring. Kevin would say he is a very private person. What he likes is the recognition, which is confirmation that he is doing well."

The 'Jessica' tattoo across his forearm is testament to his ardour for Jessica Taylor, formerly of *Liberty X* and one of the smoothest movers on the 2009 series of *Dancing On Ice*. On 22 March she came third at the season finale of the ITV Sunday night extravaganza, but, in a clear indication that a desperation to win is not just confirmed to one half of the Pietersen-Taylor marriage, stomped off the stage when it emerged she would not lift the crown. Theirs was a whirlwind romance. They met in January 2006 on a blind date at Knightsbridge restaurant Zuma, got engaged five months later and were married at a 14th-century manor house in Wiltshire on 29 December 2007. Gough was Kevin's best man.

Pietersen was only too keen to speak publicly of his love and admiration for his wife. "She understands everything that goes on," he told one interviewer. "It would have been harder for me to go out with a girl from a country village. Jess has been amazing with the support she has given me. After a hard day's cricket I can come home and speak to her about her game, about musicians and the entertainment industry." The relationship had changed his priorities, he told interviewers. He preferred a night cuddling on the sofa watching TV with his new beau and a homemade lasagne or hotpot for company to putting on his best bib and tucker and painting the town red.

Friends agree that Jessica has been a positive influence on him. "I was at the wedding and I've never seen a bloke happier in my life," says Jones. "They looked so right together and I think that's helped him a hell of a lot. It's settled him down. You can see it in him. You can see he's content with his life. He's happy in his cricket and is ecstatic with his social life and wife. That's why he is achieving as much as he is now. It has helped his cricket massively. It has settled him. When you're out on the field, you're not worried about anything else. You can go home to a happy household."

The general consensus is that Pietersen has struck gold. "His wife has brought a lot of stability to his life," explains Wayne Scott. "What a wonderful woman, an absolute cracker of a person. I can't speak more highly of her. She's a fantastic woman and people will tell you what she has done for him. He was going to nightclubs and parties and all sorts. That was his life. Then he met someone who means a lot to him and that was that. If he goes to a nightclub now, it's with her. She's not exactly low profile herself. She's actually needed now more than ever because of the nature of his position."

Jones adds: "She's a great girl. For someone who's achieved as much as she has, she's really down to earth. She's a really nice person to meet, and talkative."

The theory, propagated by tabloids, that they are cricket's answer to Posh and Becks just doesn't stand up. Aside from the belief of this writer that Kevin is a far more talented sportsman than David and that Jessica is a better singer than Victoria, their appetite for the spotlight doesn't compare to the Beckhams'. Sure, Pietersen has the bling, body art and fancy threads, but he doesn't change his hairstyle every month and showed the self-awareness to call a halt to the cringeworthy at-home photoshoots in glossy magazines. In fact, it was Jessica who persuaded Kevin to bin the gaudy hairstyles in favour of an ultra-close crop and they agreed it would be crass to sell pictures of their wedding despite being offered a six-figure fee by *OK!* magazine. A far cry from the Beckhams' ostentatious 1999 publicity-fuelled nuptials. Pietersen is now a regular on the London restaurant rather than party scene, preferring to spend time with Jessica at fine dining establishments (Brinkley's in Chelsea is his favourite) rather than cordoned off behind a rope in the VIP section of the latest trendy nightspot. Jones observes: "Do you ever see him falling out of a nightclub anymore? In life you go through stages. He was young before. He doesn't need it now, does he?"

Contrary to all expectations when he arrived in the England side, Pietersen is the model professional. All England insiders agree that he is the hardest trainer in the team and no-one thinks more deeply about their game. Furthermore, few tales of bad behaviour have emerged about Kevin, not even unsubstantiated rumour. No drunken escapades on a pedalo for him, no brawling in public, visits to lap-dancing clubs or womanising. He hasn't been seen the worse for wear in public since the Ashes party in 2005. He is an excellent role model and sponsors know it. Blue-chip brands VW, Citizen Watches, Red Bull, Adidas, Vodafone and npower have all queued up to be associated with one of cricket's most marketable figures. "Four years ago that could easily have been me on a pedalo after a few pints because I had a hectic schedule, was single and really enjoying my life," said Pietersen in an interview with the *Daily Mail* in 2008, referring to the Fredalo scandal that scuttled England's 2007 World Cup campaign. "Nowadays I try not to put myself in positions where I end up in trouble or harm's way. What I've realised is not to let my naughty activities interfere with my performance on a cricket field. I've never gone out and got smashed before I played for England."

It is instructive that after England thrashed South Africa in a one-day international at Trent Bridge last summer to win the five-match series with two games to play, Pietersen attended the celebration party in Nottingham that evening only briefly. While the rest of the squad understandably made a big night of it, Kevin had a few drinks and then got a lift straight back to London. He had sponsors commitments the following day and wanted to be in a good shape.

Pietersen has grown up. He has come to realise the responsibilities that go with being a public figure. Even his stag do was a relatively restrained affair. "We went to Edinburgh for a few days," says Jones, who was the only England cricketer able to attend as Gough, Vaughan and Paul Collingwood, Pietersen's other best friends from international cricket, all had prior commitments. "We got the train up on the Friday from London and played drinking games all the way up. Adam, his agent, is ex-army and Bryan his brother, who's a legend, were leading the way. I was in a mess. We were due to play golf the next day, but I couldn't make it because I was too rough. But Kev was alright. He can take his drink quite well." Richard Logan adds: "It was pretty low key for a stag do. We played a game of golf, had a few drinks. It was fun and quite laid-back."

Aided by his wife, Pietersen has learned to smile rather than snarl at the hordes of young autograph hunters. He explained: "I used to take things for granted and sometimes get annoyed when people asked for my autograph, but my missus has been so good in pointing out that for two seconds out of my day I can make someone so happy. These days if someone wants a picture or autograph I'll try and accommodate them. It helps to be reminded how happy I was to get autographs off cricket players as a kid." He is not embarrassed by some of his antics of the past, but has moved on. "I did my hair and wore jewellery and all that stuff," he said. "They were just lucrative things. My stupid hair didn't affect anything. It was just a phase. People grow up. People do silly things."

Nevertheless, Pietersen is still capable of the odd spot of boorish behaviour. I am told one story of when he returned to Maritzburg College a few years ago with Jessica and schoolboy friend and first-class cricketer Andre van Vuuren to donate a signed shirt. He turned up looking the part in a big car and walked over to the Goldstone's ground, where rain had interrupted a game between the first X1 and Grey College. In front of a group of awestruck boys, he said of the arena where he played his first serious cricket at the top of his voice, "I can't believe how f****** tiny this field is." Asked to pose for a picture with his then fiancée for the local paper, the *Natal Witness*, Pietersen told the reporter, who was, coincidentally, another College old boy: "I don't owe the press f****** anything in this country. They can all get f*****." The resentment towards his homeland is clearly deepseated.

Pietersen is undoubtedly a product of his time; a cricketer made for the 21st century *Big Brother* generation. He would have looked ridiculous as a Brylcreem boy in the 1950s just as Denis Compton, the Pietersen of his day, would have looked ridiculous with a diamond stud in his left ear, a watch the size of Big Ben and a left arm pock-marked with tattoos.

However, it isn't the case that KP is in the game simply for public self-aggrandisement. Just as with many of the wannabes who enter Channel 4's house for months of public humiliation each summer in the hope of becoming the 'next Jade Goody', it seems to most observers that Pietersen is motivated by the pursuit of fame. But the people who know him best tell me that it is money, and not aspirational ostentation, that really interests him. "Money is what drives him," observes Jason Gallian. "That, and being one of the best players in the world."

"Kevin is part of a new generation that plays for completely different reasons to me," observes MacGill, who is nine years his senior. "For me, it wasn't about the money, the front page the next day or about being cool. I have always felt uncomfortable about these sorts of things. As a person he is always looking for proof that he is doing okay. He is into the trappings of success. That is one of the ways he judges his success. For me, my success was judged by what I did on the field. He is very similar to Michael Clarke. They are part of the same generation. If you ask any 20-year-old today what they want to achieve in any field, they want to be rich and famous. I wouldn't say Kevin wants to be rich and famous. I would say Kevin wants to be constantly told he is successful."

The usual English conventions of humility and reluctance to talk about money do not apply to Pietersen. He is, in attitude and aspiration, much more like a Premier League footballer than a cricketer. He knows what he wants and how to go about getting it. And because he knows that he is good, and as he was not raised on the British Isles, he has no wish to disguise this knowledge with irony or false modesty. Pietersen earned £1 million in the year after England won the Ashes and is refreshingly frank about money. "It makes the world go round, but it's not my primary goal," he said. "I might only play until I'm 35, so I have to make the most of it."

By the time he joined Hampshire from Nottinghamshire, Pietersen was earning nearly six times his £15,000-a-year initial county salary, but his aspirations were always much higher. "There are so many blokes earning 20, 25 grand, it's ridiculous," he said. "I never just wanted to earn 20 grand. I wanted to be the best player I could and make a load of money out of cricket." Pietersen earns around £450,000-a-year from his central England contact and international appearances, but more than doubles that figure with his sponsorship deals.

England's cricketers paid a high price for missing out on the inaugural Indian Premier League in 2008. While other England stars cagily talked about how exposure to the IPL would help improve the team's Twenty20 performances and was not about the money, without really convincing anybody, Pietersen was honest enough to speak his mind and say what plenty of others were no doubt thinking, too. He castigated the ECB for preventing him from earning "a million dollars playing cricket for six weeks" and illustrated his point by explaining how Chris Gayle had sent him a text message littered with dollar signs after being told that England players were not allowed to milk the sport's new cash cow. Pietersen got his wish 12 months later when the second IPL auction confirmed that, for three weeks only, he and Flintoff would be able to look down on the millionaire footballers in England after securing contracts worth about £170,000-a-week, although the subsequent relocation of the 2009 competition to South Africa meant the pair would lose around one week's pay. Nevertheless, if Kevin needed any further proof of his status, it came with the knowledge that he was the equal most highly valued cricketer in the IPL, alongside Flintoff.

Pietersen's honesty about money and virtually all other matters have made him by far the favourite interviewee in the England team among the extensive press corps that follows the team home and abroad. He is polite, helpful, highly quotable and, in journalistic terms, always give reporters a 'line' from which to build a story around. Unlike, say, Wayne Rooney, Beckham or, indeed, Flintoff, sports editors don't rely on Kevin's name to carry his quotes. He is media gold.

When his *Daily Mail* contract came to an end in 2005, Pietersen switched to the red top market, not the traditional cricket demographic by any means, when he was snapped up by the *News of the World* in a deal worth around £100,000-a-year. Adam Hathaway, a respected former agency reporter who succeeded David Norrie as the paper's cricket and rugby correspondent following the 2007 World Cup, was immediately struck by Pietersen's grasp of what the paper expected from one of its star columnists. "He is brilliant," explains Hathaway. "I have worked with around 30 or 40 columnists and he is probably the best. He will talk about anything without betraying dressing room secrets and is not afraid to say what he thinks. He doesn't bomb you with platitudes and gives you a bit of insight. If you give him a topic he will think about it rather than shout off the first thing that comes into his head. If you have got an exclusive columnist you want him to give you something extra."

Hathaway's task is to use his newspaper's access to Pietersen to glean exclusive, newsworthy quotes and then ghost-write them for the player's column. It is harder than it sounds because Kevin's status means his media commitments are heavier than most. "You have to think about it a bit more," says Hathaway. "I sit in on his press conferences to see what he says and then try and get something different. We do the column basically when we need him, which is virtually every Saturday when England are playing and whenever we need him for preview material. If a game is going on I speak to him on a Friday night and get something in the bag and type up on a Saturday."

Hathaway has also been impressed with Pietersen's professionalism. "He always phones you back, which is a bit of a rarity among modern sportsmen. He asks how you are and, even if he doesn't mean it, it's nice to hear. He is polite and well mannered and knows it is part of his job. I've got to know him quite well. I wouldn't go out for a meal with him or hang out socially, but he will always come up to me and say hello. It is a good, professional relationship. If you talk to the cricket correspondents they would say the same thing about him. I don't think you would find any complaints from them."

Some of the criticism aimed at Pietersen's lifestyle, usually from non-cricket writers living in a 2005 time warp, has been completely unjustified. "What does p**s me off is the columnists who make ill-informed comments," adds Hathaway. "They just don't know the bloke. He is not like that at all. He thinks about the game a lot and probably prepares harder than any cricketer I've met."

Leading sportsmen have always gravitated towards successful people in other fields. Just as Ian Botham was close to Mick Jagger and Elton John (who could often be found babysitting in the Botham household), so Pietersen has friends in celebrity circles, including Piers Morgan, Frank Lampard and Lewis Hamilton, and has admitted to being a huge admirer of Simon Cowell. Success is what impresses him. He watched Manchester United play Chelsea at Stamford Bridge (although not a massive football fan, his allegiance is more to United than his 'local' club) last season, but the most interesting thing for Kevin that day was not the match itself, but watching Cristiano Ronaldo warm up. "I studied him for half an hour before the game, how he operates, his manoeuvres. That kind of stuff gets me going." Even on a day off, he is constantly thinking about his game.

Despite his hectic touring schedule and celebrity pals, Pietersen has not grown apart from his mates. Indeed, his oldest friends agree that one of Kevin's greatest qualities is his loyalty. Furthermore, he seems to have mastered the task of keeping his feet on the ground better than many high achievers. Whenever he goes back to Durban to see his family, he meets up with Scott, Grant Rowley, van Vuuren and Errol Stewart. Scott says: "We go out to restaurants and have a bottle of wine or a Jack Daniels and talk about the old days, nothing special. He has barbecues at his house and we get together, all his mates. He's just one of those blokes that I have a personal interest in because I have been quite close to him for the last 10 years. His roots, and all his family and friends, are still embedded in this country. To describe him is difficult, but I would say that deep down, he is a good old down-to-earth home-grown boy who loves his family, loves his friends. Whenever he is over here we get to see him. Whenever we are over there he is very happy to see us. He sorts me out tickets and I always see him and his brother."

Like Scott, Errol Stewart is a decade older than Kevin, and he now works full-time for the ICC in Dubai, but remains close to his former Berea Rovers team-mate. "He is a warm friend. It is not only me he keeps in regular contact with. He hasn't forgotten his mates and where he has come from. That happens too often with people who reach the top. A lot of people forget their roots. Kevin hasn't. He is not like that. He is loyal to his friends."

It is time for the tired stereotype of Pietersen the narcissist and devil of egotism to be put to bed. He doesn't read Dickens or Hemmingway in his spare time or listen to the *Today* programme, but does look at the world beyond himself and has a curiosity about people who intrigue him, even if Simon Cowell and Cristiano Ronaldo might not be exactly highbrow tastes. Yes, he is exceedingly driven and enjoys being the centre of attention, but who doesn't want a few extra bob and to be told they are the bees knees? Maybe Pietersen is just more honest than the rest. "People who don't know him think he is arrogant, over the top, full of himself," says Grant Rowley, who has known Kevin most of his life. "Maybe because of the way he walks, the way he dresses. But I can tell you now there is not a guy who is more down to earth. I'm still good friends with him, I'm still friends with the family. You actually need to spend a bit of time with him. You need to get to know him a bit because sometimes your first impression might be, 'Well, who's this guy?' But if you sit down with him, he's actually a world class guy. Whenever he comes back to Durban, we meet up for a drink. We've always been good mates."

Logan does not see as much of Pietersen these days because of his England commitments, but says his old mate has not changed. "When I do see him we do the same things we did eight years ago," says Logan. "We watch TV, listen to music, have a few drinks and chew the fat. We are a little bit more grown up now we're 28, although we're pretty much exactly the same. We speak to each other on the phone every now and then and have a good chat."

Logan offers a revealing insight into what it is like to be on-side with English cricket's biggest maverick. "He is brilliant. He will do anything for you. If he likes you, he really likes you. If he doesn't, he won't beat around the bush. He has a close network of really good mates and will look after those guys. He is a loyal friend. He will be very loyal to England and I think he will be remembered as a very loyal adopted Englishman."

Revealingly, Pietersen is one of only two players from the England set-up who has kept in touch with Simon Jones during the injury nightmare that has kept the fast bowler out of international cricket since the 2005 Ashes. Pietersen is the godfather to Harvey, the eldest of Jones' two young boys, and the pair are as close as when they used to hang out together during their days at the England Academy. "He's a very loyal friend, shown by the fact he has stayed in touch with me all this time," says Jones. "No-one else has, apart from [Matthew] Hoggard. All Kevin says to me is, 'Take wickets.' He keeps on saying it all the time. 'Get wickets, get wickets.' Usually by texts, generally, because we're both text freaks."

Pietersen can, though, come across as standoffish, a legacy perhaps of his four years dominating world cricket. Scott observes: "There is an element of aloofness, can I say, which is not surprising. He is an icon. The cricket equivalent of David Beckham. He has earned the respect for the position that he holds. As an individual he is highly respected. He has a lot of energy and, within certain parameters, stands out. He always wants to be at the centre of attention. He enjoys that, he thrives on it and has the ability to demand attention because he is what he is. The proof is in the pudding. There is an aura that surrounds him, which he does enjoy. When I was in London with him we were at a restaurant, but there was no drama. People will point at him, but it's not like it would be in Cannock or Nottingham."

Jones offers a completely different portrait of Kevin to the misunderstood public persona. Arrogant, he insists, is the wrong adjective. "I wouldn't say he was cocky or arrogant. He has belief in himself and without that you're nothing. Everyone has belief in themselves and just because you don't shout it from the rooftops doesn't mean you're not arrogant. I would never, ever say Kev was arrogant. I would say he's got that little presence about him that people automatically respect when they meet him. I've spent a lot of time with him and he's got a really, really soft side to him. He's a very caring person. I mean that. He'd do anything for you. If he thinks he can help you, he'll help you. If you say, 'I'm in trouble here, can you help me?' he'll come and get you. He's that kind of bloke." Just don't leave him to hold the baby. Pietersen loves to grab his godson and lift him high in the air, but Jones, aware of those six dropped catches against Australia, laughs: "I was, like, 'Hang on a minute, Kev. Calm down. With your track record . . .'"

A little Pietersen revisionism is perhaps required, although 'KP the endearing, kindly soul' doesn't make a great headline, does it? Any sports editor would tell you that.

FIGJAM

KEVIN PIETERSEN'S URN-SAVING 158 at the Oval had turned him overnight into a household name and millionaire. But it asked as many questions as it answered. How do you follow one of the most significant innings in Test history? What if that – his fifth Test match – was as good as it gets? Would everything that follows automatically be a climbdown? Few encores would have been big enough to avoid a crushing sense of anti-climax.

Shaped by his religious upbringing, Pietersen is a big believer in fate – one of his favourite sayings is, "what will be, will be" – but he also has phenomenal belief in his own ability as a plot-grabber and changer of games. He didn't just crave adulation. He wanted to be an all-time great, too. Pietersen was confident that The Oval would not represent his personal nirvana.

With his head on fire with self-esteem, Pietersen's first post-Ashes assignment was in keeping with his status as international cricket's brightest new thing. He was one of only two England representatives in a Rest of the World one-day side – the other was Andrew Flintoff – that took on Australia in an experimental three-match Super Series only 20 days after the Ashes had been reclaimed. Pietersen didn't make the cut for the one-off Test that followed, although Flintoff did, alongside Steve Harmison.

In an experiment that failed miserably, the Aussies, desperate to remove any doubt about their status as undisputed champions, treated the glorified exhibition games seriously and their all-star opponents, with no flag to play for, did not. The four games were painfully one-sided and despite a marketing campaign built around the Ashes conquerors Pietersen and Flintoff, there was little public appetite for them. Pietersen's Australian adventures failed to reproduce the dreamy heights of his 12 September apogee. Batting at No. 6, he scored two in the first one-day 'international' and pulled a hamstring in the second, during which he batted with a runner at No. 8, while making 16 from 22 balls. Succour came at the ICC's inaugural gala awards dinner. Pietersen walked off with two awards based on performances in his first year of international cricket – the Emerging Player of the Year (which he expected to win) and the One-day Player of the Year (which he didn't). The evening made a few good pictures for the newspapers back home. Every Rest of the World player was allowed a guest on tour and Pietersen, in the fashion that summed up his lust for the limelight at the time, invited a blonde celebrity – the glamour model Caprice.

If the glitz and glamour of Australia suited Pietersen, the more subtle charms of Pakistan manifestly did not. Pietersen had never previously toured what is commonly regarded as the least desirable of the destinations on Test cricket's map – certainly, for the Western cricketers – and admitted, "it's not a place I'd rush back to". As a child of Africa which has, among the white population, the same kind of sporty outdoor culture as Australia, he prefers the bounding physical life of veldt and beaches and braais and wors. Not for Pietersen the occasional Garbo-esque pleasure in solitude. He doesn't like being in hotel rooms on his own – indeed, isn't all that fussed about his own company – and finds endless rounds of darts, DVDs (*Only Fools and Horses* and *Lovejoy* were particularly popular on that tour) and PlayStation games tedious after a while. Kevin's best mates from his first two England tours, Darren Gough and Simon Jones, were not in the touring party and with few parties to attend – hobnobbing with businessmen and diplomats at official functions did not count in his book – Pakistan became a test of Pietersen's patience and tolerance.

The cricket was also considerably more low-key. After the drama of the Ashes, the crowds were down (unless national hero Shahid Afridi was batting), the intensity levels were down and so was the level of England's performance. The Pakistan tour was the first of four series against subcontinental opposition home and away before England locked horns once again with Australia for the Greatest Series Ever: Part II, to be followed by the 2007 World Cup in the Caribbean. It was like the village fete after the Lord Mayor's show. Duncan Fletcher has admitted that, try as they might, England could not forge the same spirit and togetherness in Pakistan as they had during their run of success over the previous two years. The hotels were excellent and the swimming pools and gyms inside them were superb, and the players trained hard, but there was an unmistakeable Ashes hangover, according to the England coach. "It would have been better if we had been going to somewhere like South Africa or New Zealand straight after the Ashes. After all the euphoria, excitement and fanfare of that famous victory, Pakistan was just too quiet," said Fletcher.

Pietersen's performances mirrored that of a side crippled by injuries to many of the Ashes heroes. Okay, but not quite good enough. He began atrociously in the warm-up games, stringing together consecutive scores of 2, 10, 4 and 0 and extended this run into the first Test at Multan, where he managed 5 and 19 as the visitors made a hash of a run chase and succumbed to a 22-run defeat. An unusually quick pitch at Faisalabad brought the best out of Pietersen. The highlight of a high-scoring draw was his enthralling contest with the equally charismatic Shoaib Akhtar, the dynamic but dilettante paceman who was under pressure to prove he was still committed to cricket. Kevin completed a fine second Test century by hooking Shoaib for the third six of his 137-ball knock. Next ball he tried to repeat the shot, but spliced a catch to mid-on instead. "I'd hit the previous one for six, so why not that?" was Pietersen's response. The answer was he had been suckered by outstanding fast bowling; the second bouncer was different, faster, and on to him before he could execute the stroke.

Pietersen added 42 in the second innings, but he had an anonymous game in the third Test at Lahore, scoring 34 and 1 as England were thrashed by an innings en route to a 2-0 series defeat. A rib injury curtailed Kevin's trip following the second of the five one-day internationals to bring an end to an anti-climatic tour. Even for the most one-eyed John Bull devotee it was hard to avoid the conclusion that Pietersen and England had reached the cold turkey stage of their Ashes comedown.

By his own admission, Pietersen was still learning his trade and further mixed performances came after Christmas in the cauldron of India, arguably the hotbed of international cricket. Kevin had performed outstandingly well on tour there with the England Academy two years previously, but he did not hit those same heights with the Test side against a team formidable in their own conditions. In three-match Test series he always sets himself the target of 300 runs and at least one century. He had fallen 99 short in Pakistan – despite an even hundred at Faisalabad – and fared only marginally better on the equally slow and dusty wickets of their great rivals, scoring 216 runs in six completed innings.

His best performance came in the second innings of the drawn first Test in Nagpur when he had a licence to attack as England set up a second innings declaration. Displaying the bombast and bravado of 2005, Kevin raced to an invigorating 87 from 100 balls while completely dominating a 124-run partnership with debutant Alastair Cook before selflessly throwing his wicket away with a third Test ton seemingly in his grasp. He was just about able to contain his disappointment. Pietersen added another quickfire half-century on the first day of the second Test, but once again his scores in the five-day game tailed off. Compensation came as a Johnny Cash-inspired touring team levelled the series in Mumbai when a tea-time sing-along to *Ring of Fire* imbued the flagging tourists with the togetherness to bowl out the hosts cheaply and claim a magnificent against-the-odds win.

Pietersen was back to his scintillating best in the subsequent one-day series, although, in what had become depressingly familiar fashion on tour, the switch from whites to pyjamas stripped England of their pizzazz and they were thrashed 5-1. England's No. 4 was a sole shining beacon, scoring 46 off 49 balls in Delhi, 71 off 87 in Faridabad, 77 off 82 in Cochin, 33 off 40 in Jamshedpur and 64 off 57 in Indore. His 291 runs in five innings had been delivered at nearly a run a ball and at Faridabad he became the joint fastest with Sir Vivian Richards to 1,000 one-day international runs, which he reached in 21 innings. Shaun Udal detected a more mature and serene Pietersen in India. Udal says: "He had met Jessica by that stage and she came out twice on tour. By then the skunk haircut had gone and he had grown up a bit. I didn't see him going after the limelight any more. I was really taken by how down-to-earth she was and you could see he was just getting on with his cricket."

Pietersen has always pursued greatness. There was never anything remotely half-baked about him. He always wanted to be the best and end up on the winning side. It is often a meaningless cliché when sportsmen, particularly footballers, talk about being the first on to the training ground and the last off it. In Pietersen's case, it is true. Even when he was stepping out with supermodels and fighting off the boredom in Pakistan, his preparation was first-class. Indeed, Michael Atherton once paid Kevin the huge compliment of describing him as the most professional England cricketer he had seen. Pietersen has sustained the work ethic that made him stand out from his equally talented brothers during childhood games in the back garden. Unlike all-time greats like Shane Warne and Ian Botham, who relied almost solely on inspiration, Pietersen is a big believer in perspiration. Warne rarely bothered with net practice at Hampshire, but that was one of aspect of his friend's game that Kevin had no inclination to copy.

Simon Jones reveals that Pietersen prepares in a different manner to even the most committed international cricketers. "They're not always thinking what they're going to do in a net. They'll just go in and hit a few balls whereas Kev is always thinking what to do to improve his game and will work on something specific in that whole net. The difference is even more pronounced in county cricket. He is so focused about what he is going to do. He never takes it for granted, he sees it as, 'My chance to train and improve and I'll go to bed tonight thinking, right, I've trained as hard as I can.' I admit I don't do that sometimes. I'll go into the net and bowl off a couple of yards and just do what I need to do. I'll go away and think, 'I could have done a little bit better in there, you know.' A lot of people do that, but Kev doesn't treat it like that."

Fletcher is critical of the preparation of various England players in his autobiography, *Behind The Shades*. Andrew Flintoff is famously singled out while Steve Harmison, Darren Gough, Ian Bell and Alex Tudor are among those also admonished. Pietersen is praised in unusually glowing terms by the usually taciturn Zimbabwean. Fletcher wrote: "He is an international cricketer of the highest class. Just watching him at work in the nets had told me that. He is such a smart cricketer; always thinking, always working on different facets of his game, always plotting a game plan for a particular bowler or particular pitch. His net sessions alone are worth watching, and fellow players do stop and take a look."

Pietersen is clearly a cricketer of his time. Many of the England stars of the 1980s were night animals and allergic to practice (Botham, Gower et al) and would have laughed at the possibility of analysing their performance and that of their opponent on a laptop in the middle of a Test. But Kevin is not merely a 21st century cricketer, he was also ahead of his time. He was running five to seven miles every other day – a regime he still sticks to now on the Thames towpaths near his home – at a time when Flintoff was threatening to drown his talent in a sea of takeaways and epic drinking sessions.

In the early days at Nottinghamshire, Pietersen's ultra-dedication was hardly typical of a young pro. He understood from a young age that everything was contingent upon his success as a batsman, which in turn was contingent upon the amount of hard work he put in. Mick Newell recalls: "In terms of his own training and looking after his own game he was a model professional. He was very self-motivated and interested in looking after himself. He would work harder in the gym, be fitter and stronger than everyone else. With the South African upbringing, you get this outdoor lifestyle. He was a fantastically athletic person. He did weights, he ran, he worked out. This is going back before we had full-time fitness coaches, so a lot of it was self-directed. He had obviously done it in South Africa, had a bit of a steer. He was quite mature in some ways, in terms of his fitness programme and how he would prepare."

Pietersen also put an unusual amount of thought into his game. Jason Gallian recalls a conversation in the slips involving Pietersen and Stuart MacGill during a Nottinghamshire game in 2004. "I was first slip, Kevin was second and Stuey third," says Gallian. "Kevin was asking Stuey about Shane Warne – he had never faced him before – and what Warne didn't like when he was bowling. Stuey said, 'He doesn't like being swept. In fact, he hates being swept.' This was two weeks before the game at the Rose Bowl. So Kevin practises and practises the sweep shot against MacGill in the nets, working out his strategy for Warne. At the Rose Bowl, Warne bowled two or three overs at Kevin and he kept sweeping him. In the end Warne had to take himself off and Kevin went on to get a big score. To me, that really signalled how good he is and how prepared he is. I had never seen that before. The bigger the challenge, the more he rose to the challenge. That's why we didn't want to lose him."

Pietesen didn't leave any stone unturned, as Richard Logan discovered when spending six weeks with him at Kevin's parents' home in Durban during the winter of 2002/03. Logan says: "We trained solidly the whole time. We'd go to the gym and go running. Kev never liked to do anything but running. He used to say, 'I don't cycle or row around a cricket pitch. I just run.' Normally I was running behind him. He is pretty quick. In Durban he'd run five kilometres in 20 minutes. He is definitely one of the fittest I've worked with. He is a natural athlete. He always used to be one of the top at the bleep tests at Notts and Hampshire and is still up there with the England team. He does a lot of running now."

Pietersen was not just interested in showing Logan a clean pair of heels. "We trained with the Natal Dolphins once or twice a week and when we were in Durban I would bowl at him in the nets and he would bowl at me," says Logan. "It was brilliant practise for me. The way cricket has changed with the demands of professionalism, it is a game now that you have to be totally fit for. Having played the last 10 years myself the emphasis on training has gone from 50-60 per cent to 99 per cent. Kev was different as he was always 99 per cent from the time I first knew him."

Clive Rice had drummed into Pietersen the importance of setting goals and at the start of the 2006 English season, Kevin raised his own personal bar. His first target was to translate big scores into monster ones against the tourists Sri Lanka and Pakistan, a theme strongly endorsed by Fletcher, who gathered all the batsmen together at the start of the summer and asked, "When was the last time any of you got a double hundred? It's about time you did." Pietersen's second goal was to be the No. 1 batsman in the world. He saw it as perfectly natural to announce this in his *News of the World* column. Most players would have worried that headlines spelling out their ambitions would put undue pressure on themselves. Pietersen, in typical black-and-white fashion, merely saw it as a frank expression of his desire to be the best. His response to his own clarion call was to score a flawless century in his opening international innings of the summer in the drawn first Test against Sri Lanka at Lord's. Unlike his breathless debut hundred at the Oval, this was meticulously planned. Desperate to live up to his own billing and not waste a good start by Trescothick and Cook in batsman-friendly conditions, Pietersen did not indulge himself until he had got his name on to the Lord's honours board. With neat symmetry he equalled the 158 he scored at the Oval, but rated this a more pure innings. "My knock at the Oval was played on adrenaline and emotion. I was dropped two or three times, whereas at Lord's it was a chanceless innings. I started off rock-solid and made sure that I played straight and that my concentration levels were perfect throughout the whole innings." Even when he wasn't trying to dominate, Pietersen still scored rapidly. His entire knock only occupied only 205 balls.

The abiding memory of the 2006 summer, one which turned into a personal triumph for Pietersen, was his treatment of the great Muttiah Muralitharan in the next Test. His reputation as a bold adventurer was already well established, but at Edgbaston KP demonstrated more clearly than ever before that his aggression was backed up with intelligence. On a testing track that offered bounce to the fast bowlers and spin to the slow men, Sri Lanka had been shot out for 141 and, in response, all England's batsmen struggled to cope with Muralitharan – apart from one. Pietersen is honest enough to admit that he can pick the spin wizard only occasionally "and not nearly as much as everyone seems to think I can" – so concentrates on watching Murali's wrist rather than the ball and relying on the movement of the ball off the pitch, instinct and supreme confidence in his own ability. Nevertheless, he played the Sri Lankan master-spinner with something approaching ease and cantered to a 115-ball ton even more masterful than his Lord's century.

With his second consecutive hundred secured, Pietersen set about having some fun. He took Muralitharan for three consecutive fours, had a look around a field dotted with boundary fielders and waited for the next offering. In a pre-determined move, he outrageously danced round in his stance at the last second, though not so quick to realise it was a full toss, and executed a perfect left-handed sweep for six. It landed in the notoriously raucous Eric Hollies Stand and the crowd, caught up in a white-knuckle ride of an innings, stood as one to acclaim the audacity of it. Even the Sri Lankans gasped in admiration. Andrew Flintoff, Kevin's batting partner and captain, wandered down the wicket and asked, "What was that?" Muralitharan smiled, but warned Pietersen afterwards that if he ever repeated the shot he would bowl him a bouncer or beamer.

Almost as impressive as the execution was the planning that went into the stroke. Pietersen explained: "To understand that shot you need to know that I had just come down the wicket to Murali three times; I had hit him over mid-off for four, through mid-off for four and then cut the doosra for four. So Murali moved his mid-off and mid-on back and put men deep at cow corner and deep square leg. All my options for big shots had been blocked."

Next ball he was gone, but Pietersen had again provided supreme entertainment. To put his innings into context, no other England batsman passed 34 in the match and only 35 runs were scored by his team-mates at the other end while he blasted 142, which took a mere 157 balls. Muralitharan, who took 10 wickets in the Test, was such a threat on the disintegrating surface that England stumbled across the finishing line in pursuit of their meagre victory target of 78. The unorthodox Pietersen was becoming a phenomenon. "That shot off Muralitharan was the talk of the Test," Fletcher later said. "There is no way I would ever berate him for that, but I knew he had to be careful. Sooner or later he had to go on and get the really big scores to be a great batsman. But he was still learning his trade then."

Pietersen could not continue his golden run at Trent Bridge on a pitch that seemed to be custom-made for genius wrist-spinners and Muralitharan duly wreaked havoc as Sri Lanka levelled the series. Yet Kevin's scores of 41 and 6 took his total output for the series to 360 runs from five innings, twice as many as the next best England batsman. "I felt that I took my game to a new level," Pietersen said. He was hampered by a knee injury in the humiliating 5-0 defeat in the subsequent one-day series, scoring 73 on virtually one leg at The Oval and missing two of the thrashings.

The second half of the summer against Pakistan was distinguished by England's 2-0 Test triumph, but will always be remembered for one of the sport's greatest controversies – the abandoned fourth Test at The Oval, when the visitors refused to take to the field after being accused by the umpires of ball-tampering. England's batsmen filled their boots against a Pakistan attack missing its best paceman (Shoaib Akhtar) for the entire series, and its next best (Mohammad Asif) for all but the final game. Pietersen scored 347 runs in seven innings but was not the dominant batsman on the England side. That was Ian Bell, who reeled off three consecutive hundreds from the unlikely position of No. 6, while Andrew Strauss and Cook were also marginally more productive. The divine Mohammad Yousuf, meanwhile, showed an insatiable appetite for crease occupation by creaming 631 runs. Although Pietersen missed out at Lord's (21 and 41) and Old Trafford (38), he rode his luck for a compelling and occasionally brutal first-day 135 off 169 balls at Headingley that paved the way for an emphatic series-wrapping victory. Pietersen was dismissed by Asif for his second golden duck in Tests at The Oval, but bounced back in the second innings with an exhilarating 96 that was soon forgotten in the ball tampering storm. Despite a quiet one-day series in which he didn't manage a fifty, it had been a fabulous summer for Pietersen. He responded to the pressure he had put on himself by scoring 707 runs at 58.92 in the seven Tests, including three centuries, two of which had paid the foundations for victories. He had also provided the season's champagne moment with his contemptuous treatment of Muralitharan.

Two years into his international career, Pietersen was providing a new challenge to the bowlers' brain trust. Cricket's grapevine does not have national barriers. Word was getting around about the outlandish newcomer. It was not just Pietersen's batting that opponents were hoping to find holes in, his personality, demeanour, even the way he walked, were targets. Pietersen would like to be known as 'KP' or 'PK', as Warne called him in the 2005 Ashes. Even '600' was an amusing short-term alternative bestowed by Warne as he homed on his 600th Test victim that summer. However, it is a lucky man who chooses his nickname. In Pakistan, Pietersen will always be known as 'the chicken man', a description that emerged on England's tour in late 2005 when the hosts sought to undermine England's best batsman with ridicule. The term was coined by Makhaya Ntini, who mocked Pietersen during the Super Series in Melbourne for walking like a chicken. "Everybody had a good laugh. Mind you, I can't see it myself," said Pietersen.

The chicken dance made its first appearance at the Faisalabad Test when Shoaib Akhtar celebrated Pietersen's dismissal by flapping his arms. It re-emerged in west Yorkshire the following summer, carried off with a flourish by Danish Kaneria after he had finally got one up on the batsman. "He walks with his feathers out and tries to slog the spinners," said Kaneria. "And I called him a chicken to annoy him. He wasn't going to boss me around." Pietersen's strut and swagger got the goat of opponents. The Australian players, who found England's most daring and self-confident batsman ever too cocksure even for their tastes, took to calling him 'The Ego' in 2005 and were even more inventive when England arrived Down Under for the massively hyped return series 14 months later. They adopted the witty nickname 'FIGJAM', an acronym standing for, 'F*** I'm Good, Just Ask Me', one that has also been used for the American golfer Phil Mickelson.

It was a sign of the Australians' respect for their most dangerous adversary, but, like most sledges, there was a kernel of truth behind the taunt. Pietersen is good and he knows it. He has always known it. It just took others longer to realise it. There is no self-consciousness about him on the cricket field. He swaggers about in a way that threatens to out-Richards Sir Vivian. It can attract irritation in some quarters. But he is not the only exhibitionist cricketer out there. Half of India's team are world-class strutters, while West Indies captain Chris Gayle couldn't look more cool on the field if he was lying on a hammock at midwicket in a pair of shades and boardies while a fair maiden served him Pina Coladas.

To his credit, Pietersen takes most sledges on the chin. Contrary to popular perception he doesn't take himself all that seriously – you wouldn't dare have a blue skunk haircut if you did. He also does a decent line in self-deprecation. At various times he has ridiculed his own sense of style ("it's a stupid haircut"), his captaincy ("I'm just the idiot chucking his arms around on the field") and his bowling ("my filthy off-spin"). He regards taunts from the opposition as harmless banter and, as a lover of confrontation, gives as good as he gets. He can be witty, too. After being sledged by all-rounder Shane Watson, Pietersen acerbically replied, "You're just upset because no-one loves you any more" – a reference to reports that Watson had been dumped by his girlfriend. When Andrew Symonds was called up to the Australia side mid-series he tried to get at Pietersen but immediately Kevin put him down with the line that he thought it was good that the world's best "fielding all-rounder" had at last been given a game. Every time

Pietersen hit the ball near Symonds he would yell "Fetch it! Fetch it!", the implication being that the Queenslander was only in the side for his brilliant fielding.

An amusing element of England's tour of India in the autumn of 2008 was Pietersen's running feud with Yuvraj Singh. The Indian is a brilliant strokeplayer of dubious temperament whose Test record does not match his limited-overs achievements. He took England's attack to the cleaners in the one-day series and also got some joy with his occasional left-arm spin, dismissing Pietersen on two occasions, the second of which he celebrated by wiggling his hands above his head in a bunny impression. "You are not God, you're a cricketer, and I'm a better one," said Pietersen. There was also some truth to Pietersen's retort to Yuvraj's taunts in the second Test: "I'm a little bit tougher than you, brother." It's a shame the stump microphone is muted for the sensibilities of TV viewers when Pietersen is around.

England's 5-0 Ashes whitewash in 2006/7 hurt Pietersen as much as anyone, but he still managed to confirm his advance towards the top echelon of batting. He made his reputation against Australia and South Africa in 2005, but that winter, against the undisputed world champions in their own backyard, he copperbottomed it. By the end he was "destroyed" and "mentally and physically drained", but Pietersen was the only Englishman with the desire to compete as an equal with the Aussies. When the series was 'live', he scored 16, 92, 158, 2, 70 and 60 not out. It was only when the urn had been surrendered that his performances slightly tailed off, with innings of 21, 4, 41 and 29 at Melbourne and Sydney. In the end, even he was ground down by the futility of his resistance. For the second consecutive Ashes campaign he had been England's top run-getter, scoring 490 runs at 54. Going into the series, some critics had wondered who was England's best batsman: Pietersen or Strauss? There was no doubt now and there has not been since.

The most fascinating sub-plot to cricket's oldest rivalry was Pietersen v Warne, two non-conformist attention-seekers vying for supremacy. The Australian players, stung by criticism that they had been too nice in 2005 – exemplified by the friendship between the two Hampshire men – had been instructed by team management and Cricket Australia to be as hostile to the Poms as possible. This manifested itself in some sledging which Fletcher believed to be "so foul-mouthed as to be a disgrace to the game". Warne was at the forefront of this. He decided to set aside his on-field mateship with Pietersen in favour of shredding his younger county team-mate's career. The psychological warfare began with him calling Pietersen by his Christian name, which he had never done previously. He then threw the ball at Pietersen during England's second innings in the Brisbane Test as a warning not to step out of his crease. This was brushed off. During a tense period of play on day four Pietersen pushed a Warne delivery to mid-off and stayed in his crease. Warne responded by hurling the ball at the head of Pietersen, who had to swat it away with his bat to avoid being poleaxed. From that moment, their friendship ceased to be a mutual admiration society. The red mist descended and Pietersen responded by calling Warne a "f***wit". The apprentice was outgrowing his role as Shane's little project. "You don't throw a ball at a mate," said Pietersen. "It just wasn't right. Yes, be aggressive, but I thought the extent to which Shane took that aggression was ridiculous. Players of his calibre should not be doing things like that."

The pair kissed and made up over a beer after the game, but a discernible rift had developed. Pietersen admits there was "a bit of an atmosphere" between them for the rest of the series, one that was not completely healed until Warne held out the olive branch and explained the rationale behind his actions during a two-hour chat on the phone when Kevin had returned to England.

If Warne's reckless gamesmanship hurt a friendship it did not achieve his aim of curbing Pietersen's run-gathering. Rather than hot-headedly try and belt Warne into submission, Kevin coolly ground him into dust during the second Test at Adelaide. He formed a 310-run alliance with Paul Collingwood, patiently padding away Warne's around-the-wicket offerings en route to a mature sixth Test hundred, and his third of 158. Warne was more ineffective than at any point in his career, having to wait until his 47th over before he managed a wicket, the longest barren patch he had endured in an innings, and never had he conceded more runs.

Fletcher claims the more Pietersen is sledged, the faster the ball travels to the boundary. "You're wasting your breath if you try to unsettle him. The last Ashes series was a good example. Early on Shane Warne was going very hard at Pietersen, as if he wanted to prove that he really wasn't his best mate. But Pietersen scored runs in the first couple of Tests. It was only when it quietened down that Pietersen began to drift off. If you say nothing it's almost as if you've been defeated anyway. But the silent treatment is the best way to go – don't do anything to motivate him." Nevertheless, it was the tutor who won the war at Adelaide. Warne bowled Pietersen around his legs in the second innings to set in motion a horrific England collapse that cost them the Test on the day that the Ashes were effectively handed back to Australia.

Pietersen and Collingwood were the only two England players who Fletcher felt showed any spirit and aggression towards the Australians in what was an introverted team. He particularly criticised Flintoff for failing to lead from the front and for being too friendly with Warne and Lee. The war of words between the two countries had become more competitive than the cricket by the end of the series. After England had been beaten inside three days in Melbourne, Australia coach John Buchanan suggested that Pietersen was not a team man. Buchanan offered little by way of evidence to support his theory. "Pietersen certainly talks of himself as a team player," said Buchanan. "I personally don't see any evidence of that, but that's from a distance. I don't reside in the England dressing room, but I do look at him on the field and he does seem to distance himself quite a bit from the team, in where he fields. England may want him to field out on the boundary. But he's a good fieldsman and good in the ring. It surprises me that he always seems distanced from the rest of the group."

Pietersen offered a few unflattering comments about Buchanan in return and mounted a self-defence of his own credentials. He said he offers anyone in the England team advice on batting, which Monty Panesar especially has taken him up on. During a lunch interval in Mumbai during England's 2005/06 India tour, Pietersen went out into the heat to allow Panesar to practise his bowling on the outfield, fielding the ball for him. No cameras were there to capture the moment; nothing in it for Pietersen, except if he was a team man. It is probably safe to conclude that Pietersen is as much a team man as his ego will allow – the self-esteem that makes him arguably the most exhilarating Englishman to wear flannels. Newell says Buchanan's argument does not quite stand up. "Kevin has a massive ego. He wants to be the best player and dominate games, be in the press. But it is not to the detriment of the team. KP would always be scoring at such a rate that he would never be disrupting the team's chances of winning."

Indeed, it could even be argued he is not selfish enough. Pietersen can be accused of throwing his wicket away in pursuit of personal landmarks (Oval 2006; Edgbaston 2008; Jamaica 2009), but he has also selflessly sacrificed his wicket on many occasions as England have thrashed for quick runs in readiness for a declaration (Nagpur 2006; Lord's 2007; Headingley 2007; Antigua 2009). "I tell him to get more red inkers," says Rice. "It's good for your stats and good for maintaining your dominance over the bowlers."

Pietersen returned early from the Australia tour after cracking his rib in the first match of the one-day tri-series following one sortie down the pitch too many against Glenn McGrath. He watched from his sofa as Collingwood inspired England into the best-of-three final, where they soundly beat Australia in two games to gain some compensation for their Ashes humiliation. Either side of lifting a rare one-day trophy were the two biggest global one-day competitions, the Champions Trophy and the World Cup. Australia won both competitions easily and England were an embarrassment, failing to reach the semi-finals on both occasions. Pietersen did not disappoint. He was England's top run scorer in their three games in the Champions Trophy, scoring a matchwinning unbeaten 90 against the West Indies. In the Fredalo-dominated World Cup he shone like a floodlight in a team full of oil lamps. He was one of 10 players that passed the significant 400-run barrier in the tournament, scoring 444 runs in nine innings at

55.50 to finish eighth in the run charts. Typically, he saved his best for the best. His two centuries came against Australia (104) and the West Indies (100) and two of his three fifties against Sri Lanka and New Zealand. The weakest prey in cricket's jungle – Canada, Ireland and Bangladesh – were not made to suffer by one of world cricket's fiercest predators. Although England were all at sea in the Caribbean, Pietersen reached the summit. By the tournament's end he was officially ennobled as the world's No. 1 one-day batsman, a peak achieved by only two previous England players, Marcus Trescothick in 2005 and Allan Lamb in 1989.

Having passed his pyjamas test, Pietersen settled back into his whites as easily as a businessman putting on his trusted favourite suit on a Monday morning. In terms of Test runs, the 2007 season was his most prolific to date. The West Indies brought an inexperienced attack who strived without menace and for an England top order crushed by the relentless brilliance of Warne, McGrath, Lee and Stuart Clark during the winter in front of pom-hating full houses it was like being fed candy by an army of toddlers. Pietersen had the sweetest tooth. He was the most prolific batsman on either side, plundering 466 runs in the four Tests, including a dashing century at Lord's that failed to pave the way for a last-day victory. It was followed, in the second Test win at Headingley, by his first Test double hundred – a thrilling 226 off 262 balls, above even his usual scoring rate, that demonstrated the mercilessness which Pietersen sometimes lacked. It was the highest score by an England player since Graham Gooch's 333 at Lord's in 1990. Experts were queuing up to pat him on the back. "Kevin's innings at Leeds proved to me that he has the mental strength that could make him England's highest-ever run-scorer," says Graham Thorpe.

So commonplace were Pietersen's feats becoming that there was a danger of belittling their extraordinary nature. The measure of his career was that only Don Bradman had made more runs by his 25th Test. Pieterens' tally of 2,448 runs at 54.40, including eight centuries, edged him ahead of Everton Weekes and Viv Richards. However, even KP was no match for The Don, who scored 3,194 runs in his first 25 matches at 91.25, including 13 hundreds. Pietersen also joined an exclusive club by becoming only the 21st batsman in the history of the Test cricket to have earned more than 900 points at any one time in the ICC's rankings system. Only five Englishmen have ever bettered his ranking of 909 – Len Hutton, Jack Hobbs, Peter May, Denis Compton and Ken Barrington.

The second half of the 2007 summer provided Pietersen with a more rigorous examination of his technique. The main threat came not from India's traditional stronghold – their spinners – but the banana-like swing of left-arm pacemen Zaheer Khan and RP Singh. Pietersen regards his exuberant second-innings century at swing-friendly Lord's, a chance-free but adventurous 134, as technically his most complete innings to date, although it proved in vain as England could not finish the job off on the final day. He missed out in the controversial 'Jelly Bean' Test at Trent Bridge, scoring 13 and 19 as England's top order failed to cope with the brilliance of Zaheer, but, having complained of weariness a few weeks earlier, ended the series as the sprightliest of England's batsmen with a defiant 101 to help save The Oval Test on the final day and keep the deficit down to 1-0.

Although Pietersen's one-day form had tailed off after the World Cup he ended the season on a high with 53, his first 50-over half-century in nine matches, and 71 not out as England won a compelling one-day series 4-3. In the five-day game he reigned supreme. Seven Tests against the relatively weak (West Indies) and the relatively strong (India) had yielded 811 runs from 13 innings at 62.38 and four centuries. The spectacular was becoming routine. Pietersen knew he was good. So did the whole world. "What do you do when you have played the greatest innings of your life at the age of 25?" Richie Benaud had asked. Play some more great innings, that's what.

REDEFINING THE BOUNDARIES

IT IS ASSUMED THAT Kevin Pietersen played his remarkable switch-hit for the first time in a one-day international against New Zealand, when he changed his grip to a southpaw and slog-swept Scott Styris for a brace of extraordinary sixes. Wrong. Or maybe the left-handed swipe that sent a Muttiah Muralitharan full toss into the stands at Edgbaston two years earlier? Wrong. Or perhaps in county cricket? Wrong. Or in the nets? No. Wrong again. Pietersen played the shot that delighted spectators, appalled some former fast bowlers and sent the MCC law-makers into session to decide on its legality for the first time when he was a child. In the back garden. The switch-hit had its fine-tuned international debut at Edgbaston after much nurturing in the nets, but it was in Pietermaritzburg that it was patented. Pietersen recalled: "It didn't take long before I received messages from my Dad and brother Bryan, both saying, 'You used to play that shot at home when you were a kid in the courtyard. Now you are playing it in Test cricket.'"

During his early teens, Pietersen used to mess around with grips and stances against his brothers in matches that were as competitive as an Ashes Test. "We would have some amazing games," explained Bryan. "He would nominate the player he was going to be when we played and Kevin would invariably shout out, 'I'm Brian Lara,' while I would bowl at him pretending to be Shane Warne. Kevin would try to assume the characteristics and batting style of the player, even the left-handed ones like Lara."

Doug Watson remembers Pietersen as an especially good impersonator of his team-mates at Natal. "He would take the p*** out of us," says Watson and laughs.

"When he batted he would mimic and copy our batting styles, right or left-handed. He used to mimic my batting style. I pulled quite strange facial contortions when I was at the crease so he would say, 'This is Doug Watson batting' and then mimic me to show what I looked like. It was actually pretty close to me. I was quite impressed. He would also take off a few of the other guys – Wade Winfield and Grant Rowley. He had a good sense of humour and some of his impersonations were uncanny."

Pietersen was very comfortable batting left-handed. He found he could keep his head still and maintain his balance even when hitting the ball in such an unorthodox fashion. The result was that, even though his body and hands were in unnatural positions, the ball could still be hit with great power. However, it would be some time before Pietersen began seriously practising the switch-hit to use in a match situation.

In his first season at Nottinghamshire, he would play the occasional reverse sweep or reverse pull when he had his eye in. Richard Logan recalls him taking advantage of a short boundary at Lord's to hit Phil Tufnell for six with one of these shots. It was an extraordinary demonstration of Pietersen's eye and talent, but nothing groundbreaking. Mushtaq Mohammad was flummoxing spinners with the reverse sweep in the 1960s; Mike Gatting used it to disastrous effect in the 1987 World Cup final. Indeed, Duleepsinhji, the nephew of the great turn-of-the-century strokemaker Ranjitsinhji, was said to have played a wide off-side ball 'backwards towards third man with his bat turned and facing the wicketkeeper' in a match in the 1920s.

It was in 2006 that Pietersen patented cricket's version of the switch-hit, the human in the evolution chain to the reverse sweep's ape. The term originates from baseball, where ambidextrous hitting is not unusual. It is a commonly held belief that right-handed hitters do better against left-handed pitchers and vice versa. The switch-hitter, therefore, becomes a gem of a player and can take advantage of any idiosyncrasies in the size of the boundaries. Mickey Mantle, the great New York Yankees player of the Fifties and Sixties, was one of the most famous switch-hitters. He hit 372 home runs left-handed and 164 right-handed, taking advantage of the short boundaries for the left-handed hitter at the Yankee Stadium.

Mike Young, the former Australia fielding coach whose main expertise was in baseball, named Pietersen as one of three cricketers who could make it in baseball. The others were Andrew Symonds and Dwayne Smith, the West Indian. All three, Young said, had the physical presence, ball-striking skills and speed to the ball to give it a go. Pietersen gave a sneak preview of what the future may hold during a rare appearance for Hampshire, against Essex in May 2006, in a Cheltenham and Gloucester Trophy match. Pietersen hammered a buccaneering 98 off 74 balls, at one point dancing round in his stance at the last second, switching hands and hitting Grant Flower to the cover point boundary. It was the first time he had played the switch-hit in a match.

It took bravery, bravado and self-belief – all of which Pietersen has in spades – to translate that stroke to the Test arena, as he did 25 days later against Muralitharan. The shot, played when Kevin was on 136, was remarkable not just in its audacity – the spin wizard was rated the No. 1 bowler in the world at the time – but in the perfection of its execution. Few left-handers have the strength or timing to sweep or pull so cleanly. Pietersen had extravagantly drilled the ball for six into the Eric Hollies Stand off his 'wrong' side.

"As he was running up I decided to do it," said Pietersen. "I just turned round and backed my eye and my ability, but I must admit to being surprised at how far it travelled." It was only the second time Kevin had played the switch-hit in a match, but he had got into the groove during the tour of India a few months before, where he spent an entire net session switch-hitting everything.

The stroke went in cold storage for a while. Even Pietersen dare not try it in a losing Ashes campaign. The 2007 World Twenty20 in South Africa provided the perfect stage for him to experiment. Pietersen played the shot three times in succession against the medium pace of Zimbabwe's Keith Dabengaw en route to a 37-ball 79. The result was 6-4-4, although the switch hit proved to be his undoing in that match, eventually holing out at deep point to off-spinner Prosper Utseya. Later in that tournament, Pietersen was bowled between his legs attempting the stroke to Daniel Vettori. At that stage, the shot was being referred to by commentators and onlookers as the reverse sweep and Kevin was classified with the many reverse slog/sweepers out there who now lead with their back leg (i.e. a right-hander leads with his right leg) rather than the 'normal' stance that was favoured for so many years. Where Pietersen was different, apart from the pronounced hot-step move to alter his stance, was in the change of grip.

The term switch-hit entered cricket's lexicon on a June Sunday in 2008 when Pietersen paraded the shot to such devastating effect at Chester-le-Street. The reverberations were felt around the world. Yet if Pietersen's ambidexterity had misfired, the gasps of awe from Durham to Dambulla could easily have been replaced by laughter at such cheek. Even his captain winced when Pietersen, as light on his feet as one of the professionals on *Strictly Come Dancing*, took a couple of steps to turn quickly to the left, rotated his body 180 degrees to a left-hander's stance and swapped his hands on the bat handle as Styris delivered the third ball of the 39th over. With awesome power he took advantage of the short boundary and slog-swept it for six over extra cover (mid-wicket for a left-hander). Off a delivery timed at 70.3 mph.

No other right-hander in world cricket could surely have struck a left-handed shot so cleanly. It was exhilarating. "I covered my eyes as soon as he turned his body around," Paul Collingwood admitted. Pietersen walked up the wicket and told his skipper: "I was thinking about doing that in bed last night."

Four overs later, Pietersen repeated the trick he had visualised the night before. This time Styris saw him and reacted. He held the ball back, his pace now at 52.5mph. Pietersen was probably aiming again for extra cover, but, because the ball was slower, ended up hitting it earlier. It sailed majestically over long-off (long-on). The reverse sweep may have been in circulation for more than 40 years, however no-one before had used it to smite the ball back over the bowler's head, as Pietersen did. The novelty value of the shots made them huge talking points and sent shockwaves through the cricket establishment.

Ostensibly, it was the left-handedness that polarised opinion. From the moment that the influential Michael Holding did his bit for the bowlers' union and questioned its fairness in a live television commentary, a runaway train was off. Experts on the laws of cricket sprang from every nook and cranny. The laws' guardians, the MCC, added discussion of Pieteren's shots to a previously scheduled meeting. They listened to the traditionalists' argument that the shot should be outlawed because he is temporarily turning himself into a left-hander (a bowler must inform the umpire of a hand switch), but fell in favour of innovation and, some would say, commonsense.

Others, even the man on the receiving end, preferred to celebrate cricket's first truly ambidextrous batsman. Styris said: "Sometimes you just have to take your hat off and say, 'nice shot.' There's a lot of innovation come into the game at the moment and he's obviously taken that another step further." Graeme Swann added: "We were gob-smacked. It was pure KP. For Kev to pull it off and to hit it as far as he did was laughable. I'm sure there will be other people trying it, but I'm willing to bet there won't be another person in the world who could play that shot like Kev."

There was a subtle difference to Pietersen's previous switch-hits, when the targeted area had been point (square leg). This was not mere luck. He had been planning it for some time. During the 2007 World Cup, while England were in Guyana, Duncan Fletcher suggested to Pietersen that he should practise switch-hits over extra cover rather than squarer. It requires the right leg to be cleared further out of the way, so Pietersen rehearsed this continually. After his triumph in Duham he sent Fletcher a jubilant text. It read: 'Take it as done.'

What made the shots extra special was that Styris was bowling medium pace and both deliveries were perfectly presentable. "It was ridiculous," observes Simon Jones. "The bloke bowls 75 miles per hour and Kev switch hits him for six. That just shows how naturally talented he is. The eyes of his just pick up the ball so early. You think, 'How has he done that?' It's part hard work and there is obviously a natural talent there. A normal person would think, 'Right, I'm playing for England, I'm scared of getting out here.' He is thinking, 'Right, I'm going to try the most ridiculous shot in a minute and hit it for six.'"

Reports later claimed that Pietersen was not the first to change stance and grip as the bowler is about to deliver. Martin Crowe was said to have experimented with it in the early 1980s, during his time on the MCC groundstaff. Some recalled Jacques Kallis (for Glamorgan in 1997) and Craig McMillan (during a Test match for New Zealand in 2000-01 against the occasional leg-spin of Younis Khan) doing something similar.

New or not, Pietersen's switch-hit magic caught the imagination and schoolboys and grown men around the country were soon trying to copy him. Robert Key tried it in an exhibition match and fell over in a heap. Other professionals have started to follow suit. Geraint Jones has played it with some success for Kent, as has Shivnarine Chanderpaul, who switch-hit Kyle Mills, the New Zealand opening bowler, for a six in a one-day international. Mickey Arthur, the South Africa coach who has made his team into a world-beating unit, says: "Since he has played that shot against New Zealand I have seen a lot of players across the world try it. In our domestic Pro-20 competition it has caught on – I saw one guy hit a six with a switch-hit – although I haven't seen anyone play it as well as Kevin. JP Duminy has also played a couple of switch hits. That is down to KP. There are a lot of guys trying to imitate him."

Rod Marsh, who is now director of coaching at the ICC Global Cricket Academy, says bowlers must respond with their own new tricks. "You have to think outside the box. He would never have done it to me. I would have refused to bowl. To my mind he has to let me know which hand he is batting. If the umpire says, 'You must bowl', I would say, 'Not until I know what hand he is batting.' You have always got time [to see him switching], especially when you bowl at my pace. It would be a slow old over." Styris admits he would re-think his strategy if Pietersen tried to take him on again. "Maybe I can learn. You do get a wee second to react. It does take him some time to turn and set himself. The shots came off because he was well set and playing well." What should be remembered is it is a shot laden with risk, much more so than the reverse sweep, and provides the bowler with a greater chance of claiming a wicket.

Nevertheless, the switch-hit has become an important gun in the Pietersen artillery. Not just in one-day internationals, but in the Test arena, too. His 94 against South Africa at Edgbaston later in 2008 will always be remembered for the manner in which he holed out on the boundary trying to register his century in the grand manner, but, shortly beforehand, he had slammed Paul Harris for two terrific switch-hits through backward point. Arthur recalls: "All of our guys watching it said, 'Wow, what a shot'. Firstly, to have the balls to play it and, secondly, to then execute it so well. It's a very hard shot to play." Three Tests later, the highlight of a wonderful century at Mohali was his outrageous 85-yard switch-hit for six off Harbhajan Singh. He also swept a four with the stroke. "I don't really know how to react, I'd like to hit him with the bat," quipped Harbhajan afterwards. "I haven't seen any guy coming over here and batting like that, it was tremendous. You can't do anything about that."

Pietersen says the key to the switch-hit is knowing when to use it. "This is a shot I employ when the opposition has loaded one side of the pitch with fielders to restrict my scoring, leaving space on the other side." And in a don't-try-this-at-home warning, he adds: "Not everyone can master it. I'm ambidextrous so this comes pretty natural to me." Even if the gift is as authentic as Pietersen's, it does not always work out, however.

When Pietersen had a licence to play expansively as England batted for a declaration in the re-scheduled third Test against West Indies at Antigua in February 2009 he played around a dozen switch-hits against the spinners. Some he failed to connected with, others he drilled powerfully to boundary fielders. He even played a few left-handed cover drives. It made for superb entertainment. Unusually, none yielded a boundary. His signature shot also brought his downfall for the first time in a Test. Attempting to mow a delivery from occasional left-arm spinner Ryan Hinds into St John's city centre, Pietersen edged it to the keeper. The match situation ensured he avoided any black marks against his name. Pietersen used the shot equally liberally in the second innings of the final two Tests of the series, at Barbados and Trinidad. He machined-gunned some dazzling left-handed shots in his unbeaten 72 in Bridgetown and, again, in his 88-ball century at Port-of-Spain. The spectacular was becoming the norm.

If the switch-hit for six was the firmest confirmation yet of Pietersen's outrageous talent, it was not the first demonstration of his ability to innovate. Pietersen can be said to have patented not one, but two shots. The cross-court flick – a way of countering a short-of-a-length delivery by planting the front foot on the line of off-stump and forcing the ball to the on side with turned wrists rather than risking a pull – became known as the 'flamingo shot' after Pietersen used to play it on one leg. A variation of this is shuffling a foot or two outside off-stump to work the ball through the leg side, a method perfected by Viv Richards and which has become extremely productive for Pietersen. Crucially, it also eliminates lbw. The difference is Pietersen, ever the showman, does it with his back leg raised in the air, although he noticeably plays it with less of a flourish than he once did.

Pietersen has developed other exotic alternatives to conventional shots in a bid to dominate bowlers. The top-spun cover drive, in which he can roll a ball wide of the stumps on the up and along the ground through straightish extra cover, rather than slice away square as more orthodox batsman might, has become a trademark. Like Matthew Hayden, he has used his physique to bully the faster bowlers by marching down the wicket, obscuring the stumps from view and slogging good length balls through mid-wicket. Glenn McGrath, one of the greatest line-and-length merchants the game has known, was treated with something approaching disdain. Pietersen has also used his long reach to smother spin and supple wrists to manipulate the ball and generate power.

These are all relatively modern additions to the Pietersen armoury. Grant Rowley does not recall his old schoolmate playing any outlandish shots during their days at Maritzburg College, Berea Rovers and Natal. He says: "The reverse slog, which is against all convention and the MCC law book, who plays shots like that? I never saw him do that. Not the switch-hit, where he is hitting it over mid-off or cover for six. Or the flamingo hit. That has come from practise. The more you play at that level, the more confident you get. When you are scoring runs at international level, you get more confident, and his confidence is sky high anyway."

Mike Bechet adds: "He has developed all that. He has worked incredibly hard at his batting. In England when a chap is successful they are waiting for him to fail. Right from the start the commentators were saying, 'Geez, he can't play that shot' or 'Good heavens, where did he pull that one from?' 'This flamingo, stiff front leg and whip it over midwicket for six. You can't do that.' Well, you know what? You bat how you want to. There are no rules. There is the MCC coaching manual, which says get the elbow up and the head over the ball, but he plays how he is comfortable, just like Clive Rice, whose grip on the bat was appalling."

Pietersen has developed his skill so well that he has gone from being a tailender as a youngster in South Africa to the gun batsman for every side he has played for as a professional in England. "Players who have developed organically are usually the best," concurs Stuart MacGill. "Kevin is not a coached player. You would never coach players to drive on the up like he does. The switch-hitting thing is not that remarkable to me. It's just party tricks, amazing hand-eye co-ordination. It is almost showing off. There are lots of people through history who could have done it. He could probably demoralise me as a bowler by doing other things. I love the way he plays spin around his front pad. He plants his foot down, has reasonably soft hands and once he sees it he puts his hands there. He has taught himself that. The belief in yourself to play traditional shots in an unconventional fashion, like driving on the up and pushing your hands through the ball, that's where he has changed the game."

The only rule, as far as Pietersen is concerned, is that that are no rules.

GENIUS?

KEVIN PIETERSEN HAD NOT even played a Test match before he was hailed by the England captain Michael Vaughan for possessing "a touch of genius". As a Yorkshireman, Vaughan is not given to hyperbole in his public pronouncements – Kevin is quite capable of that all on his own – but he had seen enough during Pietersen's first nine months of international cricket to put him on a pedestal. It just so happened that Vaughan's compliment came in the aftermath of Pietersen virtually beating Australia on his own in a critical tone-setting one-day international at Bristol (his first, incidentally, against England's great rivals). Four-and-a-half years of supreme achievement have endorsed the opinion Vaughan expressed at a press conference that June evening whilst sitting alongside English cricket's new star.

The opening chapter in the narrative of Pietersen's international career, against Zimbabwe in November 2004, was low key, but the rest of the story has been as compelling as any on offer from world sport. Pietersen has the aura to change the chemistry of games, to turn cricket matches into one-man shows. When he swaggers on to the stage with bat in hand and bristling with purpose there is a sense you have been conscripted into his private movie. His ability to write his own scripts, to bend the existing narrative to his own will, borders on the superhuman. Shane Warne had the same capability. So did Viv Richards and Brian Lara. Ian Botham, too. All the other actors are merely furniture, carrying out bit-part roles. "When he walks out in front of a packed house at Lord's or the Oval or wherever, failure doesn't even come into his mind at all," says Graham Ford. "He knows people have come to see a great show and he is going to put it on and pull out a big score."

Watching Pietersen bat has become the hottest ticket in town. He is what Don King, the pre-eminent boxing promoter of the modern era, would call "box office".

The paymasters of the Indian Premier League certainly thought so. KP became the joint highest paid player in the world in February 2009 when the Bangalore Royal Challengers stumped up $1.55m for him. It was comfortably the most for a player with only one specialist skill. The other headline acts were all-rounders. "Maybe I'm biased but I try and watch all his innings," says Ford. "There are only a few players in world cricket for whom you are prepared to wake up at any time of the night and make sure that you are able to watch them. For me, he is number one on the list. Probably the three that jump out at me are Kevin, Tendulkar, though he is losing some of his skills now, and Ricky Ponting. They are certainly special players and if they are playing well you don't want to leave the TV set and miss a ball."

The word 'genius' means "an exceptional natural capacity of intellect and/or ability", although the modern definition is used to denote the possession of a superior talent in any field. There is a subtle difference between genius and talent. Genius is connected more or less with the exercise of the imagination, and reaches its end by a kind of intuitive power. Talent depends more on high mental training. In other words, genius is a gift of nature and talent can be improved. Pietersen's school teachers saw a fine talent. They didn't see a born genius. It was the same at Natal, who let him go without a fight. In club cricket, at Berea Rovers and Cannock, he wasn't even the best player in the team. Had it not been for Clive Rice's talent-spotting aptitude, Pietersen might have been lost to the professional game.

At Nottinghamshire, Pietersen was driven to prove Rice correct. He soon stood out from the herd. He could play shots that no-one else could. He could construct extraordinary innings. But ability is only part of the story. It is not that he is more talented than his contemporaries. Indeed, Vaughan and Ian Bell are perhaps equally gifted, if not more so. They are certainly better technicians. Pietersen says himself that Grant Rowley is a more natural batsman. "There are still a few technical deficiencies in Kevin's game," explains Mick Newell. "He still plays around his front pad a bit, sometimes he doesn't quite get his foot to the pitch of the ball outside off-stump, but they are minor when you are as good as that."

Pietersen isn't a born genius. He is a manufactured one. If anything, this makes him more remarkable. It all looks so instinctively seat-of-the-pants precisely because of the hard graft he has put in. He has carefully constructed a game that works. Crucially, it is based on sound principles. "The basics of his technique are extremely good," argues Ford. "For me, what is interesting is the head position. Batting is all about getting your eye into the right position to hit the ball. He gets his eyes a very long way down the pitch when he's playing off the front foot, so that enables him to utilise the length of the bowler and gives him a chance to attack more balls than batters who don't get their eyes down as much."

Ford believes there is even an element of orthodoxy to the outrageous flip through mid-wicket to balls delivered a foot outside off-stump, the stroke that elevates him above the norm and clinches his genius. "He's not actually hitting across the line. Everything is still working very straight. Once he feels the ball on the bat, his eyes are over the ball and he gets right into the hitting zone which allows him to use his wrists to hit the ball into the gaps. Probably the most important thing is he keeps his shoulders really nicely aligned. Batters who have their shoulders squaring up tend to shovel across the line of the ball, whereas, essentially, because his shoulders are so good everything is working pretty straight. Because so many balls go through the leg side they all said, 'He's going to have problems because he hits across the line.' It's only the wrists that are manipulating the ball. That makes him one hell of a difficult guy to bowl to."

If Pietersen did not have a sound defence he would not have scored a century every third Test, all of them against the 'serious' cricket nations. If he wished to play in a stodgy fashion, à la Boycott, it would not be his lack of fundamentals that prevented it. Further study shows that Pietersen bats with immense power, as much perhaps as any man currently playing. But the Andrews, Flintoff and Symonds, have power too, so there is more to it. Pietersen was hungry to learn. He still is. He has watched intently, listened carefully to advice and adapted what he has learned to his own skill-set. Much of his artist-bully batting has been self-taught. "A lot of great players are very much like that," says Graham Thorpe. "They work the game out for themselves by watching other people and picking up things. People I speak to say he is an exceptionally hard worker, practises all the shots assiduously in the nets. That says to me he is exceptionally dedicated to batting. He is what I would call a natural gamesman and piles up runs on the back of confidence in his natural ability."

Writing 40 years ago, Don Bradman, who claimed not to have been formally coached, said: "A coach who suppresses natural instincts may find that he has lifted a poor player to a mediocre one, but has reduced a potential genius to the rank and file." Pietersen's coaches – or, at least, the ones he has listened to – have been intelligent enough to let his natural flair flourish. "He's got amazing talent but there's no doubt he's put in many, many hours of hard work," explains Ford. "It isn't just something that has happened. He's a smart man. He would have sought a lot of advice and ideas. He has carried a lot of information, processed the information and found out ways that work for him. During his time on the English county circuit he observed a lot of the good guys. I remember him coming back after his second season at Notts when he had scored a whole heap of runs and he said that he had gone through a bit of a barren phase and then he played against Graeme Hick. Hick made a massive score – around 300 – and he said he learned so much from watching Hick, particularly the fact that even when you have made a big score and you are on 180, you can still play out a maiden. You can still get a good over, you still get good deliveries. At that stage he felt he had been throwing it away a bit and seeing Hick made him think about compiling big, big scores. He's that kind of guy, always seeking information and I suppose it is about that burning desire to become better."

Former England batting coach Matthew Maynard gives an illuminating insight into Pietersen's desire for self-improvement. "The winter we were in Pakistan and India he told me he couldn't play the paddle sweep, as opposed to the slog sweep, but we worked on it intensely for three net sessions and he was able to take it into a game," said Maynard. "It was simply a question of working on his mindset to play the shot and he was quickly able to do it. He is like a sponge, always soaking up information and never resting on his laurels."

Nearly all of the batting greats are short men – Ranjitsinjhi, Trumper, Hobbs, Bradman, Headley, Weekes, Richards, Gavaskar, Miandad, Lara, Tendulkar, Ponting. Even Graeme Pollock, Sobers and Greg Chappell were not especially tall. At 6ft 4in and 15 stone, Pietersen is a colossus in comparison. Rod Marsh says: "Historically, the best batsmen have been shorter men. It's possibly a little bit easier to be shorter as a batsman. You are lower to the ground and your balance is better. For a tall man, Kevin's balance is outstanding. When he is on song his balance is unbelievable. To be a good first-class batsman you have to be able to play off the back foot. In my opinion, no-one is better at that than Ponting. Pietersen is a front-foot player, but he can murder bowling off the back foot, too. That is because of his balance."

He knows the value of being light on his feet. Pietersen spent a lot of time at the gym lifting heavy weights a few winters ago and became "too stocky for my liking". He gave up pumping iron. His natural agility is the key to negating some of the problem areas common to the 6ft-plus brigade. Thorpe explains: "He is one of the few tall batsmen who have really succeeded at Test cricket. That is because he is flexible. He is not a stiff or rigid tall batsman. He is on the move and has great rhythm in his batting. He bends his knees as the bowler delivers and gets low into his shots. He gets in great action positions when the ball is released from the hand. He anticipates very well and can naturally attack when the ball is off line."

Pietersen has been clever in making the best of his physical attributes. His height could have been his Achilles heel, but he has used it to his advantage. He bullies the quicker bowlers with his physical presence and uses his height and telescopic reach to smother spin. From his earliest meetings with Shane Warne Pietersen sought to counter Warne's prodigious powers by reaching far down the crease and deploying the slog-sweep (he hit Warne for eight sixes during the 2005 Ashes). "One thing better than anybody in the world are his wrists," says Shaun

Udal. "They are incredibly strong and allow him to manipulate the ball. The balls Warney was putting on a good length he was slog-sweeping for six because of his wrists and incredibly long reach."

Pietersen also possesses the hallmark of the true champion in his ability to think outside the box. A compulsive experimenter, he has been addicted to the path less travelled (even leaving his mother country for his mother's country). Independent of thought and restlessly determined, he has asked new questions and tried different solutions. Why can't I change my stance and grip mid-delivery and bat left-handed? Why shouldn't I stand outside off-stump and flip the seamers through the leg side standing on one leg? Why can't I run down the wicket to the fast-bowlers? Mike Bechet says: "Nothing is going to stop him. If you get in his way he is going to mow you over. My God, he is a determined bloke. Would Atherton or Hussain have thought of flat-batting Brett Lee back over his head for six? The only other guy I can think of doing that is Ian Botham. No other English cricketer. Don't say to Kevin Pietersen, 'You can't do that.' Cos he will just put the fingers up and show you that you are talking s***."

Pietersen is a maverick in a different sense to Botham, Sobers, Warne or Keith Miller, who were all untamed forces of nature. They would think nothing of rocking up to a day's play still drunk or having spent the night in the company of ladies, booze or cards (sometimes all three). Pietersen once hit a half-century while hungover against Surrey, but, even in the age of professionalism, he prepares and practises with near religious zealoutry.

As a determined non-conformist, he falls into another category – the dashing entertainer who created his own style. "As a developing player he got annoyed at being told that he wasn't good enough," says Stuart MacGill. "He has developed his own approach and style of batting, which is unique. He has done his own thing. He has set out to prove people wrong, as have most of the best people I have played with. When he walks out to bat he has a plan. It might not be the best plan of all time, but any plan is a good plan."

"He's brought in a whole new flair aspect to batting," adds Ford. "Guys have been playing around with reverse sweeps for some time. He took that phase further. He moves around the crease, but is still able to get into a good position to hit the ball to different parts of the ground, whereas in the old days people were told to hit the ball pretty much where it is supposed to go. This creates a lot of drama in the opposition camps. He can start to set his own fields."

Pietersen's greatest quality is his phenomenal self-belief. When asked what he thought about when the bowler was running in, he replied, only half-joking, "I feel sorry for the bowler". A lot of players can bat like kings in the nets, but they don't have the nerve to replicate that skill on the field of play. Pietersen's career has been a triumph of nerve. He is utterly fearless. The hardest thing about the stunning shots that have established his reputation is to play them in public, when the chips are down, and the game is in the balance.

From the outset, Pietersen has gambled at the crease, played his shots and dared to win. He has put runs on the board, brilliant runs scored at times of highest tension. He is able to recognise the moment when it comes and seize it. Each of his five Test hundreds, and a 94, in 2008 came when England were in strife. "He is a natural counter-attacking batsman," says Thorpe. "If England are 10-2 he comes in and counter attacks and quickly takes the game by the scruff of the neck." Pietersen almost shuns easy runs. "He is the antithesis of the flat-track bully," adds Clive Rice. "He gets runs when they matter in high pressure situations and against the best bowlers. That's what counts. He loves confrontation and loves a challenge." Tellingly, all 16 of his Test centuries up to April 2009 have been made against the major Test-playing nations. He can score all around the wicket off front foot and back, and has made runs in all parts of the world in all conditions. He scored hundreds in his first series against Australia and did the same against the attacks of Pakistan, Sri Lanka, West Indies, New Zealand and South Africa. Only India escaped a Pietersen century at the first time of asking, in 2005-06, but he atoned for that by scoring two centuries in three Tests against them in the summer of 2007. He has scored at least two centuries against each of the other seven major Test nations (there have been no 'gimme' innings against Bangladesh or Zimbabwe).

Pietersen's cavalier style belies a master tactician. "He knows when to put his foot down and take the game away from the opposition," says Mickey Arthur. "He is very tactically aware and very smart. He has thought about all the options." His explanation of why he switch-hit Muralitharan for six at Edgbaston was as impressive as the shot itself.

Pietersen provides unusual challenges for bowlers and fielding sides. There are no obvious major weaknesses in his game, unless you count an over-eagerness to bring up centuries in the grandest of manners. Kevin is susceptible to neither bombarding pace or bewildering spin, and devours medium pacers for breakfast.

Of course, Pietersen is not without some vulnerabilities. He is, as Warne once said, "a pretty average starter", although the early nervousness is less apparent than it once was. Pace bowlers have tried to outwit him by using short balls to get him onto the back foot before spearing in a straight, full, almost yorker-length delivery, as Jerome Taylor did to such spectacular effect in the infamous Jamaica Test in February 2009 in which England collapsed spectacularly to a dismal second innings 51 all out to lose by an innings. With his giant frame, Pietersen can find it harder to dig out a searing yorker than shorter batsmen. He has also been drawn into playing away from his body and pushing at wide-ish deliveries early in his innings.

During South Africa's series victory in England in 2008 their plan was to negate Pietersen's leg-side dominance and tempt him into an indiscretion outside off-stump. "We had our strategies and I don't think those strategies will change too much," explains Arthur, with half an eye on the return series in the Republic in the winter of 2009/10. "We thought that if we could swing the ball out at him, starting at 4th stump we could stop him scoring. Maybe if you stop him scoring he will do something stupid. If it is swinging away then he can't hit through the leg side. That is the key. We don't think he is comfortable driving between cover and backward point." The execution was awry in the first Test at Lord's. South Africa's seamers bowled too short and they were taken to the cleaners by Pietersen, who scored a masterful 152, with 85 of his first 103 runs coming on the leg side. "How can you be so stupid?" snorts Rice. "If you bowl short he can either leave it or whack it for four. That was an immature way of approaching it. He had the South Africans completely confused. They must bowl in the channel outside off-stump." In the second Test at Headingley, they did, and on both occasions Pietersen was caught behind the wicket playing over-aggressively. Jacques Kallis dismissed him twice in the series with his floaty outswingers and was introduced into the attack whenever Pietersen came to the crease. Arthur says: "We used Jacques. He can get it to swing away. So can Dale [Steyn], who is very dangerous with his pace, but we didn't have him for two Tests."

Pietersen's low threshold of boredom and exhibitionist streak are two areas that can be exploited. Ford says: "Patience might be a weakness because he so wants to dominate. It can lead to a speed wobble and getting himself out. He can at times try and play a shot that is not perhaps on. An area that he can maybe improve is to fight it out – all the innings that I have seen they are fantastic entertainment. There have never really been gutsy, Steve Waugh-type ugly runs. Maybe that's something – when times are tough and conditions are really tough – that he can improve on." He then pauses, before adding, endearingly: "Because he is a stubborn little fellow."

But in some ways that is the point of why KP is so magnetic when at the crease in adversity. Such is the boldness of Pietersen's batting he can change the momentum of a game in an hour. "Whenever he is at the wicket something happens," admits Arthur. "The game moves forward at pace. He has the ability to dominate and change games. If Kevin bats for two sessions he gets a hundred. That's the nature of his batting. There's not a huge amount of guys in world cricket who have that ability."

The only bowlers to have stunted Pietersen's electric scoring for any length of time are Stuart Clark of Australia and New Zealand's Daniel Vettori. "A lot depends on the surface," adds Ford. "If it's a good batting surface there's no special way of getting him out and there's no special way of containing him apart from stealing his bat. He has got these fantastic wrists and he does get into these fantastic positions and will be able to drive you on the up and if you are slightly short he will pull you. So there's no easy way. If it's seaming around a bit, then a bowler like Stuart Clark does become a factor if he can just hold that slightly back of a length for some time. Kevin, being the guy he is, will try and dominate you and drive at something and if it's nibbling around a bit, you might nick him off. If things aren't in the bowler's favour in terms of conditions, it will be a long day. He is that good."

What makes Pietersen so exotic is not so much his ability to bring a dose of high-risk endeavour to modern batsmanship – others have done that, notably Virender Sehwag and Adam Gilchrist – but the consistently captivating manner in which he has done so. His style is utterly unique; a fusion of the wristiness of the East, the flair of the Caribbean and the attitude of the southern hemisphere. Just as Ranjitsinjhi did in the 19th century, Pietersen has been at the forefront of the changing approach to 21st century batting. "In a way he has redefined modern batting," says Arthur. "He has taken batting to new heights." Mick Newell adds: "If you look at international cricket in the last 15 years and how Australia has revolutionised scoring rates, KP has taken it beyond that and taken the game to a further level. He has become the quickest scorer and most entertaining batsman in cricket and that's the way you leave a mark on the game."

Pietersen has always been different. As Rob Fuhri, one of Kevin's primary school cricket coaches, said: "Why must he fit into a little box?" Why indeed? He is so different to his contemporaries he requires his own category. Mick Newell says: "He can play shots that no-one else in the *world* can play, never mind England. If that switch-hit isn't genius, I don't know what is. To go left-handed and hit a six, that's unbelievable. With most people it would go straight up in the air and they would end up looking a Charlie. He hits it for six – in Test matches. That's genius."

Pietersen might not be a genius of natural born skill in the intuitive way that Sobers and Richards were. His genius lies in his ability to imagine the barely probable and then have the superhuman self-belief to pull it off. In a way, that is even more miraculous.

TURBULENT TIMES

ASKED TO EVALUATE KEVIN Pietersen's claims to greatness a year into an international career that had begun in such blazing fashion, Shane Warne cautioned: "My view is that once he goes through his failure period then this will be the making of KP. There really has only been one player in the history of the game who has never really failed for any length of time: the one and only Sir Don Bradman. When KP goes through this he will work out how to play different situations, he will work out who his real friends are, and he will remember what his feelings were when everything was going well. This will make him hungry and look out when this happens because we will see some very, very special innings." We are still waiting. Hurry up and fail, Kevin. We want to see how good you really are!

The roughest patch in Pietersen's Rolls Royce-smooth international ride came in 2007-8, during a sapping winter that took in three tours of varying demands – the World Twenty20 in South Africa and series in Sri Lanka and New Zealand either side of Christmas. Pietersen was the joint top-scorer in the two-week Twenty20 jamboree, but in the contrasting conditions of the subcontinent and the southern hemisphere, the runs dried up and his strike rate plummeted to something approaching mortal. The Sri Lanka Test series was the first in which he has failed to register a fifty (in 12 of his 13 other series he has scored at least one century), although he did score an unbeaten 45 to help save the second Test in Colombo. It wasn't the fierce head and humidity that was the problem. "My head was all over the place," said Pietersen, n an interview with the *Sunday Times* in 2008. "Jessica was back [in England], sorting out the wedding and I didn't play well. When the missus isn't there it's really hard." Without their star batsman to set up match-winning positions, England were inspirationless and slumped to a 1-0 defeat.

By the time he had rediscovered his cape and tights with a brilliant crisis-averting century in Napier that paved the way for a series-clinching victory – he came to the crease when England were 4-3 on the first morning – Pietersen had gone 10 innings without scoring a fifty. To put that into context, the longest period he has had to wait between hundreds, before or since, is nine innings. "Yeah, it was the first time it had happened in my career," he said. "I just had to accept it. It wasn't nice and it wasn't fun, but it made me realise that you should really, really enjoy the good days because you are going to have to deal with the bad days. I also realised that there is more to life than getting caught up and worrying about how you are playing." At the start of the tour to New Zealand, the England players were denied the company of their partners for six weeks, which encompassed the one-day series and the first Test defeat in Hamilton. The performances picked up when the WAGS arrived. Kevin's new wife stayed on with him in New Zealand rather than return home to a friend's wedding in order to keep him company.

The blip was over, though, before you could say, 'Has marriage made KP go soft?' Pietersen turned the tap back on and began drowning opponents with a torrent of strokeplay. Four months later, he was universally being hailed as the world's most complete batsman. A match-winning century against New Zealand at Trent Bridge after he had rescued England from a perilous 86-5 and his switch-hitting genius at Chester-le-Street demonstrated the size of his repertoire. These were merely the warm-ups to the main act. Everything was building towards the reunion with the country he spurned.

Pietersen was desperate to demonstrate how well the emigration had gone with a century in his first Test against South Africa and in another brilliant landmark on his path to greatness he got what he craved. South Africa's bowlers were overawed by the tradition and grandeur of the first day of a Lord's Test and the enormity of the occasion. Pietersen simply seized it. His irresistible 152 off 181 balls, a huge demonstration of willpower, quashed once and for all any lingering doubts about his allegiance. After a rapturous reception from the Lord's crowd, which he hailed as "the most emotional two minutes of my career", he declared he had never felt "so loved". "Sitting here now I have never felt so English," he told a press corps delighted to have been spoon-fed a back-page lead.

A few weeks later, in what was symptomatic of England's yo-yo summer, the wheels had come off. Pietersen failed and so did England as they were trounced at Headingley. He nearly transformed the Edgbaston Test and won England the game, but fell short and so did the team as he crossed the line between aggression and recklessness. Even Pietersen's biggest fans were disappointed when he holed out trying to hit the six off spinner Paul Harris that would have raised his century. AB de Villiers, South Africa's best fielder, had been stationed two-thirds of the way to the long-on boundary specifically for such an indiscretion. "Forget about the glory shots," says Clive Rice. "There is much more glory walking off not out having won the game. That was not professional enough." Mike Bechet adds: "I was glad I was not England coach when he played that shot. I wouldn't say I was cross because he has nothing to do with me, but I was bloody disappointed."

The winning coach could afford to be more generous. "Kevin is Kevin. He is always going to have that little streak about the way he plays," says Mickey Arthur, who detected method to the mayhem. "He thought that if he could hit Paul Harris out of the attack we would have to bring back the fast bowlers and they would still be tired. Failure would not have entered his mind. He doesn't lack confidence in terms of backing his ability. I'm not sure he rates spin bowlers too highly."

Pietersen's dismissals tend to attract excessive censure. Perhaps because he is such fun to watch, there is a greater sense of loss when it is all over. Some forget there are two sides to the coin. It's Pietersen's positive and aggressive mindset that makes him so good in the first place. Derek Pringle wrote in the *Daily Telegraph* after his Edgbaston rush of blood: "Were England's selectors made of sterner stuff they would drop Pietersen for the next Test – or make him captain – to stop him from worshipping at the temple of one." By Pringle's definition, the selectors were subsequently teak-tough. Michael Vaughan resigned in tears the following day, mentally shattered and powerless to arrest England's decline. "I want to be me again," he said. Paul Collingwood, possibly sensing the mood for change, followed suit and handed in the one-day reins. Twenty-four hours later, Pietersen was given the keys to the highest cricket office in the land.

You have to travel a long way to find anyone who saw Kevin Pietersen as a potential captain. Never mind international leader, but a captain of any team. He didn't captain his school teams – although Clarendon, Merchiston and Maritzburg College were prestigious schools and tended to field stronger teams than nearly all other seats of learning – or an organised X1 of any sort back in South Africa. "I didn't see him as a leader at school," says Bechet. Neither did Graham Ford, the coach who has known him for the longest time. "He didn't strike me as a captain. The first time I know he captained a side was England. He hasn't done much before that."

It was not that Pietersen was withdrawn or did not have appreciation of the game's tactical niceties. As a single-minded and headstrong youngster he just lacked the inter-personal skills to handle the different personalities of a dressing room. "Being a captain, jeez . . ." says Wayne Scott, raising an eyebrow and pointing at a picture of a baby-faced Pietersen celebrating winning the league with Berea Rovers. "I never would have thought he would be a captain of even Nottinghamshire. He had his fair share of mixes with people here. He was a controversial character at that stage. Not arguments. He was just in-your-face. People take offence to him."

Ford and Scott agree that Pietersen was inspirational in other ways. "He was still a highly motivated guy who showed leadership qualities," explains Ford. "He was a guy who wanted to be out in front. He talks a lot in the dressing room – always. As a young kid he used to babble away and talk about all kinds of things. Some of it – the fun side – was not sense. But when the business got serious, he got serious and certainly spoke sense. He was a guy that if you are going to go to war you wanted to have him on your side. That comes from upbringing and home and the schooling. The school was a very proud school. You wouldn't make the College first team unless you were really prepared to go to battle out there." Scott adds: "He was like that [at Rovers] as well. He would lead from the front, converting the quieter guys to raise the bar rather than go the route of fitting in and being one of the boys. He was always at the forefront of whatever occasion, he was always chatting and carrying on and talking, always picking people up."

At Nottinghamshire, Pietersen's inclination towards gaucheness disguised a deep thinker. His shrewd cricket brain was not just reserved for his batting, either. Despite their lukewarm relationship, Jason Gallian remembers Kevin being a big help to him on the field. "He was very astute," he explains. "It might be a bowling change, a fielding position or some other tactic. More times than not I would use it and it would work. I learned things from him. He is such a good player he would know how to get good players out. It was good to have someone on board like that. He has a good cricket brain. He is very methodical, very meticulous."

According to Clive Rice, Pietersen was also one of the biggest contributors to team meetings, something that can't be said of all players. Indeed, Nasser Hussain wrote in his autobiography that Vaughan was very quiet when he was in the ranks. "With him being confident like he is Kevin had a big input into team meetings," says Rice. "He had not been captain at school or anything like that, so he was relatively inexperienced at that level of cricket, but he offered ideas. I don't want someone sitting in team meetings contributing nothing."

At international level it was some time before Pietersen was viewed as officer material. He had been in the team for two years by the time of the 2006-07 Ashes, but he was not considered senior enough to be co-opted onto the players' management committee. The group who met regularly to discuss all matters cricketing on that disastrous tour were captain Andrew Flintoff, Andrew Strauss, Collingwood and Geraint Jones.

The first sign that Pietersen could be elevated from the ranks came early the following summer after Vaughan resigned the one-day captaincy on the back of the equally disastrous World Cup. Following Flintoff's pedalo indiscretions and Andrew Strauss' slump in form, there were only two serious candidates: Pietersen and Collingwood. Both men were sounded out by coach Peter Moores and the England selectors. Pietersen told them he did not feel ready. "At this stage in my career I don't think it is the right time for me," he declared in his newspaper column. "I thought about it long and hard, but right now I am happy playing."

Instead, Pietersen acted as Collingwood's unofficial first lieutenant. He became the first player that the new one-day skipper turned to for advice. Pietersen admitted that Collingwood's costly miscalculation of Flintoff's bowling allocation in the World Twenty20 was his fault. "I was in charge of counting," he said. Pietersen began to enjoy the responsibility of seniority. "I like keeping an eye out for the young guys, making sure that the Stuart Broads and Luke Wrights are okay. Darren Gough and Ashley Giles did that for me when I first came into the side and I know how secure it made me feel."

After Vaughan crashed and burned the search began for his successor. There was little time for obfuscation – a Test was beginning five days later. It was widely agreed that the ECB had only two realistic choices. But they actually had three if you discount the rank outsiders Alastair Cook and Robert Key. Collingwood was the next in line, not Pietersen or Strauss. Vaughan himself had nominated the Teeside scrapper as his heir apparent even though Collingwood's captaincy record was mixed. He had been one-day skipper for 14 months, winning two series England were expected to lose – at home against India and away to Sri Lanka – and losing three series they were expected to win – at home against the West Indies and home and away to New Zealand. Collingwood also blotted his copybook in the World Twenty20, overseeing another global failure by England and being caught by *The Sun* visiting a lap-dancing club the night before the South Africa game. He got a first-ball duck and England lost. Further question marks about Collingwood's leadership suitability were raised when he refused to recall New Zealand's Grant Elliott to the crease after he was controversially run out following a collision with Ryan Sidebottom. In a separate incident, Collingwood was hauled over the coals for England's slow over-rate and banned for four limited-overs internationals. The ECB began to have serious misgivings about his aptitude for the post.

This opened the door for Pietersen. In his own words he had "zilch" captaincy experience. The record books suggested it was limited to a single 50-over second X1 game for Nottinghamshire in 2002. He scored 113 in a convincing victory. Pietersen stood in for Collingwood in the final one-day international against New Zealand at Lord's with England needing to win to draw the series 2-2. A year after ruling himself out for the captaincy he now felt his time had come and wanted to make an excellent impression in his first game in charge. He rang Rice for advice the night before the game. Rice reveals: "I said to KP, 'You had better be asking lots of questions and of all the answers you get pick the best idea you think you get. If that doesn't work pick the next best one, then the next. Do that and create the right impression. This could be the one time you ever get to be England captain.'" Pietersen scored an out-of-character 6 off 23 balls and England lost by 51 runs, but he had eased himself into pole position for when the time came.

The wait was only a short one. Five weeks later Vaughan resigned, Collingwood followed suit half an hour afterwards and the following day Pietersen was unveiled as the unified Test and one-day skipper. His appointment was the culmination of a long, bold and sometimes hazardous journey from naturalised Englishman to captain of the England team. Mick Newell says: "The timing was right for him to be captain. He felt he should have been captain. He was now the best player in the England team. It's a bit like being at school." Gallian admits: "I thought he was a good choice. He has matured as a person and a player. He is the best player who can play all forms of the game and I thought it might take some of the self-centredness out of him. He had to work on the team, get the team up and running and managing the team."

Pietersen had clear-the-air talks with Moores at a Northampton hotel before formally accepting the post. It was at the coach's instigation. He had plumped for the maverick Pietersen ahead of the more conservative option of Strauss – a decision that was endorsed by a selection committee keen to "unite the captaincy" – and wanted to establish the kind of mutually beneficial working relationship that had hitherto been absent. Pietersen told Moores that he would drag England upwards kicking and screaming. Moores agreed to give the new captain his head. "The ECB knew what they were getting in Kevin," says Shaun Udal. "They wanted a strong, assertive Graeme Smith-type or Ricky Ponting-type. They knew he would do things his way, demand the best and upset people." "He would have taken that job and wanted to make his mark," adds Newell. The ECB knew that Pietersen's pursuit of success is total: he is unafraid of taking on obstacles, no matter the cost. Diplomacy was never on his agenda.

The manner in which Pietersen took to captaincy surprised everyone. He grabbed the reins in the same way he has seized every opportunity in his career. His first act as captain boded well. Given the task of choosing a team for the Oval Test from the squad he had been handed by the selectors, he replaced Vaughan with a bowler (Steve Harmison) rather than a batsman (Ravi Bopara). He entrusted Harmison with the first over of the match – no other captain had dared do that since that double-wide in Brisbane – and the under-achieving paceman responded with his most hostile performance for years. He even weighed in with a run-a-ball unbeaten 49, his highest Test score. Doubtless Pietersen knew that few things inspire a man as much as a sense of importance.

People wondered if the burden of leadership would affect Pietersen's majestic batting. Would it make England's finest for at least two generations go into his shell? Would the weight of responsibility strip him of his boldness? While others fretted, Pietersen had the answer already lined up in his head. He strode to the wicket at 51-2, batted in the same riveting and calculating manner as always and chiselled out an even hundred of routine brilliance. There was an inevitability about his century against his motherland at Lord's and it seemed to be written in the stars that he would do the same in his first Test in charge. "I've had a few text messages this evening asking me who writes them [scripts]," he told the press afterwards. Nothing was beyond Pietersen. He could even tamper with fate. For most players either innings would have been the crowning glory of their career. For Pietersen they were merely his most superlative feats of the month.

England's new leader followed it up with a ruthless 4-0 annihilation of South Africa in the subsequent one-dayers, which Smith later admitted had blemished his team's five-day series triumph. Pietersen was tactically smart. Knowing that match-winners are precious, he persuaded Harmison out of one-day retirement (although he tried but failed to do the same with Marcus Trescothick), backed his hunches and made the players feel 10 feet tall. Flintoff and Harmison rediscovered their lust for destruction. Promoted to his favourite No. 5 position, Flintoff was back to his box office biffing best and, in partnership with Harmison, offered a potent wicket-taking threat in the middle overs. "I haven't seen Flintoff in that sort of form for years," says Rice. "He was a powerhouse. Was KP an influence? I'm not sure, but it can't have been a coincidence."

Pietersen had dragged the team into the sphere of excellence he populates as a matter of course. "There are no half measures with Kevin," says Ford. "He will set fantastic examples because he does do things properly. He doesn't do things just to show off or to be a show pony. It's about doing things properly and if he's going to bother to do them then make sure they are done the right way."

Even the newest kids on Pietersen's upwardly mobile block that, for one pinch-yourself fortnight, strode the turf like Goliaths of the one-day game, appeared to have been sprinkled with some of the captain's stardust. All-rounder Samit Patel says: "Up in Scotland, the first day we met Kev, they named the team and I was in it. It started from there. He just said, 'Take all the opportunities you are given.' I felt confident. I was more nervous in the Lions games against South Africa than the proper games. It was knowing that you are going to play – you can't have a better feeling than that. Then, it's up to you and it's all about handling the pressure and knowing your role. Kevin Pietersen is a positive captain. England captains of the past have been negative. If you have a leader like that it reflects on everybody else. We just had no fear. English teams of the past have had a fear about who they are playing and what other people have got rather than thinking about what we've got and what we can do. He just said, 'Go out there and play how you want to play' and 'Go and express yourself.' He was very clear, it was very simple."

It was the instant success and feel-good vibes emanating from the camp that made the fall so spectacular. Pietersen was sensitive enough to the economic collapse in Britain to warn his players not to behave "like clowns" if they won the Allen Stanford money on offer in the gauche Stanford Challenge tournament in the Caribbean in October 2008. There was no danger of that. Pietersen and Moores failed miserably to deal with the many peripheral issues that surrounded the richest match in the history of team sport, including distractions about illness, floodlights, the pitch and the conduct of Stanford himself, who Pietersen later called a "sleazebag". Halfway through the week Pietersen said he couldn't wait for the $20million match against the Stanford Superstars to be over, a comment barely credible when you consider each of the players had the opportunity to become dollar millionaires for three hours work. England were trounced by ten wickets and Pietersen privately blamed Moores for the failure of the players to concentrate solely on the cricket.

The cracks that had begun to appear in the captain-coach relationship in Antigua widened beyond repair on the sub-continent. Pietersen felt exposed in the one-day series as India inflicted a similar kind of hammering on England to the one they themselves had administered on South Africa only two months earlier. The performances of England's batsmen were creditable but the bowlers – the bat-jarring excellence of Flintoff excepted – had no answer to the pyrotechnics of Yuvraj Singh, Virender Sehwag and company.

During the series Pietersen outlined to ECB managing director Hugh Morris his concerns about the guidance he was being offered by Moores. Although his own performances held up well with scores of 63, 33, 13, 5 and 111 not out, the pressure was beginning to affect him. He took England's 5-0 pasting very personally. "There is a lot of mediocrity that people settle for in England in terms of county cricket and the comfort zones of international cricket. But I am not one for settling for mediocrity, that is far from my thoughts," he thundered. And that was after England's loss in the first one-dayer. There were another four defeats to follow.

The strain was increased following the terrorist atrocities in Mumbai from 26-28 November, which killed at least 173 people. When Pietersen spoke in Bhubaneshwar prior to England's swift return home, there was some obvious weariness in his comment: "The four-year tenure that captains mostly do is now down to four months." What with all the "nonsense", as he called it, surrounding the Stanford week and then these draining negotiations maybe this was no real surprise.

It was Morris's decision for the players to catch a flight back to London so they could return to their families for a few days and clear their minds while they waited for advice from the security experts. But Pietersen displayed an encouraging appreciation of the wider picture. He said he wouldn't force any player to return against their will, but his instinct was for England to resume their tour of the sub-continent for some "unfinished business". This enthusiasm was not shared by all of his team-mates. "From early on Kevin was always up for it," explains an ECB source. "He was aware of his responsibility."

The players with young families were understandably more reluctant. Flintoff, Harmison, Collingwood and, less so, Strauss, all expressed serious misgivings, as did Jimmy Anderson, whose wife was due to give birth to their first child a month later, even though the Indian Cricket Board had announced a change in venue for the scheduled second Test from terror-stricken Mumbai to Chennai.

Hugh Morris and Sean Morris, of the Professional Cricketers Association, had two or three conversations with each of the players when they returned home to keep them updated about the situation. England announced that a full-strength squad would train for a few days in Abu Dhabi while ECB security adviser Reg Dickason ensured that all his security requirements were implemented at the Test venues in Chennai and Mohali. "Absolute assurances of high levels of security were made," the source added. "The risk was actually very low. The players had been traumatised by the pictures on Indian TV, which were much more graphic than the pictures broadcast in England, but Dickason's report said British interests were not being targeted." This contrasted starkly with the situation in neighbouring Pakistan. The 2008 Champions Trophy was abandoned because westerners were regarded as specific targets for terrorists. That touring cricket teams were targets was proved by the hideous attack on the Sri Lankan party and match officials in transit to the third morning of the second Test in Lahore on 3 March 2009.

Pietersen showed great leadership qualities at this testing time. He was in regular phone contact with his colleagues and helped to get them all on board. "Kevin has been incredibly supportive and it's nice to see the players lining up behind him," said Hugh Morris. Once the players received the all-clear from Dickason's thorough report, several meetings were held in Abu Dhabi to gauge the feelings of the squad. Despite the threat of further atrocities, Pietersen was brave enough to encourage his team to resume their tour. Following their captain's lead they all unanimously decided to return. "Kevin helped to grease the wheels," said the source. "He was important in setting the tone."

Pietersen's reputation as a leader was much enhanced by the time the squad, in its entirety, arrived back in India. This was to have a crucial bearing on later events. Emboldened by the praise he received both in England and in India, where he was given a hero's welcome, Pietersen was confident that his power base had increased. A month later his short and dramatic tenure was over.

Pietersen was under great stress in India. He recorded two single-figure scores for the first time in his Test career in Chennai – 4 and 1 – and felt powerless as India chased down their fourth-innings target of 387 on a wearing pitch with almost contemptuous ease. He lacked the nous – or experience – to alter obviously pre-determined field placings. Sachin Tendulkar was allowed to milk the bowling for easy singles. Once again, Pietersen felt poorly served by Moores.

To a backdrop of disharmony behind the scenes, Pietersen ridiculed fears that the captaincy might be stripping him of his powers with a counter-attacking century of supreme skill in the second Test in Mohali. It was as breathlessly riveting as any of Kevin's five Test centuries in 2008. Arriving at the crease only seven balls into the innings after India had stockpiled 453 and inclement weather had eaten into much of the playing time, the pressure to not surrender his wicket and yet score quickly at the same time was enormous. He batted with great fluency and showed no signs of worrying about the consequences or the perilous match situation when he switch-hit a stunned Harbahjan Singh first for a huge six and then for a four. His 144 was not enough for England to overhaul India's total and do anything other than settle for a draw, but, by any standards, it was a brilliant captain's innings.

There was no doubt who was in charge. It was Pietersen's team and he wanted a coach who he rated alongside him. Pietersen made it plain to the ECB top brass and to senior colleagues during the series that he did not feel Moores was up to the task. Mick Newell explains: "KP only respects great players or South Africans, because they are from his cricketing background. Graham Ford has played seven first-class matches but KP thinks he is the best thing since sliced bread. Me and Moores both took over from southern Africans, both of us were pretty average players and both of us took over from people he had a high regard for. He would have appreciated Duncan Fletcher's thoughts on batting and appreciated his southern African mentality. KP has a pretty low opinion of county cricket and people who exist in that world."

Moores was a lesser player than his charges were and fell into the trap of egotism by throwing his weight around. His methods were described by one team member as "in your face", a stark contrast to the calm and thoughtful direction of his predecessor. The most successful coaches have usually understood that the captain runs the show, and helped the team most through their ability to advise the skipper wisely. Moores wanted to be the boss and no-one was too big to be asked to do new things. The training was overdone and the tours of Sri Lanka and New Zealand proved to be cheerless; those who came last in drills were treated to humiliating little rituals. Moores didn't understand the needs of international cricketers and his martinet methods particularly irked the three captains he worked with – Vaughan, Collingwood and Pietersen.

Pietersen asked Moores to take more of a back seat when he took over. This appeared to be happening when Moores was seen less publicly in Antigua and India, but he maintained his style of challenging the players, however experienced, even those, like Pietersen, who prefer to be left alone to concentrate on their own games. Moores, though, stuck to his rigid egalitarian principles. He was not prepared to indulge England's match-winners or massage their egos. Senior players need careful management, but Moores treated superstars the same way he treated his county players at Sussex, where the whole added up to more than the sum of the parts.

Newell says: "Moores had to change his style of coaching. A good coach should service his captain. KP was never going to change. You don't make someone captain and expect them to change. Duncan Fletcher could have worked with KP. He got on pretty well with Michael Vaughan and Nasser Hussain. Moores' coaching is all about hard work, practise, practise and challenging the players to do different things. Be fit, be stronger. You can't scare KP with a gym session or an ice bath. He will work hard and do what he has to do to be the best. It's not about computers, that's crap. Most of us barely know how to turn one of those things on. Peter Moores is not computers obsessed. They're just to watch the highlights and analyse techniques. KP would have wanted to be in control – to decide when the practices took place, how long they went on for, who practised against which bowlers and how long for. If that's what the captain wants then let him have it. Stephen Fleming [who led Nottinghamshire to the 2005 County Championship title] didn't want that. He would just take the team on to the field at 10am and take it from there. You have to adjust your style and that's what Peter Moores should have done. I still think he was on a loser. KP would have been, 'Sussex, where's Sussex? I've never heard of the place. That's not in South Africa.'

Contrast Moores' methods with those of Arthur, who has established himself as the most-wanted coach in the world after leading South Africa through the most successful period in their troubled history. Arthur says it is vital the captain and coach establish a chemistry and are singing from the same hymn sheet. He says: "I'm a big believer that the captain is still the leader. They both lead in their own jobs, the captain on the field and the coach off the field. All off-field activities in terms of preparation are my area. Then Graeme [Smith] takes over the team meeting the night before a game and I will back him up. So we know exactly where we stand. On tour we will meet virtually every day to decide what we're going to do and who is going to say what. It's vital that we don't contradict each other. Coaches can over-complicate issues."

Pietersen and Moores were unable to strike up a relationship, and Arthur believes this would have filtered down to the players. "They must sit down and formulate the brand of cricket that they want the team to play and to pick the personnel to implement the brand. Graeme and I thrashed out our thoughts on cricket and we felt exactly the same. I'm a firm believer in the captain and coaching having the same philosophy and sharing the same methods so not to confuse the players."

While Moores had a one-size-fits-all dogma, Arthur adapts his management style to each player. "You have to deal with them differently. I try to speak to every player one-on-one for five minutes every day, either around the team hotel, at training or in the dressing room. I know exactly what makes every one of them tick. I can't speak to Hashim Amla the same as I speak to Mark Boucher. I chat to them all in a different tongue. I couldn't have a go at Hashim Amla and be stern and aggressive. I wouldn't get the best out of him if I did it that way. I have to be a lot calmer. Dale Steyn needs to be told it as it is, Makhaya Ntini the same. Morne Morkel, I have to be a bit more prickly. I can deal with Mark Boucher in strong terms. I can swear at him and be in-your-face. That is the challenge for every coach, to know your players."

It was a surprise given the complete breakdown in the relationship between Pietersen and Moores that the media touring with the party did not get a sniff of the discord in India. However, what the journalists saw was not what the dressing room witnessed. Pietersen's dealings with the media were exemplary if a little less frank than usual on that tour. An immensely assured public speaker when it comes to facing the cameras, he addressed all local questioners in India respectfully as 'Sir'. Pietersen sees it as an important part of his job to have a good relationship with the press. Like Nasser Hussain before him he became a master at switching within seconds from a seething mass of emotion in the dressing room to a polite, interesting and insightful public speaker. Wayne Scott says: "People think he is arrogant, but deep down he is a good, solid citizen. His folks have brought him up on a very strict basis and he went to a boarding establishment which I would go as far as to say is one of the top three in the country. He had a proper education. Those kids were up all brought up very well, with good morals. You can see that now. He speaks so well for a youngster. It doesn't faze him and that comes from maturity and how he was brought up."

What Pietersen's psychological range did lack was diplomacy, cunning and patience. Had he been a political animal like, say, Vaughan, and gently sown the seeds of his displeasure with Moores in a more discreet manner, he would probably still be England captain. The ECB might have requested a New Year email strategy, but Pietersen's 'me or him' ultimatum showed scant regard for niceties even if his bosses secretly shared his misgivings about the coach. Pouring petrol on the bomb with his comments in the *News of the World* and failing to return to London from his safari holiday counted against him in the final reckoning.

Graham Thorpe, who had a few run-ins himself with the England hierarchy during his rebellious younger days, says: "You always have to be careful going up against management. You don't see Kevin from the outside as a great diplomat. Maybe he was doing as he was told when he wrote the report, but the ECB realised it was out of control. No-one is bigger than the game." By attempting to unseat his line manager Pietersen thought he was merely doing what was best for England. "There is obviously a strong personality who is very single-minded in his approach," continues Thorpe. "Often when you have such high standards are you able to take two steps back and look at the situation from the outside? I thought at the time, 'why is no-one tapping on his shoulder and telling him the consequences?' You advise yourself, but you can get carried away with the emotion sometimes. I did myself when I was younger and got into arguments with the board. I was surprised no-one close to Kevin grabbed him and said, 'Just be careful, you could lose the captaincy here. If you want the captaincy so much you are putting it into doubt.' He probably misread the situation."

The ECB did Pietersen few favours by leaking the information that a group of senior players were not required to back the captain above the coach. Pietersen had overplayed his hand, but it would be wrong to suggest, as many did, that he did not have the support of the players. Flintoff and Harmison, claimed to be the biggest dissenters, are cut from very different cloth to Pietersen, but they were adamant they did not play a part in his downfall. "The idea that we told Morris we supported Peter Moores ahead of Kevin is nonsense," said Harmison. "It simply isn't true. I can say without a moment's hesitation that both Fred and I supported Kevin as our captain and leader." However, there is a subtle difference between backing the captain on the field of play and actually choosing him ahead of the coach in a kind of beauty contest. Furthermore, although Flintoff was a known endorser of Moores, injury meant that the India tour was his first under Moores' command.

The younger England players had implicitly bought into Pietersen's regime. The feedback from the Nottinghamshire quartet of Stuart Broad, Graeme Swann, Ryan Sidebottom and Patel had been very positive. Mick Newell says: "The four from here who played under Kevin all spoke well of him. They would have just got on with playing. Younger players will follow him. He will find it easier to get them on board. Samit Patel enjoyed playing for him and enjoyed Kevin's captaincy. I'm disappointed with how it all ended because I felt he could have done it, provided he had got to the stage where he could understand the other players better, which wasn't his strength when he was here. This is four years further down the line. His relationships with Harmison and Flintoff – certainly Harmison – seemed to be okay. Had he been able to rein it in, he could have been a successful captain."

Ford is adamant that Pietersen was showing a growing aptitude for the art of man-management. "In recent times, from the chats I have had with him, he has learned a lot about people. He is now able to understand the Harmisons and the guys in the set-up who do need to be handled in the right way. What Kevin has understood is that all players are different and they need different types of treatment and different buttons will switch different players on. He understands that and the difficulties some players have gone through and will go through."

Rather than an arrogant monster who impaled himself on his own ego, Pietersen was the victim of a series of indiscretions, some self-inflicted – such as allowing the dispute to enter the public realm – some not. In all the discussions about Pietersen's so-called arrogance, one question was unexplored. Was Pietersen right to try and force Moores out? Too many pundits got drawn into the debate about whether he was breaking protocol and exceeding his authority, not whether Moores was the right man for the job. His record hardly stands up to scrutiny – eight wins from 22 Tests, seven of the victories against New Zealand and West Indies. If Pietersen was wrong, why did the ECB sack Moores? If he was the man for the job, Pietersen could have been sacked and told to get on with the business of scoring runs under the man who had been appointed to coach the side. "I thought Kevin got treated terribly," says Shaun Udal. "The first time there was a problem they got rid of him. The ECB asked him for his opinion and he gave it." Udal refutes suggestions that Pietersen should have trod more carefully. "The ECB knew what they were getting – a strong-minded person who wanted things done professionally and who challenged people to be the best they could be. The ECB suddenly thought, 'Oh my God. I'm not sure we can handle this guy.'"

It wasn't clashing with the coach that cost Pietersen his job. It was clashing with the establishment, the old school committees who have run English cricket for generations. Because of the public nature of the crisis, they didn't want it to appear as though the captain was sacking the coach. That just wouldn't be right, old boy. Pietersen was appointed for being himself and then lost his job for being himself. Whether English cricket was the better for his removal from power did not seem to matter.

Pietersen left his station with plenty of 'what ifs' circling his mind. The crown had initially sat so easily before wobbling and eventually hitting the ground with a thump. Pietersen has yet to experience sustained failure in his own game, but the 'failure period' that Warne talked about came when entrusted with the captaincy. Not that Pietersen will see it like that. His record was very reasonable in his short tenure. A win, draw and defeat in his three Tests and four wins and five defeats in his nine one-day internationals was an average return at worst. Given the quality of the opposition – India and South Africa – it was arguably much better than that. Not that anyone seemed to notice. They were only interested in pointing the finger at Pietersen's failure to beat the system.

WHAT NEXT?

WHEN YOU HAVE REACHED the place where there are no more steps to climb and you have been shoved back on to the stairway that only leads down, what to do? In Australia, captains simultaneously relinquish the reins and retire from playing. Allan Border, Mark Taylor and Steve Waugh all led the team in their final Test and Ricky Ponting could well do the same. In England, the tradition is for captains to throw off the chains of office and squeeze out every last ounce from their talent while enjoying the liberation of being a footsoldier. Not since Mike Brearley in 1981 has a permanent England captain (ignoring stand-ins) discarded both crown and boots at the same time. If Michael Vaughan is eased back into the team, as he hopes to be, he will have followed in a long line that includes Bob Willis, David Gower, Mike Gatting, Graham Gooch, Mike Atherton, Alec Stewart and Nasser Hussain. And, of course, Kevin Pietersen.

Like Vaughan, Pietersen has abandoned the office at the top of the building with the panoramic views although, unlike Vaughan, he had little choice in getting the lift back down. Furthermore, the sun is not about to set on Pietersen's career. His resignation was merely a face-saving exercise. Hugh Morris told him the ECB's 12-man executive board had agreed he must go. But there was never any question that Pietersen would be welcomed straight back into the team. Pietersen was the best player; that wasn't going to change whether he was captain or not. The only question was whether he would have the desire to rejoin the England dressing room and immediately look his dissenters in the face with a tour of the West Indies on the horizon.

At this point, Jamie Fleet, the chairman of Cannock, the club where Pietersen had his first taste of the English game, contemplated having a bet that Kevin would play Test cricket for South Africa at some point in the future. Others questioned where his loyalties would lie, with the waters muddied by ongoing negotiations between the Players Cricket Association and the ECB over the participation of the A-listers, and a few B and C-listers as well, in the mega-bucks Indian Premier League. Pietersen was bitterly hurt by these accusations and the manner in which his character was, often quite wrongly, publicly dismantled day after day following revelations of the rift between him and Moores. He wanted to call a press conference to give his point of view the day after he was forced out, but 'his' newspaper would not allow him. The *News of the World* knew they had a great story on their hands and were determined to jealously guard their columnist's views until they could run them exclusively four days later. Indeed, the paper's sports editor Paul McCarthy is believed to have written Pietersen's resignation statement, anxious to avoid revealing too much information. When Pietersen did have his say, spread lavishly over five pages by the paper, he said: "I feel I've got unfinished business as captain of England – I definitely feel that. But right now I feel it is right for me to go back and just play – to do something that I totally, totally love which is scoring runs and more runs for England."

The epilogue to Pietersen being removed as captain was revealing. With him gone, the ECB went back on its commitment about having a one-day player as captain. Andrew Strauss was quickly elevated to the job and restored to the one-day side despite not having played a limited-overs international for two years. Strauss's early weeks were marked by a rebalancing of power, but not towards the coach. On the contrary, no new coach was appointed. Andy Flower, the assistant coach, took over in a caretaker capacity, but with his old job title and the ECB decided to advertise for a team director ready to take over in the return series against the West Indies in May. Strauss, having been overlooked five months previously, now took on the job on much more captain-centric terms – the kind of terms, in fact, that KP might have liked. "What I wanted, he's got," Pietersen said without rancour, but with typical bluntness, "and that is one of my frustrations."

Even a character as naturally optimistic and dogmatic as Pietersen would have had a few soul-searching moments after being stripped of the captaincy. "He is not massively outwardly emotional, but he was very hurt," says Richard Logan. "He can be a lot softer than you might think, but unless you are close to him you don't see it. Only his family really see it."

Pietersen is no stranger to rucks behind the scenes – there are plenty at Natal, Cannock, Nottinghamshire and England who can attest to that – but he is a world-beater at blocking them out when he crosses the white line. Logan recalls: "Whatever is going on off the field he would never take it on the field. That says a lot about his professionalism. A lot of the things written about and spoken about were a little bit out of proportion. The thing about Kev, though, it doesn't get under his skin. He wouldn't confide in me. He doesn't need to. You don't really get under his skin. He just gets on with it."

Consider Shane Warne's take on his one-time running mate (they are not so close as they once were) and some-time rival. "I think Kevin Pietersen's ego would have got bruised a little bit by that, but I'm sure when he woke up and cleaned his teeth the next morning and looked in the mirror he would have thought, 'I'm alright'. He would have been fine there. Deep down it'll inspire him to try to be better. To him, what's most important is scoring runs."

Yet there is no doubt that Pietersen is sensitive to the way he is perceived and that this is partly a matter of vanity. It is, too, the outcome of a reputation that precedes him everywhere. After being criticised for a 2008 magazine interview in which he made tongue-in-cheek comments about cooking in the buff and receiving explicit fan mail, he said: "You do an interview like that and everything gets picked up on. I don't want to do interviews anymore because it just becomes a burden. I'm the one that gets clattered."

One of Strauss's first acts as captain was to revive the tour management committee, a feature of life under Duncan Fletcher, but axed when Moores came along. Pietersen had intended to use it, but never did so formally. For the Test series in the Caribbean the players on it were Andrew Flintoff, Paul Collingwood, Alastair Cook and Stuart Broad. In the one-day series Pietersen replaced Cook, who was not selected. Strauss reckoned that Pietersen had enough on his plate not to be included on the committee for the main stage of the tour.

Pietersen had little time to sulk after being relieved of the England captaincy. Nineteen days later he was striding out to the middle to face St Kitts & Nevis in his first innings back among the rank and file. How would the deposed skipper react?

Pietersen's scriptwriter was in routinely resplendent form. He began the next phase of his career by blasting the ball to all parts and making an indignant century off just 90 balls. The attack was modest, but a small point was made. Speaking immediately afterwards Pietersen revealed that he remained troubled by what had been written about him. "What you guys did to me really hurt me," he told a handful of reporters. "I'd like a few questions to be answered for everything to be gone, but time is healing. Scoring a hundred is what turns me on, so that's good." Given the circumstances, a robot would have had its feelings hurt.

The healing process continued in the second warm-up of the tour against West Indies A. Pietersen larruped an even more murderous 90 off 71 balls. England's sleekest engine was fine-tuned and in prime condition. Pietersen prepared more assiduously than usual for the West Indies series, which is saying something. He watched footage on his laptop of the home side in action against Australia in the Caribbean 12 months previously. He went through the bowling actions frame by frame of Jerome Taylor, Fidel Edwards and company to see where and how the ball was leaving the hand. Their run-ups, wrist position and seam position could provide clues as to where the ball might land. Pietersen visualised the shots he would play and where he would score his runs. He trained harder than ever before, challenging himself to beat his own personal bests on his favourite runs: one through Hyde Park and the other along the Thames past Battersea Park. He would motivate himself by imagining match scenarios and reliving favourite shots while he ran. "If I get tired I ask myself, 'Do you want that hundred?' and I'll push through," said Pietersen. "I think I derive a lot of my mental strength from running." Logan adds: "Kev is a bit of a dreamer when it comes to cricket. He said to me once that he often dreams about batting, and envisages shots and innings he would like to play."

With Pietersen's phenomenal track record of performing when the pressure is at its most intense and the spotlight is shining its brightest, all eyes were thrust upon him at Sabina Park, Kingston to see if he could get runs back in the ranks. He didn't disappoint. Twenty-eight days after being deposed as captain, he brushed aside questions about his commitment by saving England's innings from disaster on a tricky surface. Pietersen made 97 and the only surprise was that he did not celebrate his 16th Test hundred. What on earth did fate think it was playing at?

This was a steely, gritty knock in difficult circumstances. Only when he was well set and in sight of a century did Pietersen throw off the cloak of caution. Sulieman Benn was hit for two thumping fours and a slog-swept six in successive balls to take him within one scoring shot of a century. A nation held its breath. What next? Pietersen, ever the adventurer, got down on one leg and tried another slog-sweep next ball in an effort to dispatch Benn to the stands. He skied a top edge and was already five yards back to the pavilion, bat tucked under his arm, by the time Dinesh Ramdin clasped the ball. It was a rare moment of flamboyance in what had otherwise been an innings of denial for him. His anguished face told a tale of its own.

Only Pietersen will know whether he would have played that shot had he still been captain. He says yes – "That is the way I play". It should be pointed out, however, that he approached the same milestone with far greater care while leader of the team. At the Oval he coolly collected a couple of singles to register his century and in Mohali he also ignored his inner daredevil. Either side of that, at Edgbaston and Sabina Park, there was only a red-blooded desire to smash the bowling to smithereens. Read into that what you will.

But Pietersen's record stands up to scrutiny. A century every three Tests, a record as good as any batsman bar Bradman, is proof of a batsman who knows how to edge out of the nervous nineties. In an interview with the *Daily Mail* towards the end of the Caribbean tour, Pietersen said: "I scored a hundred in the first match of this tour in St Kitts after I lost the captaincy, which I was desperate to do. I was desperate to score a hundred in Jamaica in the first Test, too, but I made one mistake and I was gone for 97. People called me the 'Dumbslog Millionaire' and told me I was an idiot for giving it away, but they have to remember how hard January was for me. To get so close to a hundred and then come in for a lot of criticism was hard to take."

England's premier batsman brought the best out of Taylor, West Indies' premier bowler, in the second innings at Sabina Park. Taylor cleaned up Pietersen with a stunning outswinging yorker that sent his off-stump flying for 1 as England were blown away for a humiliating 51 in the second innings that brought back memories of the bad old days. It was a thrilling moment of sport. Pietersen's technique was slightly awry – he was playing to leg – but the delivery would have done for most top order batsmen.

The drawn third and fourth Tests (after the second was abandoned just 10 balls in), on pitches as lively as plasticine, did not bring out the swashbuckling best of Pietersen. Arriving at the crease with the score on 276-2, as it was in St John's, and 241-2, as it was in Bridgetown, did not summon the fire from his belly. Perhaps mindful of the criticism that followed his first-innings self-destruction in Kingston, he dawdled his way to a pawky 51 in St John's and succumbed for a streaky 41 in Bridgetown. On flatbed pitches he can sometimes fall asleep, especially, as Duncan Fletcher has noted, if the opposition go quiet. England's fiercest beast needs a challenge to really stir him. Like Steve Waugh, he performs better at 50-3 than 350-3. There were signs of greater effervescence in the second innings of the middle two Tests. Pietersen's new favourite toy, the switch-hit, was used almost as often as conventional right-handed strokes in his 32 in St John's and his unbeaten 72, replete again with plenty of cack-handed swipes, livened up an otherwise turgid final day's play in Bridgetown. Pietersen has the *joie de vivre* to bring sunshine to even the cloudiest of cricketing scenarios.

In the final Test in Trinidad, with England needing lightning-quick runs to set a total to bowl at on the last day, Kevin provided the snap, crackle and pop. He smashed an 88-ball century, eventually succumbing for a 92-ball 102, at the Queen's Park Oval as England larruped 237-6 off just 38.4 overs. Once again, Pietersen, well aided by Matt Prior, had created a match-winning situation where none had seemed to exist. England could not prize out all 10 West Indies wickets in the remaining 66 overs, just as they had not managed to eke their stubborn hosts out on a pudding of a pitch in equally tense circumstances in the third Test in Antigua.

In a series dominated by the bat, Pietersen had performed consistently without quite hitting the heights of which he is capable. A return of 406 runs at 58 from four Tests (ignoring the abandonment at the Sir Vivian Richards Stadium) was highly creditable given the fraught circumstances leading up to the tour but, on slow, low pitches that were not especially to his liking, he was overshadowed by Strauss, Collingwood and the imperious Ramnaresh Sarwan.

Perhaps most importantly in the long-term, Pietersen's commitment to the England team appeared absolute in the Caribbean. He revels in the doors that celebrity has opened, but the currency that he luxuriates in is Test runs. No-one really expected him to lose interest in batting. If anything the captaincy saga could make him even more single-minded.

Indeed Pietersen's friends cite loyalty as one of his greatest qualities. "He will be very loyal to England and I think he will be remembered as a very loyal adopted Englishman," says Logan, who believes that, although Kevin can be touchy he is also incredibly forgiving. He prefers to look forward rather than concern himself too much with what has happened in the past. He thought he had the support of all his team-mates in his attempt to oust Moores – "he spoke to everybody and did have the backing of lots of people," claims Logan – but the dissenters in the dressing room won't trouble him. Shaun Udal points out: "Kev wouldn't have worried about it for a second. There was no rift, otherwise why did they all go back to India? He played a huge role in getting them back to India. The ECB have a lot to be grateful to him for."

Crucially, Pietersen's body language appeared to be upbeat in the Tests in the Spring of 2009. Fielding is usually a good gauge of a cricketer's commitment and Pietersen applied himself with Spaniel-like enthusiasm, most notably towards the fag end of West Indies' monumental 749-9 declared in Bridgetown when he was still zipping around the boundary and launching rocket-propelled throws back over the stumps. "The impressive thing about him is how he has got on with things," says Graham Thorpe. "He has dusted himself down as if it had never happened. The way he has handled everything has been exemplary. That is the thing about him that is impressive."

Nevertheless, Pietersen admitted halfway through the subsequent one-day series that the tour had taken its toll. "I know people have been watching me and talking about me throughout this tour," he said in an interview in the *Daily Mail* on Thursday 26 March. "It's been a heck of a tough time and I'm at the end of my tether right now. Really and truly, I can't wait to get home. Jess has been doing this television show [*Dancing on Ice*], training for it since October, and this is the longest we've been away from each other since we met. It's killing me. I'm ready to do a Robinho and disappear home! There haven't been any dramas here or any trouble with me going back to the ranks like some people seemed to think there would be. I knew it wouldn't be a problem." Nevertheless, while the players and their families, plus the entire rest of the touring party, were booked in at The Hilton during the Barbados Test, Pietersen stayed separately at the Royal Westmoreland, a fact which was not reported by the press. What did emerge was that Pietersen had been denied a request to return to England for 48 hours to meet up with his wife between the third and fourth Tests. Perhaps all this was simply because his wife could not join him due to her filming commitments and he wanted to avoid the WAGS and buggies, or perhaps because he was still licking his wounds in the aftermath of his sacking as captain.

In that same article, written by the *Mail's* much-respected Paul Newman, who also ghosted his autobiography, KP launched into a stinging and ill-judged attack on West Indian batsman Shivnarine Chanderpaul. The left-hander from Guyana, according to Pietersen, 'plays for himself', something which many observers had, in fact, accused KP himself of being guilty of, and 'never fields after making a big score'. Given that Chanderpaul had scored 299 runs in six innings in the series victory over England, including a massive 147 not out in Barbados, the comments seemed ill-timed and felt like a wounded animal lashing out.

The outburst brought a swift riposte from West Indies captain Chris Gayle, who confronted Pietersen and demanded an apology, although none was forthcoming, adding, "We're all big men. There's no need to go to that level and try and degrade other players." Critics were split between applauding his frankness and questioning for the first time whether Pietersen needed to toughen up and concentrate on his day job – playing cricket for England.

So, what does the future hold for Kevin Peter Pietersen? Plenty more runs, plenty more entertainment and plenty more headlines, almost certainly. Not the England captaincy, though. Even though he has accepted the captaincy of the Bangalore Royal Challengers in the IPL, Pietersen does not want to lead his country again, certainly in the short-term. So much so, that he would reject the opportunity to lead England again for the World Twenty20 in England in June. "I just think it's too soon after what happened between me and the ECB for me to take over the captaincy again if I was offered it for the Twenty20 World Cup," he said. "It's not something I want to go and dive into. After the way I was let down, I just don't think I want to get involved in that again. Being England captain means you have to be a politician and that's something I'm not." He also told *Sky Sports'* Nasser Hussain in a frank interview, "I've actually kept my distance on this trip because I've been so close to the captaincy in the recent past." When asked what he would have done to alter the course of what was a very disappointing winter, with no competitive victories from the Stanford 20Twenty tournament in October 2008 and the second One-day international in Guyana on 20 March 2009, Pietersen didn't exactly cover himself in analytical glory, saying, "I wouldn't have a clue. If I knew we could change things. We're trying different things in training and on the field, but really we're just not playing well enough."

Even England's narrow victory over the West Indies in Guyana was down to their opponents' failings as coach John Dyson misread the Duckworth/Lewis sheets and brought his batsmen off with 27 runs needed off 22 balls thinking they were ahead, only to discover that England had actually won by one run.

However, the 2009 Ashes will provide the stage for KP to demonstrate his excellence against England's greatest sporting rival. Pietersen is on record as saying he is desperate for revenge after Australia's 5-0 whitewash last time around, a series that temporarily looted even his ceaseless buoyancy. An intriguing sub-plot should be the private battle between Pietersen and Ricky Ponting for the unofficial title of the world's best batsman. "Kev will be the highest runscorer on either side, I have no doubt," predicts Udal. "When the big occasion comes he performs every time. He will be looking to prove a point this summer."

By the time England tour South Africa in the winter of 2009/10 – the only major Test nation where Pietersen has yet to play five-day cricket – he will be exhausted but probably rich. His itinerary would sap the energy of Ranulph Fiennes. Before the Ashes begins in July he will have taken part in the IPL for a fortnight in South Africa as one of the league's two most expensive acquisitions, followed by a two-Test series against West Indies in May, followed by the World Twenty20 in June. If that wasn't daunting enough, the ICC have also rescheduled the unwanted Champions Trophy competition in Sri Lanka for the last week of September and the first week of October. Pietersen will be sick of the sight of hotel rooms by the time he returns to his homeland. However, no international cricketer dare bleat about burnout any more, especially ones who will earn £340,000 for two weeks work in the IPL.

Pietersen turns 29 in June. Most batsmen are usually around the half-way point of their career at that stage. Given the relatively late start to his international career – he was 25 when he made his Test debut – Pietersen may only be a third of the way into his. Graham Ford says: "I think he's probably the best batsman in the world right now. You've got to believe that there's more to come from him and he's going to compete with some fantastic stats along the way. Cricket is a funny game, but all the indications are there that he is going to break some records and do exceptional things."

Statistically, Pietersen is already England's best batsman since Geoff Boycott (the Yorkshire blocker won't like to be reminded that the plunderer from Pietermaritzburg has the better stats) and his record is on a par with the greats from the first half of the 20th century. The list of the quickest Englishmen to 4,000 Test runs remained unchanged for more than half a century before Pietersen added his name during his century against India in Mohali: Herbert Sutcliffe, 43 Tests; Len Hutton 44 Tests; and Kevin Pietersen and Jack Hobbs 45. Other dusty landmarks are likely to come his way. "If he doesn't get bored with the game he can do anything he wants," says Rod Marsh. "If he wants to he can score 10,000 runs – perhaps even better."

Thorpe was England's finest batsman between the eras of the three Gs (Gooch, Gower, Gatting) and KP. He agrees with Marsh that it comes down to hunger. "The next part is longevity," says Thorpe. "When you are regularly going out there scoring runs you feel almost invincible. You have a period in your career where it might be brilliant for six or seven years. Often you are fighting your own mind to be as ruthless as you can be. But it gets harder. If Kevin gets an injury or something like that, he might have to reinvent himself like Sachin Tendulkar has. He has become even more of a fighter than a strokeplayer but has never lost his dedication to score runs. That is the next level for KP. Can he create longevity and score 10,000 Test runs? Can he keep the desire to finish his career at the highest level as one of the greatest run scorers ever? It is purely about drive and desire and not to get too complacent with the game. There is more money around now and more distractions, with the IPL and Twenty20. If he wants to be one of the best Test players ever I am sure he will get close to breaking the records."

Away from cricket, Pietersen has limited interests. A speed freak, he is a big devotee of Formula One and intends to learn how to fly. His friends say they expect him to start a family soon. But he is a narrow-minded specialist. Cricket promises to be his *raison d'etre* for many years to come. Nor, says Warne, have we seen the best of him. "No, there's still a lot more to come from Kevin Pietersen – and a lot more weird stuff, too. Reverse slogging, whatever. He'll be lying in bed thinking of things no-one else has ever thought of . . . cricket-related, I'm talking about! He'll be thinking of some weird strokes, I promise you. And you'll see them soon. We haven't even touched the surface of what he thinks about. He's one weird cat. He's a weirdo. As long as he's making runs and he's the centre of attention, he'll be fine. He likes to be the man – and he's driven. He wants to be the best in the world. And he just about is. Ricky Ponting's maybe just ahead of him at the moment, but it's a pretty close match."

Pietersen's first three coaches in England, Clive Rice, Mick Newell and Marsh agree there is one area where he can improve – the length of time he spends at the crease. "When he gets to a hundred his concentration wavers a little bit," says Rice. "If he had the mentality of, say, Boycott, in terms of going on, my goodness, the opposition would be in tears. Kevin is quite good at converting scores into big ones, but I would like to see him convert to 300 on a few occasions. When he plays against a side like Bangladesh he must take them to the cleaners." Newell is doubtful that Pietersen will ever join the ranks of triple and quadruple centurions. "I don't think he will make that sort of score. I hope he can because talent-wise he is the greatest England batsman ever. I've seen all the Notts legends down here and he's the best player we've had, ever." This is quite some compliment given that Newell was a junior member of the great Notts side of the 1980s that included Rice and Richard Hadlee. "And that was at a young age. He is a better player now than he was when he was here [but] there will always be an element of showing off about his batting. The talent of the bloke . . . he wants to impress everyone. If Boycott is on 175 you think, 'How on earth are we going to get him out?' If KP is on 175, he wants to entertain and show what he can do. That's the size of the ego, that's the talent you buy into when you get him. There is an element of risk about his batting, which means a mistake can happen."

Marsh's advice? Simple. "Get more runs," he extorts. "It's not a question of him having to play pace bowling better or swing bowling better. The way to do it is to be bloody minded about batting and not to get out. It's a mental thing, it's about how badly he wants to score runs."

Pietersen will not stop until he has fulfilled himself as a cricketer. That much is now certain. His singular pursuit of excellence has not made him loved by English cricket's establishment. They handed him the captaincy and when he behaved how they would have surely known he would behave they ran a mile. There has been something about Pietersen's individuality that has, for so many people, struck the wrong note. He makes team-mates feel inferior. He makes captains shake their heads. He makes administrators splutter into their gin and tonics. But he makes people watch cricket. People who don't even like cricket. The boy from Pietermaritzburg who dared to dream, who dared to move in pursuit of the greatness he felt within. He wanted to be exceptional and he has become exceptional.

CAREER STATISTICS

Kevin Peter Pietersen
Born: 27 June 1980, Pietermaritzburg, Natal, South Africa
Height: 6 ft 4 ins

Teams:
Natal B (1998)
KwaZulu-Natal B (1998/99)
KwaZulu-Natal (1998/99-1999//00)
Cannock (2000)
Warwickshire Second XI (2000)
Nottinghamshire CCC (2001-2004)
Todmorden (2002)
Sir JP Getty's XI (2003)
England A (2003-04)
Hampshire CCC (2005-present)
England Test (2005-present)
England One-Day (2004-05-present)
England Twenty20 (2005-present)
ICC World XI (2005-06)

England Test Career
Batting & Fielding

	M	I	NO	Runs	HS	Avge	100	50	SRate	Ct
Home	26	46	1	2598	226	57.73	11	6	63.14	17
Away	24	45	3	1847	158	43.98	5	8	63.14	14
Total	**50**	**91**	**4**	**4445**	**226**	**51.09**	**16**	**14**	**63.14**	**31**

Bowling

Balls	Mdns	Runs	Wkts	BB	Avge	5wi	10wm	SRate	Econ
735	9	518	4	1-0	129.50	0	0	183.75	4.22

Season	Opp	M	Inns	NO	Runs	HS	Avge	100	50	Ct
2005	Aus	5	10	1	473	158	52.55	1	3	0
2005-06	Pak	3	6	0	201	100	33.50	1	0	3
2005-06	Ind	3	6	0	216	87	36.00	0	2	1
2006	SL	3	5	0	360	158	72.00	2	0	4
2006	Pak	4	7	0	347	135	49.57	1	1	3
2006-07	Aus	5	10	1	490	158	54.44	1	3	3
2007	WI	4	7	0	466	226	66.57	2	1	2
2007	Ind	3	6	0	345	134	57.50	2	0	3
2007-08	SL	3	6	1	126	45*	25.20	0	0	1
2007-08	NZ	3	6	0	259	129	43.16	1	0	4
2008	NZ	3	4	0	186	115	46.50	1	0	3
2008	SAf	4	7	0	421	152	60.14	2	1	2
2008-09	Ind	2	3	0	149	144	49.66	1	0	1
2008-09	WI	5	8	1	406	102	58.00	1	3	1

Other First-class Career
Batting & Fielding

M	I	NO	Runs	HS	Avge	100	50	Ct
135	225	16	10817	254*	51.75	38	43	111

Bowling

Balls	Mdns	Runs	Wkts	BB	Avge	5wi	10wm	SRate	Econ
5539	170	3229	61	4-31	52.93	0	0	90.80	3.49

One-Day International Career
Batting & Fielding

	M	I	NO	Runs	HS	Avge	100	50	SRate	Ct
England	85	76	15	3029	116	49.65	7	20	87.77	30
ICC World XI	2	2	0	18	16	9.00	0	0	64.28	1
Overall	**87**	**78**	**15**	**3047**	**116**	**48.36**	**7**	**20**	**87.58**	**31**

Bowling

	Balls	Mdns	Runs	Wkts	BB	Avge	5wi	10wm	SRate	Econ
England	209	0	201	5	2-22	40.20	0	0	41.80	5.77

Other One-Day Career
Batting & Fielding

	M	I	NO	Runs	HS	Avge	100	50	SRate	Ct
Overall	195	177	32	6482	147	44.70	12	41	93.91	73

Bowling

	Balls	Mdns	Runs	Wkts	BB	Avge	4wi	5wi	SRate	Econ
Overall	2169	3	1920	39	3-14	49.23	0	0	55.61	5.31

International Twenty20 Career
Batting & Fielding

	M	I	NO	Runs	HS	Avge	100	50	SRate	Ct
England	15	15	1	375	79	26.78	0	1	144.23	7

Other Twenty20 Career
Batting & Fielding

	M	I	NO	Runs	HS	Avge	100	50	SRate	Ct
Overall	29	29	1	730	79	26.07	0	3	141.47	9

Bowling

	Balls	Mdns	Runs	Wkts	BB	Avge	4wi	5wi	SRate	Econ
Overall	150	0	196	9	3-33	21.77	0	0	16.66	7.84

Honours

Birmingham League 2000
Nottinghamshire cap 2002
2002 promoted from County Championship Second Division
2004 Winners of the County Championship Second Division
2004 promoted from Pro40 Second Division
Hampshire cap 2005
2005 Winners Cheltenham & Gloucester Trophy
2006 promoted from Pro40 Second Division
Wisden Cricketer of the Year 2006

(correct to 17 March 2009)